Social Ontology, Normativity and Law

Social Ontology, Normativity and Law

Edited by
Miguel Garcia-Godinez
Rachael Mellin
Raimo Tuomela

DE GRUYTER

ISBN 978-3-11-066308-2
e-ISBN (PDF) 978-3-11-066361-7
e-ISBN (EPUB) 978-3-11-066428-7

Library of Congress Control Number: 2020935446

Bibliographic information published by the Deutsche Nationalbibliothek
The Deutsche Nationalbibliothek lists this publication in the Deutsche Nationalbibliografie; detailed bibliographic data are available on the Internet at http://dnb.dnb.de.

Typesetting: Integra Software Services Pvt. Ltd.
Printing and binding: CPI books GmbH, Leck

www.degruyter.com

Contents

Contributors

Raimo Tuomela, Professor Emeritus in Practical Philosophy at the University of Helsinki and Permanent Visiting Professor at the University of Munich.

Julie Zahle, Postdoctoral Fellow at the University of Bergen

Miguel Garcia-Godinez, PhD Research Student at the University of Glasgow

Säde Hormio, Postdoctoral Researcher at the University of Helsinki

Leonie Smith, PhD Research Student at the University of Manchester

Kent Hurtig, Lecturer in Philosophy at the University of Stirling

Olof Leffler, Teaching Fellow at Durham University

Arto Laitinen, Professor of Social Philosophy at Tampere University

Rachael Mellin, PhD Research Student at the University of Glasgow

Kirk Ludwig, Professor of Philosophy and Cognitive Science at Indiana University, Bloomington

Pekka Mäkelä, Researcher at the University of Helsinki

Raul Hakli, Researcher at the University of Helsinki

Michael Schmitz, Assistant Professor at the University of Vienna

https://doi.org/10.1515/9783110663617-203

Introduction

In May 2019, the Social Ontology Research Group (SORG) at the University of Glasgow organised a two-day, interdisciplinary workshop on "Social Ontology, Normativity and Philosophy of Law". It brought together four UK PhD students and some of the international leading researchers working in each of these fields: Säde Hormio, Hans Bernhard-Schmid, Leonie Smith, Brian Epstein, Kirk Ludwig, Raimo Tuomela, Jessica Brown, Kent Hurtig, Olof Leffler, Herlinde Pauer-Studer, and ourselves (Rachael Mellin and Miguel Garcia).

This book is based on the proceedings of the workshop, along with some other contributions, all of which were written exclusively for the book. We are delighted to include papers from Pekka Mäkelä & Raul Hakli, Michael Schmitz, Julie Zahle, and Arto Laitinen.

Though each paper ranges over the topics of the workshop, we have grouped them together based on what we consider their main contribution to be. The first four deal more closely with *social ontology*, from the general discussion about collective intentionality to the capacity of institutions to be attributed with knowledge. The next four ask some questions related to *normativity*, for example, whether our ascriptions of rights can cover groups rather than only individuals, and whether we have genuine reasons to follow socially constructed norms, such as legal requirements. The last four papers take up the discussion about *law* and its ontology, including criticisms to traditional positivist views.

To help the reader navigate through all the different issues that each chapter discusses, we shall briefly present some of their main points.

Raimo Tuomela opens this book with the chapter ***We-Thinking, We-Mode, and Group Agents.*** He first introduces his now classic distinction between we-mode and I-mode group members (that is, individual agents fully functioning as group members and individual agents functioning as private persons in group contexts). He then claims that both are required to provide an adequate explanation of social life, that under certain conditions the first is preferable to the second, and that neither of them is reducible to the other. Standing on these claims, he focuses later on we-mode thinking and we-mode reasoning to argue that both are necessary for explaining cases of social construction (for example, group beliefs and social institutions), cases of joint action (such as people intentionally flitting a table together), and cases of rational choice where the group chooses what is best for the group, rather than (or even contrary to) what is best for the members (for example, in Hi-Lo games, set up for groups, where cooperation pays off better than individual, self-interest).

https://doi.org/10.1515/9783110663617-001

After presenting the three properties associated to the we-mode we-intentions, namely, that they are addressed to a certain group reason (i.e., a certain socially constructed group ethos), that they imply the collectivity condition (i.e., that the group ethos is satisfied for a group member iff it is satisfied for all group members), and that they require collective commitment (i.e., that the group members are collectively committed to their collectively accepted group ethos), Tuomela concludes that a we-mode group (i.e., an organised group) settles on the rationality criteria for group members *qua* group members as identifying themselves with the group and acting in the interest of the group (rather than in their own interest). As such, then, when explaining group action, particularly in situations of cooperation, both we-mode thinking and we-mode reasoning play a key role: They determine the conditions under which group members *qua* group members act rationally.

Considering the relevance of reductionist queries, Julie Zahle asks whether the classical methodological individualism-holism debate can be phrased in terms of lower and higher level explanations, respectively? In ***The Level Conception of the Methodological Individualism-Holism Debate***, she argues against the levels view, concluding that the debate should not be conceived of in this way.

Zahle proceeds, firstly, by introducing two conditions which a levels conception must meet: (1) The ontological level condition – individuals, individualistic properties, etc. are lower individual-level phenomena, whereas social entities, social properties, etc. are higher social-level phenomena; and (2) The explanatory level condition – individualist explanations only describe individual-level phenomena and so are lower individual-level explanations, whereas holist explanations only describe social-level phenomena and so are higher social-level explanations. Secondly, she grants that both supervenience and emergence accounts (the two main contenders of the levels conception) satisfy the ontological level condition, but denies that either can satisfy the explanatory level condition since neither account can make room for inclusive individualist positions. This is important because, according to Zahle, most contemporary methodological individualists endorse inclusive individualist notions. Yet, thirdly, she argues that these inclusive individualist explanations do not qualify as individual-level explanations. To illustrate this, Zahle considers certain elements that inclusive individualist explanations recognise when providing individualist explanations, viz., social role properties, and material and institutional context factors. However, since none of these elements suit an individual-level explanation, the explanatory level condition is not satisfied. Zahle ends the paper by refuting several objections that may be raised towards a rejection of the levels conception.

On the route towards explaining social entities, Miguel Garcia-Godinez takes up the narrower discussion about the ontology of institutional groups in his ***What***

Are Institutional Groups? and argues that we create them by taking on roles established in formal group structures. He presents this view as an improved version of Ritchie's structuralist account of organised social groups, as it introduces a further distinction, namely, between formal and informal organised social groups. Based on this improved version, he then elaborates on the conditions for institutional groups to perform intentional actions. He does so by considering Ludwig's theory of institutional and proxy agency. Although he mostly agrees with it, Garcia-Godinez claims that Ludwig's deflationary theory has problems explaining the we-intentions of institutional agents, for which a we-content account is not enough, but a more robust we-mode account is required.

Garcia-Godinez finishes his contribution by discussing different characterisations of institutions. After briefly examining their consequences and presenting some objections, he concludes that institutions (e.g., banks, universities and legal systems) are better characterised as institutional groups acting intentionally according to certain constitutive (and regulative) rules. He takes this characterisation to follow Tuomela's theory of social and institutional reality, which argues that social institutions are norm-governed social practices.

Building on work both in social ontology and social epistemology, Säde Hormio asks when can we correctly attribute knowledge to an institution? In ***Institutional Knowledge and its Normative Implications***, she argues that the conditions for institutions to have knowledge are not as demanding as for individuals. More specifically, she claims that not every member of an institution need have knowledge about something for the institution to have knowledge about it. This fragmented feature of knowledge is common as it is an inevitable consequence, particularly in large institutions with different areas of specialisation. Hormio argues that this fragmented nature of institutions is not usually problematic, as long as knowledge can be shared or accessed when needed. In other words, in order to attribute knowledge of something to an institution, it is enough that relevant members, e.g., executives, are able to acquire that information through certain roles and means of communication.

Hormio suggests further that by looking at how knowledge of climate change has evolved over time, we can distinguish between two different kinds of knowledge, viz., operating knowledge and shared knowledge, and uses this distinction to claim that certain kinds of knowledge are more robust than others, i.e., shared knowledge is more robust than operative knowledge, but shared and operative knowledge is more robust still. It is up to the executives to decide which information can remain operating knowledge within the institution and which information must be shared, i.e., made more robust. Yet, setting these parameters, Hormio admits, is not an easy task, as knowledge can be limited in different ways. Nevertheless, institutions have many means for acquiring knowledge at their disposal. Hormio argues that as a result of this, institutions have greater obligations to know about certain issues that fall within their scope of interest, e.g., states should know that climate change will likely affect their citizens since part of the reason for their continued existence is to protect the interests of their citizens. Hormio concludes by reconsidering the climate change case in order to bring out all of these distinctions.

Moving on to normative questions within an institutional context, in ***The Right to Press Freedom of Expression vs the Rights of Marginalised Groups: An Answer Grounded in Personhood Rights*** Leonie Smith argues that claims of group discrimination should be grounds for complaint against the UK press print media (PPM). Currently, she says, claims of discriminatory reporting against the PPM will only be investigated if they are made by particular individuals who are identifiable as the target of the report in question. This problem is usually framed as a "free speech vs. harm principle" dilemma where the freedom of the press needs to be balanced with the harms that the exercise of this freedom may cause to marginalised groups. Smith explores the regulations which specifically prohibit complaints of group discrimination and concludes that the reason behind this seems to be to uphold the freedom of expression of the PPM.

While Smith suggests that there are different interpretations of what the fundamental value behind press freedom is, she focuses on epistemic participation and argues that this is undermined when the PPM exercises its freedom of expression to write discriminatory reports about groups of individuals. This is because the right to epistemic participation is held by other agents, including the groups that are targeted. More specifically, when the PPM prints discriminatory reports against groups, it commits an act of epistemic injustice towards the group, which in turn undermines the individual members of that group's epistemic participation. Smith concludes by suggesting how such cases of discrimination can be adjudicated. She argues that in order to do so, we need to analyse further the value of epistemic participation, which she does in terms of performative personhood.

Continuing the normative discussions, in ***Consent and Normativity*** Kent Hurtig asks what is consent and suggests that there are two broad answers to this question. What he calls (1) Mental State Views of Consent take consenting as being in a certain state of mind, and (2) Communicative Act Views of Consent take consenting as engaging in a particular communicative act. The first purpose of Hurtig's paper is to cast doubts on the plausibility of (2) and offer some considerations in favour of (1). The second (and main) purpose is to challenge the widely-accepted idea that consenting is normatively transformative: A's consenting to B's φ-ing changes the normative situation from its being impermissible for B to φ before A consents to its being permissible for B to φ after A has consented.

Hurtig begins by considering Kleinig's account of consent – what he takes to be a strong version of a Communicative Act View. He identifies three central elements to Kleinig's view: (i) To consent is to perform a communicative act; (ii) Consent is necessarily normatively transformative, and (iii) The two previous claims are conceptual truths. Hurtig swiftly rejects (i) as it cannot account for cases of uncommunicated consent. As for (iii), he appeals to Moore's open question argument to show that it is not a conceptual truth that consent is a performative speech act. Against (ii), Hurtig offers two reasons: first, due to certain restrictions, it is not easy to identify possible actions which are impermissible before consent and permissible after consent; and second, it is not clear how an agent's consenting to the performance of an action can reshape the balance of reasons for/against the performance of this action since there are also antecedent, consent-independent reasons involved, i.e., reasons that obtain prior to, and independently of the consent to perform the action. Based on these reasons, Hurtig concludes that consent is necessarily *not* normatively transformative.

Olof Leffler follows with ***Reasons Internalism, Cooperation, and Law***, where he argues that some moral norms depend, ultimately, on fundamental reasons to cooperate. Building upon an internalist theory of reasons, namely, that there is a necessary relation between a reason for action and a person's psychology, he develops a desire-based account of reasons: If an ideal (or fully functional) agent desires to φ, then a non-ideal agent has a reason to φ.

His argument also reveals interesting features of ideal agency, for example, that ideal agents do not only have beliefs, but true beliefs, that they must be under relevant circumstances (which, in the case of ideal agents close enough to the non-ideal agents of our actual world, include the circumstances of justice), and that they possess instrumental rationality (not just to take the means to an end, but to deliberate, e.g., about the best means to a certain end). When added to these features, a further condition, viz., that ideal agents are embedded in contexts of social interaction, the requirement of cooperation (at least to the extent that other ideal agents cooperate back) is in place. In other words, to exercise its ideal (fully functional) agency, an ideal agent positioned in a social context that includes the circumstances of justice is required to cooperate. This cooperation, however, is constrained. It rules positively to cooperate (if others do so), and it rules negatively not to prevent others from cooperating (for example, by satisfying important anti-social desires). Based on this, Leffler suggests that certain moral norms can be explained in terms of the desire of ideal agents to cooperate, which, for non-ideal agents (if reasons internalism is correct), constitute a reason to cooperate. This, he also affirms, can be a fresh starting point for a natural law theory.

When accounting for what there socially is, i.e., our social ontology, we can come across facts that involve a certain normative component. In ***Varieties of Normativity***, Arto Laitinen distinguishes several ways or senses in which these facts can be normative. Arguably, not all normative facts are normative in the same way. Laitinen considers, for example, the normativity of oughts and reasons, and wonders whether legal requirements and other socially constructed norms are normative in the same way.

He, firstly, presents four senses of normativity. The first corresponds to the good or sufficient reasons we have, e.g., to do something or to believe something or to intend something, etc. The second is about the norms, expectations, standards, etc. that we are meant to satisfy on pain of punishment or another way of social retribution. The third has to do with rational or logical normativity, such as the 'ought' in "one ought to accept the conclusion if one accepts the premises". The fourth sense covers what Laitinen calls "ought-to-be norms", that is, norms that establish that such-and-such state of affairs ought to obtain, rather than one ought to do such-and-such. The 'ought' in "legal systems ought to be morally just" is an example of this. After discussing in depth these and other senses of normativity, he takes up the question about the normativity of law and concludes that, although it is by definition normative in the second sense, it is worth examining whether and when it is normative in the first sense.

From the normativity of law to the nature of law, in ***The Metaphysics of Legal Organisations*** Rachael Mellin engages with Scott Shapiro's account of the nature of law which begins with an inquiry into the nature of legal organisations. This, in part, involves identifying the properties of legal organisations that distinguish them from other similar kinds of groups. In her chapter, Mellin argues that Shapiro fails to do this. She considers a similar objection raised by Kenneth Ehrenberg in order to elucidate exactly why Shapiro is unsuccessful, although disagrees with the alternative Ehrenberg suggests for two reasons. Firstly, despite his intentions, Ehrenberg's proposal is incompatible with Shapiro's project as he undermines the priority of legal organisations in giving an account of the nature of law. Secondly, because Ehrenberg's account introduces complexity and further questions which, in order to answer, will partly require him to elaborate on the nature of legal organisations.

Though Mellin takes seriously Ehrenberg's challenge against Shapiro, she claims that the main problem for Shapiro lies elsewhere. She argues that his conceptions of both *nature* and *identity* are problematic and incomplete. Rather than abandoning Shapiro's project, Mellin suggests that these notions can be clarified and an account of the nature of legal organisations can be given by using Brian Epstein's metaphysical framework for understanding the nature of groups.

Staying within social ontology and philosophy of law, Kirk Ludwig examines both what legal systems (particularly, legal norms) are and how they can be distinguished from other normative systems. In ***The Social Construction of Legal Norms***, he sets out the precise way legal norms are socially constructed: They derive from rules that specify status roles in legal systems, the general point of which is to solve large-scale coordination problems (without this implying, though, that each of these rules solves a coordination problem).

Status roles, Ludwig argues, are a variety of status functions, the existence of which requires collective acceptance, that is, that someone or some group be collectively accepted as having such a status. However, adds Ludwig, since status roles are defined by constitutive rules, i.e., the kind of rules that specify the functions that those having the status role are to fulfil, but without these rules specifying who is to have such a status, people must coordinate in their social transactions on who is to hold the role. This coordination, says Ludwig, constitutes a convention (in a Lewisian sense). Thus, playing a role in social transactions has a conventional nature, which depends on the collective acceptance of someone or some group as having such a status. Yet, collective acceptance does not come in only one way. Ludwig distinguishes formal from substantive acceptance. For one thing is to participate in the formal process of assigning someone or some group a status role, and another is to participate (however loosely) in the general practice of sustaining status roles. In the case of law, the assignment of status roles to individuals and groups is both formally and substantively accepted. For this reason, those individuals and groups, when acting upon their roles, are proxy agents, i.e., they act not only in the interest of the community which collectively accepts their having such a status, but in the name of the community. They are, in other words, authorised by the community to act for itself. Grounded in a distinction between internal, definitional and external authority, Ludwig contrasts his view to Hart's, for whom only the official acceptance of a secondary rule (that is, the rule of recognition) would be enough to explain the authorisation of proxy agents (legal officials) to act for the community. This, Ludwig says, is an external form of authority (which does not require the community's acceptance). According to his view, on the contrary, the community's internal acceptance is also essential. The community collectively accepts a constitutive rule (Hart's rule of recognition) which articulates the functions (rights and duties) of certain roles in a legal system (e.g., the role of citizen, the role of judge, etc.). Thus, there being a legal system, Ludwig concludes, is not there being a network of externally authorised legal officials, but there being a network of internally accepted status roles. Legal norms, on his view, are socially constructed by specifying the functions of those roles.

On a critical note, Pekka Mäkelä and Raul Hakli raise some objections to Kirk Ludwig's (2017) deflationary account of corporate agents in their ***Identity of Corporations: Against the Shareholder View***. His account, they say, takes institutional actions (of which corporate actions are particular cases) to be analysable in individualistic (rather than collectivist) terms: Corporations *qua* institutions act through their proxy agents (that is, agents fulfilling a collectively assigned status role), which strictly speaking act as representatives of the shareholders. Thus, according to Mäkelä and Hakli, Ludwig seems to defend a corporate agency theory that, firstly, identifies corporations with their shareholders, and, secondly, assumes that proxy agents act in the interest of the latter.

Under this characterisation, Ludwig's theory may not be as strong an argument for individualism as first thought. On the one hand, because it seems to neglect one aspect of social constructivism. Mäkelä and Hakli argue that social constructivism does not consist only in internal, but also in external social construction. In the case of corporations, the first takes the form of collective acceptance of status roles (which are specific types of status functions), whereas the second involves societal (for example, political, legal and economical) recognition. Both, in other words, are constitutive elements of corporations. However, they argue, Ludwig's corporate agency theory seems to neglect the external social construction of corporations. His theory is focused on the internal acceptance of status roles (for example, managements and employees) but does not say much about the external recognition of corporations nor the implications they have at the large-scale social world. On the other hand, Mäkelä and Hakli raise a red flag in Ludwig's theory, as it seems to presuppose, contrary to some empirical evidence, that proxy agents act for the interest of shareholders (that is, as maximising return on shareholders' investment). Yet, they show how this general policy for corporations is not the best strategy in the long run. As such, however committed Ludwig may be with this general policy, his theory seems to be better off if it does not rule out that proxy agents can act not only for the interest of the shareholders, but for the interest of the corporation itself. But in this case, contra Ludwig, his theory will not be as individualistic as originally claimed.

The book closes with a layered account of collective intentionality. In ***Of Layers and Lawyers***, Michael Schmitz aims to both characterise law in terms of such an account and use it to shed new light on an old debate between legal positivism and natural law. Roughly, the debate concerns if and how morality enters into the law. Natural lawyers take law to be necessarily moral whereas positivists deny this. Schmitz declines to align himself with one side or another, instead proposing that the best way to think of law is as an institutionalised form of morality (meant in a broad sense to include mores and conventions) whichever side of the debate this view falls.

Schmitz begins by presenting his account of collective intentionality. He takes it to be essentially layered, where these layers can be understood in terms of the structure and format of the representations involved. He distinguishes between three layers: (1) the nonconceptual, (2) the conceptual, and (3) the institutional. He then introduces four criteria (or parameters) that can be used to differentiate between these layers. These parameters, he says, distinguish between layers since they come in different degrees which correspond to the representations involved in each layer. That there are relations between these parameters is a central hypothesis of Schmitz's layered account. He demonstrates this correlation by describing how a moral practice, which falls within layer (1), can become a legal practice, which is paradigmatic of layer (3). Another claim made by Schmitz is that higher-level legal representations depend on lower-level ones, e.g., moral attitudes. All of this is then used to argue for the thesis that law consists in institutionalised, codified moral rules.

Before getting to this and the other discussions presented above, we wish to thank all of the contributors for their joint commitment in writing this book. We give special thanks to Raimo for his kind support in funding it. We hope it can be of interest to philosophers and legal scholars alike.

Miguel Garcia-Godinez and Rachael Mellin
Glasgow, 2020

Raimo Tuomela

We-Thinking, We-Mode, and Group Agents

PART I

Introduction: Sociality, The We-Mode and the I-Mode

The present paper focuses on giving a brief and idealized sketch of the central features of the conceptual framework of "we-thinking", the strongest form of which is called the "we-mode" in contrast to the individualistic "I-mode". Some remarks will also be made about the explanatory power of the we-mode concerning cooperation in social action dilemmas. The general underlying assumption of this paper that grounds the motivation of human sociality is this: Human beings need and tend to desire to live in orderly groups for enhancing the well-being of their members.

Strong collective intentionality, termed the *we-mode*, concerns functioning fully as a group member and is distinguished from weak collective intentionality, called the *pro-group I-mode* that concerns functioning as a private person, although being a member of a group.

General theses of the we-mode approach: It is argued that

1. an adequate description and explanation of social life requires we-mode thinking in addition to I-mode thinking which represents a central way of thinking and theorizing in the social sciences, and that
2. in several contexts the we-mode is to be preferred to the I-mode on conceptual and philosophical grounds and often also on functional, action-related grounds.
3. We-mode thinking and reasoning is not reducible to I-mode reasoning, i.e. it is not definable by, or functionally construable from, I-mode notions. This is in part because it employs a different reasoning mechanism that relies on groups as the basic agents of reasoning.

We-mode we-thinking: We-mode thinking is a group's and its members' thinking and reasoning in terms of the thick "togetherness" notion of "we" about attitudes, actions, and emotions attributable to a social group and its members.

Groups as social systems can function in ways resembling the functioning of individual agents, and this gives justification for the attributions in question. (Note that in democratic groups, authority is given and justified from below, by the members.) The "switch" from the I-mode to the we-mode means

https://doi.org/10.1515/9783110663617-002

both a change of agency from individual agents to collective (quasi-) agents and a change of I-thinking and acting to we-mode thinking and acting (and not only to mere we-thinking, viz. use of the word "we").

The core of the we-mode: The we-mode framework of concepts is based on collective acceptance ("construction") of attitudes and other group properties by the group members. Here are three central framework features:

1. The members are supposed to take the accepted attitudes or contents to be (authoritative) group reasons for their proper functioning *qua* members.
2. These contents are assumed to satisfy a collectivity condition expressing the idea of necessarily "being in the same boat."
3. The members are collectively committed to what they have accepted. Accordingly, every group member is to an extent responsible for every other member's actions *qua* group member, and alike the whole group is responsible for its members' actions.

The we-mode is to be understood as a top-down notion, viz. the group level properties ("the cake") are conceptually prior to the member level properties ("the slices").

Methodological individualism in social science:

a) Conceptual understanding of an individual's action must be based on either the individual's own attitudes or reasons or some other agent's (individual's or group agent's) attitudes and reasons as its ground. (*Meaning*)
b) Explanation of an individual's action must have either the individual's own attitudes and reasons or some other agent's (individual or reducible group agent's) attitudes and reasons as its explanatory basis. (*Explanation*)
c) The basic ontology of the best explaining social scientific theory must consist *solely* of the activities, properties and interactions of either individuals or groups referred to in (a) and (b). (*Ontology*)

Why we-thinking?

1) We-thinking in the full we-mode sense is *in some cases conceptually necessary*, e.g. in contexts where the members construct (through their we-mode thinking and acting) *full-blown group notions – collective artifacts* – such as group beliefs and social institutions.
2) It is *functionally required* in many contexts, especially in cases of joint action requiring *synergy effects* for collectively (and individually) *beneficial* results.
3) The we-mode gives a different solution to the Hi-Lo game than the pro-group I-mode. It solves the dilemma because the group chooses what is best for the

group, contrary to the members of a pro-group I-mode group where the members make their choices as individuals.

Extrinsically intentional group agents: Group members form a group mind (collective attitudes, etc.) e.g. by their relevant kind of collective acceptance or some related group-internal process or mechanism such as collective attribution of mental states to group members and group attitudes to groups. An organized group (e.g. a we-mode group) can functionally be taken to be an agent (person) if it is goal-directed and if it can also be taken to reason and reflect upon its activities through its members. Its mental states are functionally construed as *group-level states*.

In simple cases, a group agent is (possibly "emergently") constructed on the basis of the members' properties and relations. In the case of group agents with normatively characterized positions (e.g. corporations and states) a top-down kind of construction may be used. We can thus have both a *group-level* and a *member-level* description of collective intentions and beliefs. A group agent exists as a functional social system capable of producing group action – not as an intentional agent with phenomenal features. It can only function via its members' functioning appropriately. In many cases a group agent involves some fictitious and irreducible constructed elements and it seems that it cannot be fully accounted for by individualism (see Tuomela, 2007, Ch. 4).

A *we-mode group*: A person functions in the we-mode if she functions as a group member and in the I-mode if she functions as a private person (possibly in a group context). A group is in most contexts below assumed to be a *we-mode group*. It is assumed to commit itself to a group *ethos* (viz. certain constitutive goals, beliefs, standards, norms, etc.) and to relevant we-reasoning and we-acting. A we-mode group is taken to be able to reason and to act as a unit through its members. Even a fleeting table-carrying group can be a we-mode group and thus a group agent.

A social group's ethos ("constitution") and its fulfillment and promotion may be governed by an *external authority* that has the power to coerce the group. In some cases it is still possible for the group members to reason and act in the we-mode (e.g. a military unit). Yet the external authority retains its power to change the group's activities. Such a group is a "quasi-we-mode" group.

Three central we-mode criteria: The we-mode involves the following three central criteria on the member level (see Tuomela, 2013):
1. *group reason,*
2. *collectivity condition, and*
3. *collective commitment.*

We-mode mental attitudes are had in the way or mode satisfying the above requirements for thinking and acting with the full we-perspective with a "togetherness-we". (People can e.g. carry a table either in the I-mode or in the we-mode. A content can thus be intended in various modes.)

I-thinking and we-thinking in the I-mode versus the we-mode: In general, there can be we-thinking and we-action, etc. in the we-mode but also in the I-mode (even for the benefit of the group's goals and interests). On the other hand, there can be "I-thinking" and "I-action" in the we-mode (conceptually group-dependent thinking), e.g. I we-intend to participate in joint action or in the I-mode ("private" I-thinking without conceptual dependence on the group).

PART II

The Three We-Mode Criteria: Group Reason, the Collectivity Condition and Collective Commitment

Before the we-mode criteria are presented some general remarks about the we-mode will be made. The idea of a group agent capable of acting as a group can in part be based on an intuitive analogy of intentional action (as action for a reason) in both the individual and the group case. Analogously to typical intentional action by an individual agent, intentional action by a group agent (through its members) is normally based on the members' (group) reasons for actions. Analogously to an individual's having to coordinate the movements of her body parts, the members of a (we-mode) group coordinate their activities (including mental ones) in order to achieve group goals. Analogously to an individual agent committed to her intended actions, the group members are committed as a group, i.e. collectively committed, to the group's actions. These ideas can be summed up as an *analogy argument* for the we-mode criteria.

The following *distinctions* concerning *collective intentions* (a generic term for several kinds of social intentions) are appropriate:

1) *Group intention*: intention attributed to a group (e.g. a group's intention to paint a house).
2) *Joint intention*: intention attributed to a collection of individuals; e.g. John and Tom jointly intend to paint the house together. When a group intends to paint a house, in general at least some if not all of its members have to share the joint intention to do it.

3) *We-intention*: intention attributed to an individual taking part in a joint intention, the individual's "slice" of the joint intention in question (e.g. John we-intends to paint the house together with Tom). It is an *intention to perform one's part* of the participants' joint action in accordance with and partly because of the participants' joint intention to perform the joint action: A we-intention can be generic or specific. A generic we-intention is an "unspecified" we-intention.

Examples:

a) Group g intends to paint the house. (*group intention*)
b) We (the members of g) jointly intend to paint the house together. (*joint intention*)
c) I, *qua* member of g and a participant in joint intention we-intend to paint the house together with the others. (*we-intention*)
d) I, *qua* member of g and a participant in our joint intention to paint the house together with the others, intend to perform my (so far unspecified part) of our painting the house. (*generic part-performance intention*)
e) My part being to paint the front of the house, I intend to do it and set myself to do it. (*specific part-performance intention.*)

The three we-mode criteria

1. Group reason

In general, the group members function as group members in accordance with the group ethos (the group's fundamental goals, beliefs, etc). This ethos gives them their central reason for acting as a group member in group contexts.

The reason is an authoritative one if the group members *qua* group members have freely accepted the ethos for their group. In some cases they have authorized some members to act for the group and in other cases they share the tasks in an informal way.

A group reason is a reason based on what the group believes, intends, wants, demands (etc.). In a formally structured group an authority (e.g. a leader of the group) instructs the members in their actions by giving them directives for how to act, the members' having given him or her part of their "natural" authority to make decisions and act. These directives give group reasons for the members. For instance, in the case of a state the goals and values, e.g. concerning human rights and justice, that its ethos may contain, is taken to require authorized group action; and this serves substantively and socially to justify state authority.

In cases where the group members act as a group, but cannot freely choose the group's ethos and leaders, we speak of an "externally authorized" group. (In some of those cases the group may choose its "lower level" leaders.) In such externally authorized groups, the members are at least in some cases not free to enter or exit the group. An example of externally authorized groups is a military unit (in a state with mandatory conscription). As was mentioned above, a quasi-we-mode action within the group is possible and here the group reason is externally decided.

2. The collectivity condition

Because of being members of a group (as an agent), the group members will necessarily "be in the same boat," and the "collectivity condition" is satisfied. Formulated for goals, this condition is as follows: Collectivity Condition for Goals: Necessarily (for conceptual reasons), as based on the group members' construction of a goal as its goal, the goal *is satisfied for a member if and only if it is satisfied for all members.*

3. Collective commitment in the We-mode

The we-mode group's commitment to its ethos from the members' point of view basically amounts to their collective commitment to it (with the world-to-mind direction of fit).

The group commitment is based on the members' performative *collective acceptance* of an ethos as the group's ethos. The members collectively commit themselves to the ethos and might not be released without sanctions by the group. (The sanction may merely amount to social disapproval.) Collective commitment also involves the members' being socially committed to each other to function as group members. Collective commitment entails "group-social" (e.g. quasi-moral) obligations (see Tuomela 2007, Ch. 1).

Three features that distinguish *collective commitment* from collective or *"aggregated" private commitments in the I-mode case* are these:

(i) We-mode collective commitment is *derived from a group reason* (recall the "top-down" feature of the we-mode).

(ii) *Qua* being based on the group's commitment, a member, at least ideally, *should not give it up without other group members' consent.* This is because it is a ground principle that both on conceptual and functional grounds all the group members ought to be collectively committed when the group is committed to some content *p* – where the group's commitment is based on its intending to bring about *p* or to uphold *p*.

(iii) Another central difference between I-mode and we-mode commitment is this: In the pure I-mode case a person is committed to herself to further her *own interests*. In the pro group I-mode she is committed to herself to further *the group's interests*. In the we-mode she is committed to the group to further *the group's interests*.

To end Part II, let me say a few words about the key notion of *collective acceptance* and about a *group's intention*. The next part will consider group agents in detail.

In general, we-mode thinking, "emoting," and acting presuppose *the group's reflexive collective acceptance* of appropriate contents. Such group acceptance centrally involves the members' (or representatives') collective commitment with the right attitude-based direction of fit to the accepted contents (see Tuomela, 2013, ch.5 for group acceptance). The collectively accepted contents are primarily for the "use" of the group.

Finally, *a (we-mode) group's intention* to see to it that something X will be the case is based on its members', or at least some members' relevant *joint intention*. In simple, e.g. egalitarian, cases this kind of account creates a group-level attitude by aggregation from member-level attitudes. Here members' having a joint intention is normally equivalent with the group's having the intention with that content. The other members – because of their membership – *ought to* accept what the operatives have accepted as the group's intention, and all this is assumed to be mutual knowledge.

(GI) Group g *intends to see to it* that X obtains (or comes about, etc., where X is an action or state) as a group if there are authorized operative members of g such that

1. these operative agents, when acting as group members in the we-mode or in the quasi we-mode sense, have the joint intention toward X (e.g., involving acceptance of the conative expression "Our intention as a group is to see to it jointly that X") and are collectively committed to bringing about X;
2. there is a mutual belief among the operative members to the effect that (1);
3. because of (1), the (full-fledged and adequately informed) non-operative members *qua* members of g tend (explicitly or implicitly) to accept with collective commitment – or at least group-normatively ought so to accept – that their group g intends to perform X (as specified in clause (1));
4. there is mutual knowledge in g to the effect that (3).

PART III

Group Agents

As we have seen, there is weak and a strong collective intentionality. Strong collective intentionality, termed the *we-mode*, concerns functioning fully as a group member and is distinguished from weak collective intentionality, called the *pro-group I-mode*, concerned with functioning as a private person, though as a member of a group.

General theses of the we-mode approach: It is argued that

1. an adequate description and explanation of social life requires the we-mode (involving we-thinking and we-acting) in addition to the I-mode (involving individualistic thinking and acting), which represents the dominant way of thinking and theorizing in the social sciences, and that
2. in several contexts the we-mode is to be preferred to the I-mode (both private and pro-group I-mode) on conceptual and philosophical grounds and often also on functional, action-related grounds (Tuomela, 2013).
3. We-mode thinking and reasoning is not reducible to I-mode reasoning, i.e. it is not definable by, or functionally construable from, I-mode notions. This is in part because it employs a different reasoning mechanism that relies on groups (collective agents) as the basic agents of reasoning.

According to the we-mode approach, to think and act in the we-mode is to think and act fully as a group member. This involves identification with the group, involving at least accepting the ethos of the group and acting according to and because of it. The we-mode approach is conceptually based on the intuitive idea that a group, not its individual members, is the primary agent. In contrast, to think and act in the I-mode is to think and act individualistically as a private person. The I-mode divides into pro-group I-mode and plain I-mode. The pro-group I-mode is concerned with promoting the group's interests (while reasoning individualistically), whereas the plain I-mode concerns promoting the interests of individuals. As *a group's action* must be based on its members' actions, *collective agency* requires that the individual agents *act as group members* by performing their parts in the satisfaction of a group-preferred alternative. In the fullest *case the members act in the we-mode.*

We-mode thinking is a group's and its members' thinking and reasoning in terms of the thick, non-distributive "togetherness" notion of "we" about attitudes, actions, and emotions attributed to a social group and its members by the members and others. Groups as social systems can function in ways resembling the functioning of individual agents, and this gives justification for the attributions in question. In democratic groups, the members give to some operative members the authority to decide and/or to act for the group.

The we-mode framework of concepts is based on *collective acceptance ("construction")* by the group members of attitudes and other group properties for their group. Here are three central framework features:

1. The members take the accepted attitudes or contents to be *group reasons* for their proper functioning as members (see Tuomela 2007, Ch.1 and 2013, Ch. 4).
2. These contents are assumed to satisfy a *collectivity condition* expressing the idea of necessarily "being in the same boat".
3. The members are *collectively committed* to what they have accepted. Commitment means binding oneself, generally with a normative bond.

Accordingly, every group member is to an extent responsible for every other member's actions *qua* group member, and the whole group is responsible for its members' actions.

We-mode versus I-mode: functional differences in the case of rational groups: In the (2010) Hakli, Miller, and Tuomela paper and in Tuomela's book (2013, Ch. 7) one of Bacharach's (1999) mathematical game-theoretic results applying team reasoning is used to show that the *(pro-group) I-mode* and the *we-mode*, probabilistically construed concerning mode adoption, in many cases do not entail the same equilibrium behaviors. The pro-group I-mode admits Pareto-suboptimal equilibria (e.g. Lo-Lo in Hi-Lo) that in many cases will not be equilibria in the we-mode case. The above result applies to common interest (Paretian) game situations with strong interdependence (such as, the Hi-Lo game and the PD). In Hi-Lo a full-blown group "framing" obviously makes the joint outcome Hi-Hi (rather than Lo-Lo) a rational group's choice.

A simple Hi-Lo game:

	Hi	Lo
Hi	3,3	0,0
Lo	0,0	1,1

This Hi-Lo game (a coordination game without effective communication) has two equilibria, HiHi and LoLo, of which HiHi dominates over LoLo. Classical game theory cannot recommend HiHi over LoLo in situations where agreement making is not allowed, but group game theory (in our present sense) can. The general result about differences between action equilibria gives an argument against individualism.

Group reasoning schema:
1. Group S wants (or has as its interest) to maximize the value of utility U.
2. We are the members of S.
3. Each of us identifies with S.
4. Each of us wants the value of U to be maximized.
5. A uniquely maximizes U.

Therefore, (i) S should choose and perform A and (ii) each of us should thus choose and perform her part of A. Here S is a group and A its relevant choice protocol.

We-mode group as a group agent: A person functions in the we-mode if she functions as a group member (as one of "us") and in the I-mode if she functions as a private person, possibly in a group context. A group is in most contexts below assumed to be a *we-mode group*. It is assumed to commit itself to a group ethos (certain constitutive goals, beliefs, standards, norms, etc.) and to relevant we-reasoning and we-acting. A we-mode group constructs itself as a group in a quasi-entifying sense and can be viewed as a (functional) group agent. Because of group membership the members of a we-mode group ought to *identify with the group* and hence act as group members.

Here the argument for employing the notion of *group agent* is that it is *explanatorily, predictively, and descriptively useful* as well as *epistemically convenient* for theorizing about the social world – especially in the case of large groups (e.g. corporations as group agents for the purposes of macroeconomics and political states for the purposes of the study of international relations). The group-level description of the social world making use of notions like that of a group agent (instead of trying to get along with micro-level notions involving individual human beings) helps a researcher to get knowledge about e.g. a large group's properties (attitudes and actions) and intergroup relationships. Having both detailed micro-level and macro-level information is more desirable. The conceptual necessity of the we-mode is in part based on the fact that we-mode thinking and reasoning is not reducible to I-mode reasoning, i.e. is not definable by, or functionally construable from I-mode notions. This is in part because it employs a different reasoning mechanism that relies on groups (collective agents) as the central agents of reasoning. In addition to this, the we-mode is needed for an adequate description and explanation of social life.

While any group that is organized for action and thus can act purposively can be viewed as a group agent, an organized group (e.g. a we-mode group) can, furthermore, be functionally taken to be a "proper" agent if it is goal-directed, and if it can be taken to reason and reflect upon its activities. Its "mental" states are extrinsically functionally construed *as group-level states* in terms of world-mind, mind-mind, and mind-world relationships. In simple cases, a group agent can be constructed on the basis of individuals' properties and relations. However, top-down construction is typical in the case of corporations and states and other group agents with normatively characterized positions. We thus can have a group-level description of collective intentions and beliefs, etc. and a member-level description of them. E.g. our group performs x, and my part is to perform x1 as my part of x.

A group agent exists as a functional social system capable of producing uniform action, not as an intentional agent with phenomenal features. It consists of its members and can only function via its members functioning appropriately. In many cases (e.g. corporations) a group agent involves some fictitious and arguably irreducible constructed elements. It cannot be fully accounted for by individualism – which on conceptual grounds cannot incorporate irreducible groups and group properties.

Theses:

a) Collective minds can exist in the extrinsic sense that mental states can be extrinsically (and functionally) attributed to group agents on the basis of their actions (and, more broadly, behavior). E.g., a group might believe that the mark is the official currency in Finland.
b) Collective minds can exist in the extrinsic sense that the group members can jointly have an attitude of a certain type (e.g. that we jointly intend to go together to the movies tonight) while the members' tokens of that attitude type are different.
c) Group agents do not have conscious phenomenal mental states, although their members of course individually do have such mental states (e.g. each of them intending that they will go together to the movies on Friday). Those member-level states yet do not together amount to an intrinsic conscious state of the group agent.

Group agent as a collectively constructed functional social action system: A group agent as an (extrinsically) intentional agent is a collectively constructed and partly "fictitious" functional entity with real features:

1. The "mental" attitudes and actions of the group agent are generally extrinsically constructed, typically by the group members (or their leaders) and attributed to it by them and are mainly their construction of those group level states. In many (but not all) cases the group agent's "mental" properties supervene on the members' joint mental states and actions. This functional construction involves world-mind, mind-mind, and mind-world connections (typically both causal and normative ones) largely in analogy with how

individual-level functionalists typically bring about the construction in the single-agent case.

2. A group agent is functional *qua* having functional states and also in that it functions in many contexts as if it were a person.
3. Features (a) and (b) involve postulating group attitudes which in some organizations, such as business corporations, serve to *explain* the individual group members' activities.
4. From the naturalistic causal point of view, a group agent is constituted by a collection of interdependent and interacting individuals and it acts as a group in virtue of its members' actions.

Group agent as an action system and agent with the power to act: Despite being a partly fictitious agent with extrinsic intentional features, a group agent can have *causally objective existence* as a social action system based on intentional member actions and *also epistemically objective existence* as an extrinsically intentional group agent. A group agent *qua* social action system may amount to a group of (individual) agents capable of joint action and control over the group's performance. A group agent can act only indirectly through its members' actions. A joint action is a causally objective event that is brought about by an epistemically objective group agent that has been collectively constructed (collectively accepted to be a group agent) by the group members. A group agent's power to act involves the capacity to act *qua* group and the capacity to interact with other groups. An (extrinsically) intentional group agent's action is mainly guided by its ethos as well as its contextual goals and beliefs (and possibly other partly fictitious, constructed attitudes and properties – e.g. liability features, its capacity to own, buy and sell property).

A group agent has *derived intentionality and lacks phenomenal properties. A functional group agent has only derived, extrinsic intentionality* and, as bodiless, it lacks the phenomenal features of normal individual agents (e.g. shared feelings or qualia are not possible phenomenal group agent states). Group agents do not have intrinsic conscious minds.

Emergence with respect to individual members' we-mode "proposals" and their I-mode properties: A functional group agent in the we-mode sense may be emergent (in a stronger sense than provided by supervenience) with respect to the group members' private, I-mode properties and also with respect to the members' we-mode proposals for what the group should do and which attitudes it should accept. The group agent may have attitudes that none of its members has in the I-mode as her purely personal attitudes – e.g. compromises are a trivial example, and there may also be other kinds of discrepancies between the group level and the member level.

Some social organizations (e.g. business corporations) can act as groups (units) partly in virtue of having a *collective decision making system* (an implicit or explicit one). Furthermore, e.g. business corporations and firms typically have a hierarchical structure that involves a normative system of division of labor and tasks.

Group agent as an economical explanatory system especially in the case of large groups: At least in the case of large groups (e.g. states and countries) a theorist's employment of the notion of functional group agent may e.g. in the case of some organizations be employed to *causal-intentionally* explain (a) its members' actions and outcomes that they produce as group members rather than as private persons and (b) intergroup cooperation and conflict (and other intergroup relationships and activities) and may do all this in a more *economical* and *epistemically tractable* way than does an individualistic theory that rather operates in terms of members' interaction and interdependence. Of course, the individual level is important as well, but here the thing to be emphasized is the group level.

Example: Some people are found spying against a state. Perhaps there is a network of spies involved. A simple explanation might be that they belong to a certain spy organization of a foreign state. Thus that state is at least partly responsible for the spying activity, and it also serves as a partial causal explanans of the spying activity. The important thing in this kind of case is that a valid explanation of the explanandum requires describing it as action *qua* member of a certain group (here the state). The spy activity can be explained at least in part by reference to a group agent and its extrinsic mental states. But the group does not directly cause the explanandum action – it does it only vicariously. The direct causation is due to the group members *qua* group members. We are dealing here with a kind of downward explanation: The group explains its members' actions *qua* members but it does it, so to speak, through its "arms and legs", i.e. through the actions of some of its members (e.g. those state officials who ordered the activity).

Attribution of "mental" states from outside the group: In addition to group members in some cases (e.g. when the group members are deluded) also group-external agents (e.g. theoreticians dealing with group agents or people from the surrounding society) may explanatorily and predictively attribute "mental" states to group agents – typically on the basis of the very actions of the group agents (cf. the "behavioristic" attribution of mental states to individuals).

Autonomous versus non-autonomous group agents: As we-mode groups can generally be viewed as present kinds of functional agents, the classificatory distinctions of Tuomela (2013, Ch. 2), concerning power and autonomy in we-mode groups apply to group agents. Especially, the distinction between *autonomous* and *non-autonomous* we-mode groups yields respectively autonomous and non-autonomous group agents.

Joint states versus group states: Consider this example. John and Jane jointly intend to paint their house together. This joint intention can be regarded as constituted by real states (perhaps their brain states) in them. Consider also the dyad, a group agent, consisting of John and Jane. This group agent is collectively constructed. John and Jane form a group roughly because they and others take them to constitute a group. The fact of their being a group is ontologically grounded by their relational state of joint intention (i.e. their we-intentions and their mutual awareness of them) and their joint action dispositions. (Note that joint intention and action as such do not conceptually require describing the participants as constituting a group agent.)

Grounding does not entail reduction in the present case. What the dyad involves in addition to the joint states and activities and their relevant dispositions is the members' (and/or perhaps some group-external others') collective construction (under their own conceptualization) of their together constituting a functional group agent. Here the ontological gap between the non-fictitious joint states and actions and the fictitious intentional attitudes and actions attributed to the group agent figuratively speaking is rather "small" in relation e.g. to the case of a corporation that is partly defined in legal terms. But the gap is still there.

Basic views summarized:

1) For the purposes of philosophical social action theory, joint actions and joint intentions can be regarded as real – although dependent on the employment of the intentional stance.
2) Social groups can be assumed to be real *qua* being full-blown existents in the causal realm (through their members' actions).
3) Social groups can have intentional properties only extrinsically on the basis of attribution to them by their members.
4) Social groups (including corporations and political states) may be able to act *(extrinsically) intentionally.*
5) Applying the intentional stance to social groups *qua* interaction and dependence systems of individuals (and in some cases subgroups) generally involves treating such social groups as group agents.
6) When viewed as extrinsically intentional group agents (and thus organized for action) social groups can be taken to act through their authorized members who are generally assumed to act *on behalf of* and *for the good of* the group members *qua* group members (but not necessarily *qua* private persons). All members are assumed to act so as to promote and "obey" the group ethos.

Note that it is ultimately the members acting as group members who have the *motivation* that acting for reasons requires. The members jointly have the causal power to bring about the group's outcomes.

7) The attribution of a *joint we-mode intention* to some group members obviously involves treating the participants as intentional agents. Joint we-mode intentions do not differ much from *intentions attributed to social groups*. Intentions ascribed to social groups are viewed as extrinsic, and joint we-mode intentions are also extrinsic. The difference lies in the level of description.

PART IV

Concluding Remarks

The we-mode versus the I-mode:

a) A group thinking and acting as one agent (*we-mode group*) contrasts with a collection of agents acting and interacting in pursuit of their (shared) private goals (*I-mode group*).
b) We-mode group reasons and I-mode reasons for acting and having attitudes are different in kind.
c) It is argued that only the we-mode can properly account for the generality, openness, and "member interchangeability" that the group level involves.
d) In the I-mode case the members function as private persons on the basis of their *private* (purely personal, I-directed) attitudes.
e) The members' "collective commitment" is different in the we-mode and I-mode cases (cf. the three differences discussed earlier).
f) Group-based reasons can contingently be involved but only as based on private acceptance → *pro-group I-mode.*

As was pointed out above, one of Bacharach's (1999) results can be applied to show that the (*pro-group*) *I-mode* and *the we-mode*, probabilistically construed concerning mode adoption, do not entail the same equilibrium behaviors. This holds also for cases (even) where the choices, utilities and the probabilities of the players acting for their own benefit instead of the group's benefit are the same: The pro-group I-mode admits Pareto-suboptimal equilibria (e.g. Lo-Lo in Hi-Lo) that in many cases will not be equilibria in the we-mode case. The above applies to Paretian game situations with strong interdependence (such as, the

Hi-Lo game). In Hi-Lo a full-blown group "framing" obviously makes joint outcome Hi-Hi (rather than Lo-Lo) a rational we-mode group's choice.

Summary: The we-mode, as contrasted with the I-mode, at least ideally involves the following features:

1. It is conceptually top down.
2. It involves group agency and we-reasoning.
3. The notions of group, group's goal, etc. are collectively constructed and fail to be reducible to individualistic notions (see Tuomela, 2007, p. 99).
4. It satisfies the collectivity condition.
5. It involves collective commitment to the group's ethos.
6. There is an authoritative group reason for group members' actions.
7. There is collective and individual order and stability, possibly with changes of members through time.
8. There is proper group responsibility and the members' presupposed right and responsibility to help and sanction.
9. The group can be trusted – and its members can trust as a group.
10. It is capable of handling large groups.

Acknowledgement: I wish to thank my wife, Dr. Maj Tuomela for excellent comments on this text.

References

Bacharach, M. 1999. "Interactive Team Reasoning: A Contribution to the Theory of Co-operation", *Research in Economics* 53, 117–147.

Hakli, R., Miller, K., and Tuomela, R. 2010. "Two Kinds of We-Reasoning." *Economics and Philosophy* 26, 291–320.

Tuomela, R. 2007. *The Philosophy of Sociality: The Shared Point of View*, New York: Oxford University Press (paperback ed. 2010).

Tuomela, R. 2013. *Social Ontology: Collective Intentionality and Group Agents*, New York: Oxford University Press (slightly improved paperback edition 2016).

Julie Zahle

The Level Conception of the Methodological Individualism-Holism Debate

In this paper, I argue against the common view that the classic methodological individualism-holism debate in general may be conceived of in levels terms, that is, as a dispute about whether to offer only individual-level explanations in the social sciences, or both individual- and social-level explanations.

I begin by offering a brief introduction to the debate. Next, I point to two conditions that must be met in order to phrase the dispute in level terms and I present the two standard defenses of the level conception. On that basis, I go on to show that the level conception fails to encompass widely endorsed individualist positions. For this reason, I maintain, it is inadequate, and hence should be rejected, as a characterization of the general methodological individualism-holism debate. Subsequently, I discuss three objections to this finding and then conclude.[1]

1 The Classic Methodological Individualism-Holism Debate

The methodological individualism-holism debate is a dispute about the proper focus of explanations in the social sciences. In this paper, I am concerned with the classic version of this debate. Accordingly, methodological individualism is the view that *only* individualist explanations (explanantia) should be offered. These explanations solely describe individuals, their actions, beliefs, desires, etc. In contrast, (moderate) methodological holism is the position that *both* individualist *and* holist explanations (explanantia) should be advanced: sometimes it is in order to offer individualist explanations, other times holist explanations. The latter are explanations that solely describe social phenomena like social entities (e.g. universities), social processes (e.g. revolutions), statistical properties of groups (e.g. the unemployment rate), and mental properties ascribed to social entities (e.g. the university's desire to enroll more students).

---

1 This paper extensively draws on, as well as expands on, Zahle (2019).

https://doi.org/10.1515/9783110663617-003

2 The Level Conception of the Methodological Individualism-Holism Debate

When the classic methodological individualism-holism debate is conceived of in level terms, it is taken to revolve around the question of whether to use individual-level explanations only (the methodological individualist stand) or whether to employ both individual-level and social-level explanations (the standpoint of methodological holists). This way of phrasing the debate typically rests on the view that the following two conditions may be met:

1. The ontological level condition: individuals, individualistic properties, or the like, are lower individual-level phenomena and social entities, social properties, or the like, are higher social-level phenomena.
2. The explanatory level condition: individualist explanations qualify as lower individual-level explanations because they only describe individual-level phenomena (they don't describe phenomena at other levels); and holist explanations qualify as higher social-level explanations since they only describe social-level phenomena (they don't describe phenomena at other levels).[2]

The two standard defenses of the level conception maintain that both these conditions may be fulfilled. I now examine each in turn.

3 The Supervenience-Based and the Emergence-Based Level Conception

The two standard ways in which to underwrite the level conception appeal to supervenience and emergence respectively. The supervenience-based level conception began to appear in the 1980s. It is particularly popular among philosophers. The emergence-based level conception goes back to the mid-1970s while being currently associated with the influential social scientific school of critical realism and its followers.[3]

---

2 It may be noted that the conditions are in line with standard discussions of ontological and explanatory levels in science more generally. See, e.g., Craver 2007, Kim 2002, and Oppenheim and Putnam 1958.

3 Important proponents of the supervenience-based level conception include Jackson and Pettit 1992, Kincaid 1995, 1996, and Sawyer 2002, 2003. Important proponents of the emergence-based

Supervenience accounts begin by drawing a distinction between individualistic properties and social properties. Individualistic properties are often identified with individuals' bodily movements and mental states or, more broadly, with individuals' properties that do not presuppose the existence of social entities or processes. Social properties are taken to comprise both the properties of social entities and processes, and individuals' social role properties as exemplified by being a nurse, being a politician, voting and firing. Supervenience accounts continue by maintaining that social properties supervene exclusively on individualistic ones. Roughly, this means that there can be no change at the level of social properties unless there is also a change at the level of individualistic properties. Moreover, these accounts contend, because of the relation of supervenience, social properties should be viewed as higher social-level phenomena relative to individualistic properties that are lower individual-level phenomena. Hereby, the ontological level condition is met.

On this basis, supervenience accounts make it clear that individualist explanations solely describe individuals with their individualistic properties. Consequently, since individualistic properties are individual-level phenomena, these explanations qualify as individual-level explanations. Similarly, holist explanations only describe the social properties of social entities, processes, and individuals. Because social properties are social-level phenomena, holist explanations qualify as social-level explanations. In this manner, the explanatory level condition is met too. Thus, the classic methodological individualism-holism debate is apt to be phrased in level terms: it turns on whether to use individual-level explanations only (the methodological individualist view) or whether to employ both individual- and social-level explanations (the methodological holist position).

Emergence accounts vary as to how they spell out the notion of emergence.[4] For this reason, I focus on David Elder-Vass' account as it is particularly clear (Elder-Vass 2007, 2010). The account also draws a distinction between individualistic and social properties. Individualistic properties are the properties that individuals have in isolation or as part of an unstructured collection of individuals.

level conception include Archer 1995, Bhaskar 1978[1975], 1998[1979], and Elder-Vass 2007, 2010.

4 Despite their differences, emergence accounts rely on a similar conception of what constitutes individual- social- and other-level phenomena and this places their accounts within the scope of the criticism that I raise below. Also, note that critical realists use the notions of methodological individualism and holism differently than I do here. I am describing their positions using *my* understanding of these notions.

Social properties come in two varieties. Resultant social properties are the properties that social entities have in virtue of the aggregation (simple addition) of individuals' individualistic properties. Emergent social properties are ones which social entities have in virtue of individuals (with their individualistic properties) standing, at that moment, in certain relations to each other. Some emergent social properties are possessed by social entities *qua* wholes whereas others, like social role properties, are exercised by individuals. Unlike resultant social properties, emergent social properties are not possessed by their parts, viz., individuals, in isolation or as parts of an unstructured whole. The account goes on to maintain that because social properties are either resultant or emergent relative to individuals with their individualistic properties, social properties should be viewed as higher social-level phenomena and individualistic properties as lower individual-level phenomena. In particular, the account emphasizes this point in relation to emergent social properties as these, alone, are novel properties compared to those found at the individual level. For this reason, I refer to the account as an emergence account. In any case, it meets the ontological level condition.

Similar to supervenience accounts, Elder-Vass' account links these considerations to questions of explanation. More precisely, the account makes it plain that individualist explanations only describe individuals with their individualistic properties. Since individualistic properties are lower individual-level phenomena, individualist explanations qualify as lower individual-level explanations. In the same vein, holist explanations solely describe social entities with their social properties.[5] Therefore, as social properties are social-level phenomena, holist explanations qualify as social-level explanations. Thus, the explanatory level condition is satisfied too and, as a result, the methodological individualism-holism debate is apt to be conceived of in level terms.

4 A Rejection of the Supervenience- and Emergence-Based Level Conception

The level conception of the general methodological individualism-holism debate may be rejected by showing either that the ontological or explanatory level condition cannot be satisfied. For the purposes of this paper, I grant that the

5 Since social role properties are emergent properties of social entities (though exercised by individuals), explanations that describe individuals with their social role properties should be regarded as holist explanations too.

supervenience and emergence accounts each fulfill the ontological level condition: they are right to hold that individualistic properties are lower individual-level phenomena and that social properties are higher social-level phenomena. Thus, I focus exclusively on establishing that the accounts are wrong to hold that the explanatory level condition is satisfied. To this end, recall the rough characterization of individualist explanations as explanations that only describe individuals, their actions, beliefs, desires, etc. In what follows, I point to three different ways in which methodological individualists have elaborated on this specification by defending inclusive notions of individualist explanations. Moreover, I argue that these inclusive individualist explanations fail to qualify as individual-level explanations.

Since the 1950s at least, methodological individualists have mostly adopted the view that individualist explanations are allowed to describe individuals' social roles and role actions. For instance, Watkins – a key protagonist of methodological individualism in the 1950s – offers such explanations (see, e.g., his 1952 and 1957). And, in his classic 1968 paper, Lukes observes that these explanations are widespread among methodological individualists (Lukes 1968). Keeping these points in mind, consider that supervenience and emergence accounts both regard social role properties as higher social-level phenomena. Hence, inclusive individualist explanations that mention individuals' social role properties do not describe individual-level phenomena only and, for this reason, they do not qualify as individual-level explanations.

Moreover, going much further back than the 1950s, many methodological individualists have taken it that individualist explanations are permitted to describe material factors that, as part of individuals' context of action, constrain or facilitate their actions (Agassi 1960). For example, in some of his writings, Watkins is representative of this trend too (see Watkins 1957:106). Now, the supervenience and emergence accounts typically take it that below the social and individual levels, there are further levels including a biological, a chemical, and a physical one. It is reasonable to think that the accounts view material factors (physical resources, the material environment, etc.) as belonging to one or several of these additional levels. In consequence, inclusive individualist explanations that describe material context factors refer to phenomena at a different level than the individual one. Therefore, they do not qualify as individual-level explanations.

Finally, around the 1940's, the position of institutional individualism made its first appearance. According to it, individualist explanations may not only describe material context factors, but also institutions that, as part of individuals' context of action, constrain or facilitate their actions. By institutions, institutional individualists mean, among other things, social entities like schools and states. Moreover, they think that explanations may describe these using terms like "school" and "state." Popper's writings from the 1940s and onwards contain the first explicit, though highly sketchy, formulation of institutional individualism (see Hedström et al. 1998 on Popper's position). Since then the position has become widespread as also testified by Udehn's remark that institutional individualism is the dominating individualist position in political science and institutional economics (Udehn 2001:348). Returning once more to the supervenience and emergence accounts, they take institutions, like schools and states, to be social-level phenomena. This means that inclusive individualist explanations, which describe institutional context factors, fail to mention individual-level phenomena only. By implication, the explanations fail to qualify as individual-level explanations.

These reflections bring out that, at least since the 1950s, most methodological individualists have endorsed one or several of the inclusive notions of individualist explanations. These notions license individualist explanations that do not qualify as individual-level explanations and for this reason supervenience and emergence accounts are wrong to maintain that individualist explanations, *in general*, qualify as individual-level explanations. Due to the existence of the inclusive notions of individualist explanations, the explanatory level condition is not satisfied. Accordingly, the level conception of the general debate between methodological individualists and holists should be rejected: it is inadequate because it fails, to repeat, to encompass widespread inclusive individualist positions (that endorse one or several of the inclusive notions of individualist explanations). Against this background, it is no surprise that the supervenience- and emergence-based level-conception has first and foremost been advocated by methodological holists.

5 Objections to the Rejection of the Level Conception

One way in which to dispute the dismissal of the level conception is by arguing that the inclusive individualist positions should *not* be counted as part of the general debate: participants in the methodological individualism-holism debate are not allowed to rely on inclusive notions of individualist explanations. Obviously, if that were the case, the inclusive individualist positions would no longer constitute an obstacle to conceiving of the general debate in level terms.

A number of different arguments along these lines have been offered (see, e.g., Hodgson 2007, Lukes 1968, Elder-Vass 2010, Kincaid 1995, Udehn 2001).

I have elsewhere discussed these objections one by one and shown that inclusive methodological individualists may convincingly respond to them (see Zahle 2003, 2014, 2019). Here, I adopt a different approach by pointing to considerations, which show that the very idea to dispel inclusive individualist positions from the general methodological individualism-holism debate is a bad one.

To this end, recall that, since the 1950s at least, methodological individualists have mainly relied on inclusive individualist explanations. Accordingly, while some methodological individualists may in the past have endorsed narrow notions of individualist explanations, that is, notions such that individualist explanations qualify as individual-level explanations, few, if any, current methodological individualists do so.[6] This being the case, imagine that inclusive individualist positions are excluded from the debate. In that case, the debate would be turned into a rather outdated dispute: there would no longer be any, or only very few, active participants in the debate who would want to defend the methodological individualist side to it since this would mean the advocacy of narrow individualist positions (i.e. ones endorsing narrow notions of individualist explanations).

Moreover, and independently of their engagement in the dispute, social scientists may perhaps in the past have implemented narrow methodological individualism, that is, proceeded by offering narrow individualist explanations only. Today, though, few, if any, social scientists do so. In contrast, many offer inclusive individualist explanations. For instance, as Jarvie observes, social scientists constantly refer, in their explanations, to institutions as part of individuals' context of action (Jarvie 1998:374). Consequently, insofar as inclusive individualist positions were dismissed from the methodological individualism-holism debate, the debate would no longer have much, if any, bearing on social scientific practice: the dispute would become largely irrelevant from the perspective of social scientists who are engaged in offering social scientific explanations. In view of these considerations, proponents of the level conception are better off not to pursue the strategy of arguing that inclusive individualist positions should not be counted as part of the general methodological individualism-holism dispute.

Another way in which to challenge the rejection of the level conception might be to contend that instead of the conception being supervenience- or emergence-

6 Thus, methodological holists are presently the main proponents of narrow notions of individualist explanations and, as shown in the foregoing, they often do so as part of their endorsement of the supervenience- or emergence-based level conception.

based, it should be underwritten by an alternative ontological account that meets the ontological level condition. Relative to this alternative account, it might be argued, the explanatory level condition may be satisfied.

In this spirit, note that the individual and social level are sometimes referred to as the micro and macro level respectively. This makes it natural to venture that the alternative ontological account should be scale-based.[7] A proponent of this view might say the following: Individuals are within a smaller size range than social entities and processes and, this being the case, individuals should be viewed as lower individual-level phenomena relative to social entities and processes that are higher social-level phenomena. Further, since individualist explanations solely describe individual-level phenomena (viz., individuals), individualist explanations qualify as individual-level explanations. Similarly, as holist explanations only describe social-level phenomena (viz., social entities and processes), they qualify as higher social-level explanations. In this manner, both the ontological and explanatory level conditions are met; the methodological individualism-holism debate is apt to be conceived of in level terms.

However, the scale-based account only fares slightly better than the supervenience- and emergence-based level conception. More precisely, inclusive individualist explanations that describe individuals' social role properties no longer pose a problem. Since it is individuals (and so individual-level phenomena) who have social roles and perform social role actions, individualist explanations that describe individuals' role properties seem to qualify as individual-level explanations. In contrast, inclusive individualist explanations that describe material factors or institutions as part of individuals' context of action still cause trouble. Material factors are not necessarily individual-level phenomena since they may be within a different size range than individuals. To see this, just think of an ant and a forest both of which may be part of an individual's context of action. In a similar vein, institutions, such as schools and states, are social entities and hence they are, by the lights of the scale-based account, social-level phenomena. It follows that inclusive individualist explanations, which describe material factors not within the same size range as individuals and/or social institutions, fail to qualify as individual-level explanations. And this, in turn, means, that due to these inclusive notions of individualist explanations, the scale-based level conception fails to satisfy the explanatory level condition: individualist explanations in general do not qualify as individual-level explanations. The scale-based level conception should be rejected too.

7 For a presentation of scale-based levels more generally, see Craver 2007:180ff.

In fact, any alternative ontological level account will run into trouble. To see why, assume first that an alternative ontological level account *does not maintain* that social role properties, material factors, and institutions are all individual-level phenomena. If so, at least one of the inclusive notions allows individualist explanations to describe phenomena that are not individual-level ones and, as a result, these explanations do not qualify as individual-level explanations. Alternatively, suppose that an alternative ontological level account *holds* that social role properties, material factors, and institutions are all individual-level phenomena. In this case, all inclusive individualist explanations do indeed qualify as individual-level explanations. However, standard holist explanations that only describe institutions create a problem instead: they fail to qualify as higher social-level explanations (as institutions are individual-level phenomena on this view). Thus, either way the explanatory level condition is not satisfied. Therefore, the level conception may not be salvaged by opting for an alternative account that meets the ontological level condition.

One final way to respond to the rejection of the level conception might be to point out that this conception need not assume that the ontological and explanatory level conditions are fulfilled. The conception may equally be underwritten by alternative conditions that revolve around descriptive, rather than ontological, levels. Relative to these alternative conditions, it might be claimed, the inclusive notions of individualist explanations do not pose a problem.

This line of approach may be illustrated by the suggestion that because descriptions of individuals, individualistic properties, or the like, are more fine-grained than descriptions of social entities, social properties, and the like, the former are lower individual-level descriptions and the latter higher social-level descriptions. Further, it might be carried on, individualist explanations qualify as lower individual-level explanations because they contain (fine-grained) individual-level descriptions only (they don't contain descriptions belonging to any other levels) just as holist explanations qualify as higher social-level explanations because they solely contain (coarse-grained) social-level descriptions (they don't contain descriptions belonging to any other levels). In this fashion, the methodological individualism-holism debate turns on whether to use individual-level explanations only (the position of methodological individualists) or whether to employ both individual-level and social-level explanations (the stand of methodological holists).

For the present purposes, there is no need to spell out the notion of more or less fine-grained descriptions or go into other ways in which to cash out the idea of basic descriptive levels. In any case, the approach runs into difficulties similar to those detected above. On the one hand, such an account may hold that descriptions of social roles, material factors, and institutions are not all social-level descriptions. As a result, at least some inclusive individualist explanations contain descriptions that are not individual-level ones. These explanations do not qualify as lower individual-level explanations. On the other hand, if the account categorizes all descriptions of social roles, material factors and institutions as individual-level descriptions, this difficulty is solved: all inclusive individualist explanations qualify as individual-level explanations. However, standard holist explanations that contain terms like "government" and "school" (and no descriptions at other levels) then fail to qualify as higher social-level explanations (since "government" etc. are individual-level descriptions). Either way, therefore, individualist and holist explanations, in general, fail both to qualify as lower individual-level and higher social-level explanations respectively. Accordingly, this approach must be found wanting too.

6 Conclusion

In this paper, I have argued that the level conception of the classic methodological individualism-holism debate should be rejected: the conception is inadequate as a characterization of the general debate because it fails to encompass widespread inclusive individualist positions. Thus, the general debate should *not* be conceived of as a dispute about whether to use individual-level explanations only, or whether to employ both individual-level and social-level explanations. Rather, it should be conceived of in traditional terms, namely as a discussion about whether solely to use individualist explanations, or whether to employ both individualist and holist explanations. In this way, individualist positions that subscribe to inclusive notions of individualist positions are also recognized as partakers in the debate.

By way of ending, it is worth stressing that it has only been shown that the level conception is inadequate as a characterization of the *general* debate. This is compatible with the contention that the level conception is adequate in relation to *some versions of* the classic debate, namely versions in which methodological individualists and holists endorse a narrow notion of individualist explanations. However, as noted above, few, if any, current proponents of methodological individualism subscribe to these narrow notions just as few social scientists today proceed by offering narrow individualist explanations. This does not only make it a bad idea to contend that inclusive individualist positions should not be viewed as participants in the general debate. Also, it raises the question as to why we should take an interest in those versions of the classic debate that are aptly conceived of in level terms.

References

Agassi, J. (1960). "Methodological Individualism," *British Journal of Sociology* 11:244–270.

Archer, M. (1995). *Realist Social Theory: The Morphogenetic Approach*. Cambridge: Cambridge University Press.

Bhaskar, R. 1978[1975]. *A Realist theory of Science*. Brighton: Harvester Press.

Bhaskar, R. 1998[1979]. *The Possibility of Naturalism. A Philosophical Critique of the Contemporary Human Sciences*. London: Routledge.

Craver, C.F. (2007). *Explaining the Brain*. Oxford: Oxford University Press.

Elder-Vass, D. (2007). "For Emergence: Refining Archer's Account of Social Structure," *Journal for the Theory of Social Behaviour* 37(1): 25–44.

Elder-Vass, D. (2010). *The Causal Power of Social Structures. Emergence, Structure and Agency*. Cambridge: Cambridge University Press.

Hedström, P., Swedberg, R., Udehn, R. (1998). "Popper's Situational Analysis and Contemporary Sociology," *Philosophy of the Social Sciences*, 28(3): 339–364.

Hodgson, G.M. (2007). "Meanings of Methodological Individualism," *Journal of Economic Methodology*, 14(2): 211–226.

Jackson, F. & Pettit, P. (1992). "In Defense of Explanatory Ecumenism," *Economics and Philosophy* 8:1–21.

Jarvie, I.C. (1998). "Situational Logic and Its Reception," *Philosophy of the Social Sciences*, 28(3): (365–380).

Kim, J. (2002). "The Layered Model: Metaphysical Considerations," *Philosophical Explorations* 5(1): 2–20.

Kincaid, H. (1995). "Reduction, Explanation and Individualism" in *Readings in the Philosophy of the Social Sciences*, Michael Martin and Lee C. McIntyre (Eds.). Cambridge MA: The MIT Press, pp. 497–513.

Kincaid, H. (1996). *Philosophical Foundations of the Social Sciences. Analyzing Controversies in the Social World*. Cambridge: Cambridge University Press.

Lukes, S. (1968). "Methodological Individualism Reconsidered," *The British Journal of Sociology*, 19(2):119–129.

Oppenheim, P. and Putnam, H. (1958). "Unity of Science as a Working Hypothesis" in *Concepts, Theories, and the Mind-Body Problem, Minnesota Studies in the Philosophy of Science II*, Herbert Feigl, Michael Scriven, and Grover Maxwell (eds.). Minneapolis: University of Minnesota Press, pp. 3–36.

Sawyer, R.K. (2002). "Nonreductive Individualism: Part I – Supervenience and Wild Disjunction," *Philosophy of the Social Sciences*, 32(4):537–559.

Sawyer, R.K. (2003). "Nonreductive Individualism: Part II – Social Causation," *Philosophy of the Social Sciences*, 33(2): 203–224.

Udehn, L. (2001). *Methodological Individualism. Background, History, and Meaning*. London: Routledge.

Watkins, J.W.N. (1952). “Ideal Types and Historical Explanation,” *The British Journal for the Philosophy of Science*, 3(9): 22–43.

Watkins, J.W.N. (1957). “Historical Explanation in the Social Sciences,” *The British Journal for the Philosophy of Science*, 8(30): 104–117.

Zahle, J. (2003) “The Individualism/Holism Debate on Intertheoretic Reduction and the Argument from Multiple Realization,” *Philosophy of the Social Sciences*, 33(1), pp. 77–100.

Zahle, J. (2014). “Holism, Emergence and The Crucial Distinction” in *Rethinking the Individualism-Holism Debate. Essays in the Philosophy of Social Science*, Julie Zahle & Finn Collin (eds.). Dordrecht: Synthese Library, Springer, pp. 177–196.

Zahle, J. (2019 – online first). “Limits to Levels in the Methodological Individualism-Holism Debate,” *Synthese*.

Miguel Garcia-Godinez
What Are Institutional Groups?

1 Introduction

We are all members of some institutional group or another, and we may all be members of different institutional groups at the same time (e.g., someone can be a faculty member, the goalie of a football team and a UK citizen simultaneously). Since being a member of an institutional group involves occupying a certain role assigned with certain normative attributes (viz., rights, duties, powers and responsibilities), our institutional membership shapes to an important extent the way we interact with each other in our everyday life.

Crucially, though, institutional groups cannot exist independently of our social interaction. On the contrary, they exist as particular forms of social organisation. In this paper I present an ontological analysis of institutional groups that elaborates on this idea and shows how, when so organised, we can create more complex and sophisticated social entities, e.g., institutions.

In the following sections, I introduce and argue for three main theses. In **§2** I claim that an institutional group is a realisation of a formal group structure. In arguing for this thesis, I improve on Ritchie's ontological structuralism. In **§3** I hold that institutional groups can perform intentional actions. This thesis results from an ontological analysis of institutional and proxy agency akin to Ludwig's theory of collective action. In **§4** I distinguish between institutions and institutional groups and state that the former are institutional practices. I take up this issue here, firstly, because I consider misleading some of the characterisations of institutions that prominent social ontologists have recently offered (e.g., Searle, Guala and Ludwig), and, secondly, because I think it is important to clarify the way institutional groups create institutions. By following Tuomela, I argue that institutions consist in institutional activities conducive to the realisation (or "satisfaction") of institutional activity types. Since this realisation is carried out by institutional groups, our having an answer to *what are institutional groups?* is a necessary step towards a better understanding of what institutions are and how we create them.

2 Institutional Groups

I introduce in this section a structuralist account of institutional groups. I do so by discussing Ritchie's ontological structuralism about social groups, as developed

https://doi.org/10.1515/9783110663617-004

in her (2015), (2018a) and (2018b). Although she does not consider institutional groups *per se*, she does discuss organised social groups, which I take to be the genus to which institutional groups belong. The thesis I argue for here is

Th 1 An institutional group is a realisation (or an instantiation) of a formal group structure

This thesis improves on Ritchie's structuralist account of organised social groups as it introduces a further distinction, viz., between formal and informal group structures. This distinction, I show, represents the structural difference between institutional groups and other kinds of organised social groups. Her account, I argue, does not recognise this difference.

Despite improving Ritchie's account, I am not committed to her view, nor is my goal to defend her project. Although I take it to be worth pursuing (in spite of the objections it has been already subject to, e.g., Epstein 2019, 4901–4904), a further supportive argument will not be given. My contention will be, instead, that her structuralist account is a good starting point for a more detailed ontological analysis of organised social groups.

In any case, my **Th1** results from a much narrower ontological investigation. One that also aims to further our understanding of institutional agency, i.e., the capacity of institutional groups to act intentionally. If **Th1** is true, then this structuralist position will provide us the ontological background against which we can explain how institutional groups can create certain, complex social entities, particularly institutions.

2.1 Organised Social Groups

In contemporary social ontology, almost everything is related to groups. Though not just any kind of groups (e.g., a group of chairs or a group of particles arranged tablewise), but a group of people organised in such a way that they can do something together (*as a group*). The notion of group that interests social ontologists, to put it otherwise, is that associated to group agency. This notion, then, is different from that of a mere plurality of individual agents. A plurality does not act as a group (i.e., it does not perform group actions). A plurality is identical to its members, whereas a group is not. A group can survive a change in its membership, while a plurality cannot.

Yet, the fact that groups (and group agency) are not so easily reducible to individuals (and individual agency), does not lead us immediately to accept that they exist over and above their individual members. The literature on this topic ranges over different ontological positions, viz., from those who deny the existence of groups (e.g., Quinton 1975) to those who attribute them with a mind of their own and are, thereby, able to have all sorts of mental attitudes, such as beliefs, desires and intentions (e.g., List and Pettit 2011).

In this paper I do not address all of these positions. I simply show, following Ritchie, that groups are not (nor reducible to) their individual members. With this, however, I do not mean to support the extreme alternative, viz., that groups are minded entities. To begin with, let me state clearly what pluralities are. A plurality is a mereological sum of individual agents. For example, Mario and Luigi compose the plurality Mario&Luigi, of which they are all and the only essential members. If either of them leaves this plurality, then it no longer exists. If either of them is replaced by someone else, then it no longer exists (though another plurality comes about). Moreover, two pluralities composed of exactly the same individuals are necessarily one and the same plurality, whereas two groups with exactly the same members are not necessarily the same group (Ritchie 2018a, 23–24).

Of course, that Mario&Luigi is a plurality does not mean that it cannot perform certain actions. Indeed, as Ludwig has shown, it can perform plural actions (Ludwig 2016). For example, the plural action sentence "Mario and Luigi carry a table together" seems to attribute to both of them, collectively, an action.[1] What happens in this case is that Mario and Luigi each make a direct contribution to the realisation (or the obtaining) of an action. (Notice here, though, that I am not saying anything as to whether this action is performed intentionally or not). What makes true this plural action sentence, in any case, is that the action (i.e., the event) is performed (i.e., brought about) by both of them acting in a certain way so that the result of their acting is (or amounts to) their carrying the table together (see Ludwig 2016, 138–144).

Yet, there is nothing special about this. Any plurality can be attributed with a plural action in this very simple way. For instance, my writing this paper and your reading it (however distant in time) can be described as a plural action, say, "our discussing about institutional groups" (with 'our' involving the plurality composed by you&me). Any plural action, thus, is exhaustively reducible to (or analysable in terms of) mereological sums of actions performed by a plurality.

---

1 On the difference between the distributive and collective reading of plural action sentences, see (Ludwig 2016, Ch 9).

When a plurality acts intentionally, though, things get more complicated. Let me return to this point later (see **§3** below). For now, the only point I want to emphasise is that groups are not pluralities. There seems to be something distinctive about the former that makes us think of them as having additional properties – beyond that of just being arbitrary collections of people, as Ritchie puts it (2018b, 2). In this respect, I take her ontological analysis of social groups to help us identify what that is. In a nutshell, that the group consists in a collection of people who satisfy (or are taken to satisfy) either a certain socially constructed feature (e.g., being black or being lesbian) or the requirements for occupying a role in a socially created group structure (e.g., the role of goalie or sweeper in a football team).[2]

Ritchie calls the first "feature social groups"; and the second "organised social groups" (2018b, 9–19). Women, black men and LGBTs are paradigmatic examples of the former; a group of friends, the UK Supreme Court justices and the French women's National Football Team, on the other hand, are of the latter. Although this distinction has been challenged on different grounds (e.g., Epstein 2019, 4901–4904), I take it here at face value. It is not my business, in other words, to test it against any objections. What I want to do, instead, is to focus on the second kind of social groups that she recognises, viz., organised social groups, and show that, after introducing a further distinction, we can use it to account for the ontology of institutional groups. To do so, I need first to present her view.

According to Ritchie, an organised social group is a structured whole, i.e., a realisation of a social structure (2018b, 9–10). With this, however, she does not mean that organised social groups are identical to their social structure. A social structure is a *type* of social organisation, whereas the organised social group is a *token* of it. What makes the latter exist (at a certain time at a certain possible world) is that some individuals instantiate (at that time at that possible world) the social structure. I clarify what 'instantiation' means below. In any case, the idea of the group being a realisation (or instantiation) of a group structure prevents us from taking groups to be fictional entities (i.e., uninstantiated types of groups) (Ritchie 2018a, 27).

Now, since this kind of groups have certain social structures, they are not identical to the individuals who instantiate them either (i.e., unlike pluralities, organised social groups are not identical to their members). For example, a certain collection of individuals standing at a certain distance from each other

2 On the difference between *socially constructed* features and *socially created* group structures, see (Ritchie 2018a).

does not instantiate a group structure (unless, of course, this organisation, i.e., their being standing at that distance from each other, is socially created, e.g., because they are playing a game which requires them to be standing at that distance from each other). If they only happen to be so standing (e.g., because they are waiting for a train to come), their 'organisation' is only causally produced (perhaps as a result of intentional actions). Yet, there is no type of social organisation here that this collection of individuals instantiates by their standing at that distance from each other.

"On [Ritchie's] view both members and structure are relevant to a group's synchronic and diachronic identity conditions" (2018b, 8). Although this is the expected result, the fact that organised social groups are not identical to either their members or their structures, taken individually, explains why group agency is a complex social phenomenon. Firstly, because group agency (or the capacity of groups to act) is not simply analysable in terms of group structure: Types of groups do not act, but only tokens of them do. And secondly, because group actions are not reducible to individual actions: Although groups act through their members, since groups are not identical to them, something special about the latter's actions makes them constitute group actions. When discussing institutional agency in **§3**, I shall address this puzzle directly.

To understand Ritchie's structuralism, then, it is crucial to have a clear idea of what social structures are and what role they play. For Ritchie, "a social structure is a structure that is constitutively dependent on social factors" (2018b, 6) and that captures the "functional organization" of the group (2018b, 10). Let me unpack this.

A social structure consists in certain roles (or positions) and the relations between them. Those roles are defined in terms of relations to other roles and the conditions (or requirements) for role occupancy (Ritchie 2018b, 4). For example, a faculty member is someone who occupies a role, e.g., a lecturer, in a group structure. To occupy this role, it is expected that the person satisfies certain conditions, e.g., to have relevant qualifications for teaching and pursuing independent research.

The relations that hold between roles, on the other hand, can be characterised as deontic powers, viz., rights, duties, powers and responsibilities, that one carries as role-occupant (Searle 2010, 9). These powers determine normatively the types of actions that group members *qua* group members may, may not, ought to and ought not to perform. For example, the relation between a lecturer and the Dean of the faculty is a normative relation which specifies, amongst others, the power of the latter to require from the former an academic report, and the obligation of this to comply with the requirement. By specifying the deontic powers associated to a role, we can determine what kind of normative relation holds between this and other roles, e.g., if it is symmetric or asymmetric (Ritchie 2018b, 4).

That social structures consist in roles and relations, however, is not enough to individuate them, i.e., to distinguish them from other kinds of structures. Two other aspects are important. Firstly, they must relate social entities (particularly individuals, but it can also be other groups); and, secondly, they must be not only causally, but constitutively dependent on social factors, e.g., beliefs, desires, intentions, habits, practices, etc. (Ritchie 2018b, 6).

Ritchie characterises *constitutive dependence* in terms of a disjunctive view:

A structure S constitutively depends on social factors just in case:
(i) in defining what it is to be S reference must be made to some social factors or
(ii) social factors are metaphysically necessary for S to exist or
(iii) social factors ground the existence of S (or the fact that S exists). (idem)

By the obtaining of any of these disjuncts, we have that the structure (i.e., the type of organisation which consists in certain roles and relations) is a social creation. Thus, to the question *what brings into existence a social structure?*, Ritchie would answer that (partly at least) its being constitutively dependent on beliefs, intentions, habits, practices, and the like.

This disjunctive view of constitutive dependence is meant to make room for all the different forms in which a structure can be socially created, where this does not just mean socially causally produced. The structure of a football team is socially created in this sense, whereas the structure of a plurality of individuals who find themselves standing at a train station is not (notwithstanding this may be the result of a series of actions – perhaps intentional – that cause them all to be there).

With this, we have that a social structure is a type of social organisation that relates social entities and that is constitutively dependent on (as opposed to simply causally produced by) social factors. Now, if we have a social structure (i.e., a type), then we can have an organised social group (i.e., a token). As already mentioned, this happens when the social structure is instantiated (i.e., when the roles are occupied at a certain time at a certain possible world). Yet, instantiating a social structure is not something that individuals do on their own. This is rather a collective action (in some cases, it is also an intentional collective action). For example, if Hegel, Marx and Engels instantiate (possibly intentionally) a social structure (e.g., the social structure of a football team), then this instantiation is something that Hegel, Marx and Engels do together (i.e., collectively). It is not that Hegel instantiates the social structure, or that Marx instantiates the social structure, etc. They collectively instantiate the social structure by each occupying the corresponding roles. Their instantiating this structure is, in other words, a plural, rather than an individual action.

Nevertheless, although it is a plurality which instantiates a social structure (at a certain time at a certain possible world), this again does not mean that the organised social group is identical (or even reducible) to this plurality. This is so, because it is always possible for a different plurality (e.g., Hegel, Marx and Adorno) to instantiate the group structure, without this implying any change in the group. What is more, even if Hegel, Marx and Engels were the very same members of two groups (e.g., the football team and the chess club), since these groups have different structures, this would not make these groups one and the same group.

Although quite schematic, all this should give us an idea of what Ritchie's structuralist account of organised social groups is. Her account, I believe, is very promising and can help us understand better the ontology of structured groups. Nonetheless, it is not yet fine-grained enough to accommodate a further distinction between organised social groups. Particularly, her account (as it is) does not explain the nature of institutional groups (as distinct from other organised social groups). The reason she falls short of noticing this may be that her main purpose is to distinguish between feature and organised social groups, but not to go any further as to find that different kinds of groups may fall within each of those general categories.

Be that as it may, what I think is missing from her account is a distinction between *formal* and *informal* group structures (i.e., a distinction between two forms of social organisation). Once properly distinguished, we can explain the structural difference between institutional and other organised social groups. I presently discuss this.

2.2 The Formal Structure of Institutional Groups

In this subsection I give some reasons to support **Th1** (i.e., that institutional groups are realisations of formal group structures). To begin with, let me introduce a distinction between two kinds of organised social groups, viz., social and institutional groups. The former, e.g., an ordinary group of friends, a mob, or a group of street musicians, are groups organised according to a certain informal group structure. By this, I mean two things. That the group structure is informally (as opposed to formally) created and that it is informally (as opposed to formally) instantiated. Let me explain.

An ordinary group of friends, for instance, has a certain group structure (i.e., roles and relations) upon which its members can perform certain group actions. This structure, however, is informally created: It is based (or constitutively dependent) on common beliefs about what it is to be someone's friend. Importantly, though, no official creation is required here, i.e., no authoritative act specifying the conditions for being someone's friend must be priorly performed. Additionally, when some individuals instantiate this structure, they do not do it by making explicit through any formal process of recognition their collective attitudes of acceptance towards occupying the corresponding roles (e.g., by signing a contract or paying a registration fee)[3]; rather, they do it simply by taking each other as friends (e.g., by caring and carrying some other good feelings towards each other).

Yet, this group, despite its informal structure, is not a plurality. That is, it is not identical to its members. Let us suppose that the group has four members (at a certain time at a certain possible world), viz., John, Paul, George and Ringo. Since the group structure imposes requirements for role occupancy, viz., the conditions for being someone's friend, it is always possible for the group of friends to have more members at a different time, e.g., Yoko, or to lose some of the current members, e.g., John, depending on whether Yoko is taken to be another friend or John is dismissed, respectively. In any case, though, it would be a mistake to think of any of these changes as implying a group change. Occupying a role, however informal, is something that can happen at some point, but that can also no longer happen.

Depending on the group structure, however, a change in membership can prevent the group from continuing existing. For instance, a couple, which has an informal group structure (socially created based or constitutively dependent on common beliefs, practices and, ultimately, attitudes about what it is to be someone's partner) establishes roles that, once occupied, the role-occupants become essential members. Think, e.g., of Grace and Jill. As a couple, both are the only and essential members of this group: If either is replaced by someone else, e.g., Laura, then there is another couple. Also, if Laura joins Grace and Jill, then the couple ceases to exist. Nonetheless, since this feature is due to the group structure (rather than just to the fact that Grace and Jill actually occupy the corresponding roles), the group is still not (nor reducible to) a mere plurality. A full account of social groups should deal with this and other distinctive features (for a more complex analysis of groups, see Epstein 2015 and 2019).

Of course, social groups can become institutional (without this meaning that all actual institutional groups are social groups that became institutional).

3 On 'collective acceptance', see (Tuomela 2002, Ch 5).

This happens when their group structures and their corresponding instantiations acquire a formal character. For example, a group that plays football in a street every other weekend can become a proper football club, or a couple can become a married couple, or a community can become a nation-state (with its own legal system), etc.

The reasons for institutionalising a social group are several (and practically impossible to classify them all). For instance, although an unmarried couple may perform a great number of group actions (e.g., celebrating anniversaries), it may not be able to perform some others (e.g., adopting a child) unless it becomes institutional, that is, a married couple (in Ukraine, e.g., foreign citizens can adopt only if they are married couples).

Regardless of which reason(s) motivate(s) the institutionalisation of a social group, my claim here is that this institutionalisation occurs when the group structure and its instantiation get formalised. The informal group of football players that becomes a formal club satisfies this condition. While informal, the group membership of this group is determined, e.g., purely in terms of reciprocal attitudes, viz., shared beliefs about each other being interested in playing football every other weekend. Because this membership is specified by a socially created group structure, the social group (as we saw above) is not a mere plurality. However, when it becomes institutional, this group is officially (as opposed to simply socially) created. By this, I mean:

(i) that the group structure has been created by an authoritative act (i.e., by someone or some group exercising the power to create certain roles and relations). Thus, unlike the informal structure of social groups, the formal structure of institutional groups require a certain authority to exist (i.e., to be created). To be clear, by 'authority' I do not mean (only) legal or political authority, but an individual or group which is collectively recognised as having the power to create a group structure (Searle 2010, 102–104). As such, then, there is not anything extraordinary about this authority. For example, the group itself can agree that joining the club will require filling in a form and paying a registration fee. They can also agree that the money collected will be used mainly to rent a proper football ground and other facilities. Assuming that they give a name to this club, e.g., the Footy Club, they (i.e., the plurality then instantiating the informal group structure) will thereby causally fix its reference. That is, their naming the club "the Footy Club" will start its causal chain of reference (Ludwig 2017a, 166). In this case, the informal group is the authority that creates the formal group structure of the Footy Club, whose instantiation (at a certain time at a certain world) will require the satisfaction of the authoritatively created membership requirements (viz., filling in a form and paying a registration fee).

As mentioned above, however, not all institutional groups are institutionalised social groups (i.e., social groups that become institutional); there also are institutional groups which are created from scratch by other institutional groups. For example, the current UK Supreme Court justices is an institutional group whose structure was authoritatively created in 2005 by the House of Lords and the House of Commons approving a Constitutional Reform Act, likewise the institutional group that now carries out the activities of Tampere University was authoritatively created in 2019 by the merger of the University of Tampere and Tampere University of Technology, after this merger was approved by the Finnish Parliament in 2017.

Additionally, there are mixed cases, i.e., where the creation of a formal group structure involves both a social and an institutional action. The Royal Society is a good example. It was founded in 1660 by "the Invisible College" (an informal, social group) when granted a royal charter by King Charles II.

Anyway, whether a group structure is the result of an institutional rather than a social action, or the result of a certain combination of both, the important thing to notice here is that what makes the structure of institutional groups different from that of social groups is that the former is formally (i.e., authoritatively) created.

Perhaps when Ritchie says that certain social structures are overt (as opposed to covert) and intentionally (as opposed to unintentionally) socially created (2018b, 7), she tries to accommodate this feature. That is, she may say that exercising this authoritative power amounts to intentionally creating an overt social structure. However, I think this is not enough. Both formal and informal structures can be overt, in that it is openly known that they are constitutively dependent on social factors (e.g., the informal structure of an ordinary group of friends is as overt as the formal structure of a football club), and both can also be intentionally created, in that they are the product of intentional actions (e.g., the informal structure of an unmarried couple is as intentionally created as the formal structure of a married couple). The difference between them, instead, is that they have different structures, some have formal and others informal structures.

(ii) that the group structure is formally instantiated. That is, that the individuals or groups that take on the corresponding roles do so by making explicit their collective acceptance attitude through performing certain actions, e.g., by signing a contract, filling out a membership form, making an oath, etc. These actions, unlike those required for a collective agent to instantiate an informal group structure, are formally or officially regulated (e.g., by academic or legal rules). One cannot be a UK Supreme Court justice or a lecturer just by being taken to be so, but only by fulfilling all the academic or legal requirements to occupy the corresponding institutional role.

Ritchie also seems to be aware of this, especially when confirming that structures can be intentionally or unintentionally instantiated (2018b, 7). Yet, as before, this is not enough to distinguish between social and institutional groups. Both the informal structure of social groups and the formal structure of institutional groups can be intentionally instantiated. For example, one participates in the instantiation of the informal structure of a group of street musicians as intentionally as one does in the instantiation of the formal structure of the Royal Philharmonic Orchestra. The difference between them is that the latter is instantiated by individual agents collectively performing certain formally or officially regulated actions.

This formal instantiation explains why the individuals occupying the corresponding roles in the formal group structure are both internally and externally recognised as institutional group members. There is *internal recognition* when group members take each other as group members. This kind of recognition is enough for a great number of social groups, e.g., friends, couples and communities. In all these cases, it is not necessary that other people (i.e., non-group members) recognise them as instantiating social structures. There is *external recognition*, on the other hand, when some people are taken to be group members, regardless of their accepting themselves to be group members. Feature social groups, e.g., race and gender groups, seem to ultimately depend on such kind of recognition. One does not need to take oneself as a woman, black or LGBT, for instance, for one to be recognised as such. Since enrolling in institutional groups entails making explicit having a collective acceptance attitude towards contributing to the instantiation of a formal group structure, both group members and external people can take those occupying such roles as institutional group members. For example, whoever occupies the role of USA President or the role of Pope is taken to be an institutional group member (a member of the USA Government, or a member of the Catholic Church, respectively), though not only by other group members, but by non-group members as well.

Being recognised as an institutional group member involves having (and being taken to have) certain deontic powers determined by the corresponding institutional role. Based on these deontic powers, the role-occupier is normatively committed to (not) performing certain intentional actions, which can contribute to the realisation of an institutional group action. To distinguish institutional roles (i.e., roles in formal group structures) from non-institutional roles (i.e., roles in informal group structures), I shall say that the former are associated with *job-descriptions* that specify both the requirements for role-occupancy and the deontic powers attached to it. Thus, we can re-describe now the formal structure of an institutional group as a formal network of job-descriptions.

Think e.g., of a corporation. A corporations consists, roughly, in shareholders, a board of directors, officers and employees. To be a shareholder, an officer (e.g., a Chief Executive Officer or CEO) or even an employee, one needs to satisfy certain conditions. These conditions as well as the deontic powers attached to the roles are (however vaguely) established in their associated job-descriptions. For example, a CEO is responsible for making major corporate decisions, managing the day-to-day operations and resources of the company, being its 'public face', etc. So, whoever takes on the role of CEO will hold such responsibilities.

A lecturer is also a role associated with a certain job-description, which establishes as a requirement for occupying it, e.g., to have expertise and proper qualifications for teaching as well as for undertaking research projects. It also establishes the deontic powers related to it, e.g., the obligation to supervise students' research activities, and the right to receive a fair payment. By generalising, we can say that the institutional roles and relations that correspond to a certain formal group structure are normatively determined by the whole network of job-descriptions. This network, in other words, establishes the normative boundaries within which the institutional group members can perform certain actions, including their contributing to the obtaining of group actions. This is perhaps a case of what Thomasson identifies as the function of social group concepts, viz., "to give normative structure to our lives together" (2019, 4830).

3 Institutional Agency

In this section I explain and argue for the following thesis:

Th 2 Institutional groups can perform intentional actions

Although a platitude, this thesis (and the more general: Groups can perform intentional actions) has been under the philosophical spotlight since the origins of analytic social ontology. My purpose here, however, is not to present, let alone examine, the different accounts that social ontologists have offered. Instead, my focus is only to answer *what is it for an institutional group to act intentionally?* from a very well-developed theory of institutional agency, viz., the one that Ludwig has introduced in his (2014, 2017a; and 2017b).

While considering his theory, nonetheless, I also raise an objection: His notion of we-intentions does not distinguish between people acting in informally organised social groups from those acting in formally organised social groups. For the latter, I claim, a more robust notion is required, viz., the one that Tuomela labels "we-mode".

To start seeing the problem of institutional agency, let me state again the puzzle I mentioned in the previous section. As follows from the structuralist account of institutional groups that I presented above, this kind of groups consists in a formally created group structure that is formally instantiated by a collective (or plural) agent (at a certain time at a certain possible world). Thus, its properties (including the agency property) must be related to both the group structure and the collective agent (i.e., the group members). Taken separately, these two elements do not account for its capacity to act intentionally. Firstly, because a group structure, which is a type of group organisation, does not act, but only a token of it does. Secondly, because the group is not identical to its members, which means that the fact that group members are agents and can perform intentional actions does not itself ground the fact that the group is an agent and can perform intentional actions (e.g., the fact that Rachael and myself are currently the only members of the Social Ontology Research Group or SORG, is not enough to ground the fact that, when she and I go for lunch together, the SORG also goes for lunch).

The approach I take here to discuss this puzzle follows Ludwig's deflationary theory of group agency, viz., that we can attribute intentional actions to groups, though they are not genuine agents (in the sense that individual agents are). This theory, I show, is still compatible with the structuralist account of institutional groups that, following Ritchie, I submitted above.

3.1 Institutional Intentions

Although we may think that Ludwig has a different understanding of institutional groups than the one I have here, upon closer examination, it should not be difficult to appreciate that we indeed share a common background. He takes institutions to be "systems of status roles", and those roles to be "a special type of status functions [. . .] in which the collectively accepted function is expressed in part through its occupier's intentional expression of her agency in that role" (2017b, 271). I contest his characterisation of 'institution' below (**§4**), but for now let me just highlight our commonalities.

Both Kirk and myself take institutional groups as concrete (as opposed to abstract) objects: They are realisations or systems of group structures. Both rely on institutional roles to explain institutional membership: For him, an institutional group member is an agent occupying a certain status role, which is attributed with a certain collectively accepted function; for me, an institutional group member is an agent occupying a role in a formally created group structure, which is associated with a job-description that establishes both the requirements for role-occupancy and the deontic powers attached to it.

Working on this and his theory of institutional agency, I presently show how institutional groups can perform intentional actions. The first thing to discuss is what it is for a group to be an agent, i.e., able to perform intentional actions. To do this, as Ludwig acknowledges, we require a notion of we-intentions (2017b, 275). To say, e.g., that we intend to bake a cake together (as a group), we are ascribing a certain shared intention to the group, viz., that the group bake the cake. "The group then bakes the cake intentionally (as a group) when it carries out its shared intention successfully" (idem).

Ludwig's notion of shared intention boils down to this:

> Shared or joint intention in a group is just a matter of each member of the group having a we-intention directed at the group doing a particular thing together (2017a, 22).

Thus, in the case of our baking a cake together (as a group), we each intend to do something that contributes to the obtaining of our baking a cake together. When this obtains, we can say that we bake a cake together, i.e., that there is an event (viz., our baking a cake) such that all and only each of us are the sole agents of it.[4]

One can be an agent of an event in different ways, e.g., by causing it to happen (directly or indirectly), by doing something that constitutes it (in whole or in part), by producing something that is conceptually sufficient for it to be the case, etc. (Ludwig 2016, 76).

What matters here, however, is that when we do something together (as a group), we do it based on our we-intentions. Ludwig has an account of collective intentionality that distinguishes we-intentions from I-intentions purely based on their content, viz., we-intentions are addressed to a shared content, e.g., a joint plan (2017b, 275). I challenge the application of this account to institutional agency below. But before, let briefly present another element of his explanation of institutional group action.

A group can do something intentionally or not. For example, a group can push a car up a hill intentionally (if each group member has appropriate

4 For simplicity, I am leaving out tense and other important qualifications. See (Ludwig 2016) for a detailed, logical analysis of plural action sentences.

we-intentions addressed to a shared content, viz., that the group push the car up the hill) or unintentionally (if they do not have any relevant we-intentions towards realising this group action, but still they are all and the only agents which contribute to its realisation, e.g., they were all pushing a car but without noticing that they were all pushing the same car). Although many group actions admit of these two possibilities, some do not. Playing chess, playing tennis, having a conversation, getting married, etc. are the kind of group activities that can only be collectively intentionally performed. There is no way we can play chess without doing it intentionally. The reason for this, as Ludwig has clearly shown, is that playing chess is an essentially intentional collective activity type, which can only be instantiated by a group following intentionally the constitutive (and regulative) rules that define it (2017b, 276).

Thus, when we play chess, we each are constitutive agents of an essentially intentional collective activity token. 'Constitutive agency', as we saw above, is only one of the different ways we can be agents of an action. This is my focus for the rest of this paper. Being a constitutive agent of an essentially intentional collective activity token means that one intentionally makes direct (or unmediated) contribution to the performance of the joint intentional action by partially constituting it by following the relevant constitutive (and regulative) rules (Ludwig 2014, 84–86).

Since following these rules is something we do intentionally, this is where our we-intentions become crucial. What ultimately grounds our performing an essentially intentional collective activity token is that we have appropriate we-intentions addressed to our making direct contribution to the realisation of a joint activity, e.g., our playing chess by partly constituting it by following appropriate constitutive (and regulative) rules, i.e., the rules that define what playing chess is.

This general framework is meant to account as well for institutional group actions. Ludwig considers 'trial' as "an essentially collective intentional action type" (2014, 85). This type of action, I take, is institutional, in that its constitutive (and regulative) rules are formally or officially (rather than simply socially) created. Participating in a trial, to put it otherwise, requires following certain formal rules. The people playing a role in a trial, e.g., the judge, the clerk, the barristers, the solicitors, the witnesses, the jury, etc. are all participating in bringing about an essentially intentional collective action token by following legal rules (i.e., the rules that formally define what a trial is).

Again, since following these rules can only happen intentionally, we can attribute to those people appropriate we-intentions, i.e., they each we-intend to make a direct contribution to the performance of a trial by partly constituting it by following the trial rules. Another example will be an academic group organising a workshop. Let us say that this academic group organises a workshop on social action. For this institutional group to do so, and given that organising a workshop is an institutional essentially intentional collective action type, the institutional group members must do it by each intentionally making direct contribution to the obtaining of an event that counts as (or constitutes) their organising the workshop. They each, then, we-intend to perform certain actions (e.g., booking a room, sending out invitation letters, applying for funding, etc.) that contribute to the realisation of this action type. Their we-intentions, thus, are addressed to a certain shared content, viz., their bringing about (as a group) an event that constitutes the organisation of a workshop.

So far, so good. Ludwig's account of group agency, which builds on his account of plural agency, can also be extended to institutional agency: "Institutional agency ought to be continuous with informal collective intentional activity" (2016, x). Moreover, since accepting plural agency does not commit us to the existence of groups (over and above their individual members), Ludwig ends up with an individualistic account of groups and their capacity to perform intentional actions. Although I do not contest here his individualism (as I mostly sympathise with it), I think there is something important to discuss around his notion of we-intentions when applied to the institutional context. I do so here, though very briefly.

As seen, Ludwig takes we-intentions (and conditional we-intentions) to be some of the building blocks upon which we can explain more complex forms of social organisation, e.g., institutional organisation (2017b, 275). Yet, his notion does not distinguish between we-intentions in informal and formal contexts. For the latter, I believe, we need to consider a more robust notion, viz., a we-mode we-intention. By this, I mean an intention of fully acting as a group member (Tuomela 2013, Ch 2)

When participating in bringing about an institutional essentially intentional collective action token, we each have we-intentions addressed to a certain shared content (viz., that the institutional group brings about an event that constitutes the action token) by following the appropriate constitutive (and regulative) rules (i.e., the rules that define the corresponding institutional essentially intentional collective action type). Yet, there seems to be more to these we-intentions than just their content, viz., they are held (or taken to be held) in a certain way by all the individuals participating in bringing about the institutional essentially intentional collective action token. Let me explain.

As mentioned above in relation to occupying an institutional role in a formal group structure, when the individual takes on the role, she does so by making explicit through a certain formal process of recognition (e.g., signing a contract or making an oath) her collective acceptance attitude towards contributing to the realisation or instantiation of the group structure. Making explicit this attitude is what allows (at least *prima facie*) not only other group members, but also non-group members to recognise her as occupying a role in an institutional group. Since occupying this role comes with having certain deontic powers (established, however vaguely, in its associated job-description), her acting within the normative boundaries of these powers is (taken to be) intentional. When she participates in an institutional essentially intentional collective action as a role-occupant, she does so based on appropriate we-intentions, which are not only addressed to a certain shared content (as Ludwig says), but also held in a certain way (as Tuomela argues). That is, she has we-intentions *qua* role-occupant, which represents a strong commitment to acting as a group member. Since the notion of 'group' is irreducible here, this would be a case against thinking of we-intentions as providing enough resources to build up an individualist analysis of institutional group action that does not require in the analysans any mentioning of groups whatsoever. This, again, is only a hint of an objection, a full development of which goes beyond the scope of this paper.

3.2 Institutional Proxy Agency

No theory of institutional agency would be complete without analysing the special case of proxy agency, i.e., when an authorised individual or group acts for an institutional group. In developing his theory, Ludwig has thoroughly advanced an account of this social phenomenon that appears consistent with his overall project, viz., to explain institutional group action in terms of plural action, where all and only institutional group members (i.e., the plurality instantiating the formal group structure at a certain time at a certain possible world) participate in its obtaining.

Proxy agency (or proxying), as Tuomela presents it, involves an action generation that takes place by another (individual or collective) agent's action (1984, Ch 6). This phenomenon, as Ludwig says, "is pervasive in institutional action" (2014, 75). In his words,

> Proxy agency is a common instrument in institutional action. When the Congress passes a Joint Resolution to declare war, the United States thereby declares war. When a corporation's lawyers file bankruptcy papers, the corporation thereby declares bankruptcy. When a jury foreman announces the verdict at a trial, the jury thereby announces its decision. And so on (2014, 76).

All these cases have in common that at first glance the institutional action (declaring war, declaring bankruptcy or announcing a verdict) does not seem to involve all and only the institutional group members (i.e., the plurality instantiating the formal group structure) doing something intentionally together. Were this the case, we could not account for this kind of institutional actions by only applying the structuralist account developed thus far.

The social phenomenon of proxy agency, however, is not exclusive of institutional contexts. For example, a couple (which is an informal or social group) can agree that one of the partners will decide where to go for dinner tonight. In this case, the partner is a proxy agent *internally* authorised to act for the group. If the couple agrees, instead, that a friend of them will make the decision, then the friend (assuming that she accepts the role) will be a proxy agent *externally* authorised to act for the group. The difference between internal and external authorisation depends on whether the authorisation comes from the group one is a member of.

'Authorising' can be either an individual or a collective action. If you hire an attorney to deal with tax problems, your authorising him to act for you in the appropriate social transactions is an individual action. When a group authorises someone or some other group (or proper subgroup) to act for it, then its authorising is a collective action. In the institutional case, this authorising is formally or officially regulated. That is, there are certain rules that need to be observed in order to *validly* authorise someone or some group to act for an institutional group.

Putting these rules aside, what is key to understanding the role of proxy agents in institutional group actions is that their authorisation is both a causal and constitutive element of what makes them what they are (i.e., individuals or groups acting for an institutional group). Their being this kind of agents, in other words, depends on the authorising institutional group attributing them with a status function in social transactions (particularly, in the performance of institutional essentially intentional collective actions) (Ludwig 2014, 89).

Now, since the institutional authorisation itself is an institutional essentially intentional collective action (which is to be performed according to certain rules), then it can be explained (or analysed) in terms of the general framework introduced above, viz., as all and only the institutional group members making direct contribution to its realisation. When the institutional group authorises someone or some other group (or proper subgroup) to act for it, the plurality of individuals instantiating the formal group structure performs an action that constitutes the institutional group's authorising a proxy agent. Because being a proxy amounts to holding a role in group action, it is expected that this authorisation establishes (however vaguely) the deontic powers associated with it. Thus, although a proxy may not be authorised to act in a very specific way for the group (i.e., some proxy's actions may not count as intentional group actions under certain, specific descriptions), it may be authorised more generally to perform, still within certain limits, an action or types of action for the group. See (Ludwig 2014, 89–92) for a detailed analysis of a spokesperson delivering a message for a group.

Three more things must be discussed before getting the idea of proxy agency right. Firstly, that authorising the group does not require that all and only the institutional group members agree on who the proxy agent will be and which particular actions it will perform for the group, etc. (Ludwig 2014, 96). In larger institutional groups, it is enough that operative members authorise someone or some group (or proper subgroup) to act for them, while the non-operative members only accept, as in go along with, this authorisation. Secondly, although the proxy agent executes the institutional group action (e.g., giving expert testimony in a courtroom), the action is still attributed to the authorising institutional group (e.g., the Crown Prosecutor). The reason is that the proxy owes its agency property to the authorising group (i.e., its authorisation is both causal and constitutive of its having the corresponding role). When the proxy acts *qua* proxy its action does not constitute by itself the group action; it is only a constitutive (though the most salient) part of it. The prior authorisation is also constitutive of the group action. To put it otherwise, while the proxy agent makes direct realisation of the group action, the authorising group makes indirect contribution to its realisation (Ludwig 2014, 91). Thirdly, a proxy agent can also be authorised to further authorise other proxy agents (Ludwig 2017b, 283). For example, an academic group can hire (thus, externally authorise) a company to organise a workshop; and this company can in turn also delegate (thus, internally authorise) a proper subgroup to organise it. Although, in the end, the organisation of the workshop (i.e., the action under this description) is only correctly attributed to the initially authorising group (i.e., the academic group), it can also be attributed (under a different description) to the subsequently authorised groups (e.g., the company's organisation of a workshop for an academic group).

To conclude this section, let me consider again the objection sketched above regarding Ludwig's notion of we-intentions. As mentioned, what ultimately explains in his theory of collective action that certain individuals are acting collectively intentionally (as opposed to individually intentionally) is that they each have appropriate we-intentions. The difference between we-intentions and I-intentions, says Ludwig, is that the former are addressed to a certain shared content (which is neutral regarding mutual cooperation). In the case of institutional proxy agents, however, a more robust notion of we-intentions is needed. Institutional proxy agents are formally authorised, which means that they make explicit through a certain formal process of recognition their collective acceptance attitude towards taking on the institutional role and acting for the group (according to and within the normative boundaries of the corresponding authorisation). When they do something intentionally for the authorising institutional group, they do it based on their we-mode we-intentions addressed to a certain shared content. This 'we-mode' explains their acting *qua* institutional proxy agents, which involves just as strong a commitment (and accompanied responsibility) as the one that institutional group members have. An institutional proxy agent, in this sense, identifies itself with the institutional group (Tuomela 2013, 11). Again, this kind of we-mode we-intention involves an irreducible notion of group that Ludwig seems reluctant to accept.

4 Institutions and Institutional Groups

In this final section, I take up how institutional groups are related to institutions (e.g., banks, universities and legal systems). I do so with a twofold intention. Firstly, to show that the ontological analysis of institutional groups is only a first step towards the ontological analysis of our institutional reality. Secondly, to make clear that institutional groups and institutions are not one and the same thing (they actually belong to different ontological categories). The thesis I want to argue for here is

> **Th 3** Institutions are institutional practices, which consist in tokens of institutional activity types

As I presently show, **Th3** differs from some other characterisations of institutions that prominent social ontologists have offered when analysing our social reality. Although we may accept this diversity as it reflects the different aspects of what these social ontologists are focused on, I think it is important to share an understanding of *what it is* under analysis. To be clear, let me highlight that **Th3** is not about the meaning of 'institution', but about what an institution is.

The literature about institutions is abundant, and it is almost impossible to categorise all the different views that philosophers and social scientists have therein developed (though, for an overview, see Miller 2019). Here I shall only consider three of them and claim that the last one fits better the reality of institutions.

Institutions as abstract objects. The first view corresponds to those who claim that institutions are a certain kind of abstract object. With this, however, I do not mean that they intentionally claim that institutions are abstract objects, but only that this follows from their characterisations. For example, in his *What is an institution?*, Searle says

> An institution is any system of constitutive rules of the form *X counts as Y in C.* Once an institution becomes established, it then provides a structure within which one can create institutional facts (2005, 10).

If "an institution is any system of constitutive rules", then it is an abstract object. Rules, that is, are not concrete (spatiotemporally located) objects. They exist as types, but not as tokens. What we report when someone follows a rule is an intentional action or behaviour, but not the rule itself. Under this Searlean characterisation, we shall have problems conceptualising, e.g., what it is for someone to participate in an institution, or what it is for certain artifacts or ordinary objects (buildings, tables, cars, etc.) to be part of an institution, etc.

Despite these problems, however, Searle is not alone in thinking of institutions as rules: In several parts of his *Understanding Institutions*, Guala has also claimed that institutions are rules, e.g., "Institutions [. . .] are rules that people are motivated to follow" (2016, xxv), and "The conception of institutions as rules is intuitive, and fits with our pretheoretical understanding of many paradigmatic institutions" (2016, 4). Again, were institutions rules, conventions, patterns of behaviour or the like, it would not make sense to say, e.g., that we participate in such-and-such institution, or that such-and-such artifact is part of the institution, etc., as we, our actions and those artifacts are concrete, spatiotemporally located objects.

Although true that institutions also incorporate abstract objects, e.g., rules, conventions, statuses, etc., they are not identical to these. For an institution to exist, certain constitutive rules must exist, but the rules do not constitute by themselves the institution: The intentional following of these rules is also required, which in turn implies there being people performing essentially intentional collective activities (which is precisely what I have defended here).

Institutions as organisations. The second view of institutions that seems at odds with our understanding of their ontology, is the one that suggests that institutions are indeed concrete objects, but the kind of objects that are composed by people, viz., organisations. In his *Do corporations have minds of their own?*, Ludwig endorses this view by identifying "institutions as systems of status roles" (2014, 271) and then systems of status roles as organisations (2014, 279).

Although this accounts better than the previous view for the necessary relation between people and institutions, it still gets things wrong. Particularly, it commits a category mistake: Organisations are a particular kind of organised groups, which are realisations (or instantiations) of group structures. They can be attributed with attitudes (e.g., intentions, beliefs and desires) and actions. However, to say that organisations are institutions leaves unclear how particular activities can be part of the latter. The only way to make sense of this is to say that organisations perform those activities. So, e.g., when a group follows the rules of trial, they are not instantiating an organisation, but a certain type of activity. Although the group is necessary for the instantiation, it does not constitute on its own the activity. Simply put, organisations and institutions belong to different ontological categories, viz., the former, to groups; the latter, to activities (or practices). Making this mistake, as before, implies having problems conceptualising what it is for certain concrete objects (e.g., buildings, tables, cars, etc.) to be part of an institution.

Institutions as practices. The third view I consider here is the one that takes institutions to be (a certain kind of) practices. Tuomela has hinted at this view in several works. For example, in his *Social Ontology*, he says:

> Social Institutions [. . .] basically consist of a *norm* system and a system of *social practices* conducive to the satisfaction of these norms (2013, 214).

This view has also been endorsed by other social ontologists, e.g., Hindriks (2018, 353). Although this requires more refinement, the idea is simply that an institution, e.g., a university, a bank, or a legal system, is an institutional practice. The Bank of Scotland, for instance, is an institution which consists in all those institutional actions that are correctly attributed to the commercial banking company (i.e., the institutional group). As we saw in the last section, the company can also act through a proxy agent, but still the action performed is correctly attributed to the company (i.e., the authorising institutional group). This is the way we can individuate those actions. Moreover, for the institutional group (and its proxies) to perform the corresponding actions, they must follow intentionally the corresponding constitutive (and regulative) rules that define the institutional action types. Their successfully performing those actions, as Tuomela would say, amounts to their realising (or satisfying) the norms that govern the institutional practice.

To conclude, let me just consider three elements of institutions (characterised as institutional practices) to show that this view is not subject to the objections raised against the others. An institution (e.g., the Bank of Scotland, the University of Glasgow, or the UK Supreme Court) is related in specific ways to

(a) some ordinary objects, e.g., tables, chairs, buildings, cars, etc. These objects are constitutive elements of institutions, because institutions consist in institutional groups performing institutional (and social) actions, some of which require their using (or treating) these objects according to certain institutional rules, i.e., by imposing a status function on them.

(b) some abstract objects, e.g., rules, concepts, roles, etc. These objects are also constitutive elements of institutions, because they provide participants with the types of actions, objects, groups, etc., that are to be realised, used, instantiated, etc., in order to carry out an institutional activity.
(c) some individuals and groups. Since the institutional groups that perform the institutional actions that bring about institutions interact with individuals and groups (of a different kind), and those interactions are constitutive parts of the realisation of those institutional actions, they also contribute to the existence and persistence of institutions.[5]

References

Epstein, Brian. 2015. *The Ant Trap. Rebuilding the Foundations of the Social Science.* New York: Oxford University Press.

Epstein, Brian. 2019. What are social groups? Their metaphysics and how to classify them. *Synthese* 196, pp. 4899–4932.

Hindriks, Frank. 2018. Institutions and Collective Intentionality. In Jankovic, Maria and Ludwig, Kirk, *The Routledge Handbook of Collective Intentionality*, New York: Routledge.

List, Christian, and Pettit, Philip. 2011. *Group Agency. The Possibility, Design, and Status of Corporate Agents*, Oxford: Oxford University Press.

Ludwig, Kirk. 2014. Proxy Agency in Collective Action. *Nous* 48, pp. 75–105.

Ludwig, Kirk. 2016. *From Individual to Plural Agency. Collective Action: Volume 1.* Oxford: Oxford University Press.

Ludwig, Kirk. 2017a. *From Plural to Institutional Agency. Collective Action: Volume 2.* Oxford: Oxford University Press.

Ludwig, Kirk. 2017b. Do Corporations have minds of their own? *Philosophical Psychology* 30(3), pp. 269–301.

Miller, Seumas. 2019. Social Institutions. In Zalta, Edward. *The Stanford Encyclopedia of Philosophy*, https://plato.stanford.edu/archives/sum2019/entries/social-institutions/.

Quinton, Anthony. 1975. "The Presidential Address: Social Objects". *Proceedings of the Aristotelian Society* 76, pp. 1–vii.

Ritchie, Katherine. 2015. The Metaphysics of Social Groups. *Philosophy Compass* 10(5), pp. 310–321.

Ritchie, Katherine. 2018a. Social Creationism and Social Groups. In Hess, Kendy, et al. (Eds.). *Collectivity: Ontology, Ethics, and Social Justice.* Rowman & Littlefield.

Ritchie, Katherine. 2018b. Social Structures and the Ontology of Social Groups. *Philosophy and Phenomenological Research*, pp. 1–23. doi:10.1111/phpr.12555.

Searle, John. 2005. What is an institution? *Journal of Institutional Economics* 1(1), pp. 1–22.

5 Thanks to Rachael Mellin for helpful discussion and comments.

Searle, John. 2010. *Making the Social World. The Structure of Human Civilization*. New York: Oxford University Press.
Thomasson, Amie. 2019. The Ontology of Social Groups. *Synthese* 196, 4829–4845.
Tuomela, Raimo. 1984. *A Theory of Social Action*. Dordrecht: Reidel.
Tuomela, Raimo. 2002. *The Philosophy of Social Practices. A Collective Acceptance View*. New York: Cambridge University Press.
Tuomela, Raimo. 2013. *Social Ontology. Collective Intentionality and Group Agents*. New York: Oxford University Press.

Säde Hormio

Institutional Knowledge and its Normative Implications

> For over fifty years, the United States of America has known that carbon dioxide ("CO_2") pollution from burning fossil fuels was causing global warming and dangerous climate change, and that continuing to burn fossil fuels would destabilize the climate system on which present and future generations of our nation depend for their wellbeing and survival. Defendants also knew the harmful impacts of their actions would significantly endanger Plaintiffs, with the damage persisting for millennia. Despite this knowledge, Defendants continued their policies and practices of allowing the exploitation of fossil fuels.
>
> First Amended Complaint for Declaratory and Injunctive Relief, *Juliana v. U.S.* 2015

We attribute knowledge to institutions on a daily basis, saying things like "the government knew about the threat" or "the university did not act upon the knowledge it had about the harassment". Institutions can also attribute knowledge to themselves, like when Maybank Global Banking claims that it offers its customers "deep expertise and vast knowledge" of the Southeast Asia region, or when the United States Geological Survey states that it understands complex natural science phenomena like the probability of earthquakes occurring along a given fault line.

This chapter aims to discover when we can correctly attribute knowledge to an institution. I find this an interesting question, especially because when something does go wrong, all too often the official line of response from institutions is that they were unaware of the situation: in other words, they did not have enough information at their disposal. I will argue that institutions have fewer excuses for being ignorant than individuals do, and that many admissions of institutional knowledge are too modest. I begin by discussing a real-life example of the latter, before turning my attention to the usually fragmented nature of institutional knowledge. I also discuss the robustness of this knowledge, offering a distinction between two types of institutional knowledge. I then discuss knowledge parameters and why institutions have fewer excuses for not knowing about something than individuals do. I round off the chapter by examining institutional knowledge on climate change.

A clarificatory note is in order: by 'institutions' I refer throughout to large organisations, and not to the wider meaning of institutions as shared and established social practices and laws, although legal institutions are naturally included. Other examples of institutions include universities, governments, art establishments, and insurance companies. What these types of large organisations have in

https://doi.org/10.1515/9783110663617-005

common is that they are established to be more or less permanent in nature. Hence, enterprises and other temporal organisations with short-term goals do not qualify as institutions.

1 What did the USA Know?

In September 2015, a group of 21 young people and children brought a lawsuit against the United States of America. The First Amended Complaint for Declaratory and Injunctive Relief filed by Kelsey Cascadia Rose Juliana et al. (henceforth Juliana) argues that the state has acted indifferently in a deliberate way to the known peril of climate change, which they have been involved in creating. According to the plaintiffs, this infringes on their constitutional rights to life, liberty, and property. In addition, they argue that the state has also failed to protect land, water, air, and living things – the heritage of the whole nation.

Juliana is coordinated by Our Children's Trust, a non-profit organisation with several cases pending, and inspired by the *Atmospheric Trust Litigation* (ATL) approach, originated by Mary Christina Wood, Professor of Law at the University of Oregon.[1] ATL draws on the public trust doctrine, which was first articulated in Roman law. At its heart lies the idea of designating government actors as trustees of essential natural capital, which is viewed as "an enduring ecological endowment".[2] ATL applies public trust principles to the atmosphere and adopts a fundamental rights approach to climate change.[3] The plaintiffs do not seek damages for themselves, but rather for the court to order the state to draw up a plan to phase out fossil fuels and reduce excess carbon in the atmosphere, and to monitor compliance with the same.[4] Juliana et al. argue that the

1 Wood 2013.

2 Blumm and Wood 2017: 22.

3 Although the atmosphere has not traditionally been thought of as a natural resource in the public trust context, "air" is mentioned in the Institutes of Justinian, the Roman sixth-century recodification of an ancient law, and it has been affirmed as public property by the U.S. Supreme Court in an earlier decision (Rubinton 2017). The denial in 2016 of motions to dismiss in Juliana v. U.S. by U.S. District Court Judge Ann Aiken made history by asserting that a climate system capable of sustaining human life is a fundamental constitutional right.

4 This is why it is unlikely that the case will go to trial: appellate courts are reluctant to allow district courts to tinker with standards set by the Environmental Protection Agency, holding that the juridical branch should not be setting its own standards. Regardless of what happens, the case has still opened up interesting avenues for future climate change litigation by linking climate change to the public trust doctrine.

current actions of the state favour "the present, temporary economic benefits of certain citizens, especially corporations" over those of the plaintiffs' constitutional rights.

The U.S. Department of Justice responded to the case on behalf of the federal defendants in January 2017, just before the Obama administration was leaving office, and admitted that current and projected greenhouse gas emissions "constitute a threat to public health and welfare". They also agreed with the plaintiffs that carbon emissions from the United States accounted for more than a quarter of cumulative global CO_2 emissions from 1850 to 2012. What is more, they admitted that they had known about the issue for a long time:

> Federal Defendants admit that for over fifty years some officials and persons employed by the federal government have been aware of a growing body of scientific research concerning the effects of fossil fuel emissions on atmospheric concentrations of CO_2 – including that increased concentrations of atmospheric CO_2 could cause measurable long-lasting changes to the global climate, resulting in an array of severe deleterious effects to human beings, which will worsen over time. Juliana v. U.S. 2017

It is clear that the U.S. Department of Justice is not trying to question climate change science in their response. Rather, what they deny is the plaintiffs' claims that they have ignored expert warnings and have wilfully ignored the impending harm to future generations.[5] The response also stated that the term "United States" is "vague" and "ambiguous" and that the "Federal Defendants cannot attribute knowledge to it". From the list of defendants, which includes both state departments and individuals in their official capacity representing various state branches, it is clear that what is at stake is the knowledge that the Federal Government possessed about the issue. What they contested in many places was having sufficient information or knowledge. While some of these relate to accusations that are perhaps too vague to obtain knowledge about in the sense required, I find the admission of knowledge too modest in the quote above.

Note how in the quote the admission is that "*some* officials and persons employed by the federal government have been aware" (emphasis mine) of the

5 At the same time, they admit that they "permit, authorize, and subsidize fossil fuel extraction, development, consumption, and exportation" while knowing that these activities produce CO_2 emissions and increase the atmospheric concentration of CO_2. They also acknowledge, as shown in the quote above, that this could result in many severe harmful effects for human beings, and is set to worsen over time. The apparent contradiction can be explained by what the costs and benefits of these activities are estimated to be, but I set that issue aside here.

issue for many decades. For an institution to be said to have knowledge about an issue, not every member needs to have knowledge about it. It is not even necessary for the knowledge to be widely distributed within the institution, or for it to be readily available to interested members, or so I will argue below.

2 Institutional Knowledge

Knowledge is not evenly distributed within institutions. It would be totally implausible to demand that for an institution to have knowledge about an issue, all of its members should duly have knowledge about it. It is economical for an institution to consist of groups of experts that can work together when needed, as this allows for a wide range of skills and expertise to be employed. In fact, the capacity for an institution to have broad and deep knowledge is based on their ability to pool together knowledge from various individuals and sources. Institutions require specialisation to be able to have all the skills and knowledge they need, so fragmentation of knowledge is an inevitable consequence of this.

If we consider an educational institution like a university, it is composed of several specialised faculties and departments consisting of experts in a given field.[6] Only a fraction of the knowledge found within the institution is acquired by the university's top management, or shared among the faculties (even given the inter-, multi- and transdisciplinary research that is in vogue with funders these days). This does not mean that the information cannot be accessed when necessary, for instance when a journalist or a government agency contacts the university to obtain information about the latest research on some issue.

In general, highly fragmented information within institutions is fine as long as groups of experts are willing to share their knowledge if and when needed. They should also share with others information that affects the institution as a whole, unless there is a policy by the upper levels of the institution to supress this knowledge.[7] For an institution to be said to have knowledge about something, not every member of it – or indeed even the majority – need to have knowledge about it. Nor does the availability of the information need to be widespread. It is enough that

6 University is a special kind of institution when it comes to knowledge, as knowledge is at the core of its existence. Universities create new knowledge and teach students this knowledge: their activities are all about knowledge.

7 There may be cases where they should arguably share the information even in the event of ongoing knowledge suppression, but I will not go into these whistleblower cases here.

those who are working in areas requiring this knowledge possess it or, at least, that they *could* possess it if the executives so wished.

It is important to distinguish between when an institution has knowledge about something through its members, and when members have knowledge that cannot be attributed to the institution. After all, institutional knowledge is not as simple a matter as a certain percentage of members knowing something. Instead, in order to count as institutional knowledge, the knowledge must be attached to the relevant roles and communication lines. Therefore, in an institution with 500 members, the institution does not know *X* even if 300 of its members know *X* as individuals, that is, without having an awareness of each other's knowledge or sharing their knowledge with the executive members. However, the same institution can be said to have knowledge of *Y* even with only one member knowing *Y*, as long as it is known to the executives (or the relevant manager in the communication line) that the member has this knowledge. An example of the latter could be a lone researcher within a university biology department focusing on some obscure species of frog. No-one else in the university knows anything about these frogs, but as long as the expertise is known to the relevant people along the lines of communication, then this knowledge is available within the institution. Often, institutional knowledge is distributed knowledge, meaning that the individuals who possess the institutional knowledge do not have to be gathered together into a task force or a panel of specialists; rather, they do what they do and the institution has the knowledge because of this. The frog specialist is just such an example.

It should also be noted that institutional knowledge may be more than the sum of its individual parts. Imagine a group of people with varying fields of expertise, and/or epistemic access, thinking together a solution to a problem facing the institution. Together, they can come up with an answer for the institution that is novel and innovative, exceeding the aggregate knowledge of the individual members.

Much institutional knowledge is of course documented in different texts or encompassed in files, software programs and so on. This knowledge can be part of institutional knowledge as long as it is accessible to the executives, senior managers or the people working in areas that need it. (If the files are buried in a basement somewhere, they are lost institutional knowledge). Hence, not all of the building blocks of institutional knowledge are traceable back to the knowledge that the individual members currently have.

The fragmentation of knowledge and information can go too far, however, and this is when the institution is no longer able to make the best decisions as a collective. In these cases, there is either a systematic fault in the lines of communication, or knowledge is suppressed, whether through denials, taboos or secrecy.[8] Still, for an institution to have knowledge about something, it holds that this knowledge does not have to be shared among all, or even most, of its members. For example, when a group of experts is tasked with finding out about the state of climate change science, and duly reports back to the executives of an institution (or the management level deemed appropriate by the top-level management), the institution has knowledge about the issue. This is so even if the institution in question decides to hide the findings from its regular members or just decides not to take any further action on the matter.

3 Robustness of Institutional Knowledge

While it can be said that the USA has known about climate change for many decades, it is clear that not everyone in the federal government, let alone the citizens or denizens of the USA, knew about the issue in the 1970s or 1980s. These days general knowledge about climate change is widely shared (although expertise about the science is not). Looking at how knowledge about climate change has evolved over the years, there seems to be different degrees of institutional knowledge at play. In this section, I will distinguish between two types of institutional knowledge, which I term *operating knowledge* and *shared knowledge*.

Let us start with an example of operating knowledge in a group setting. Imagine a spy ring, where the spies do not know the identity of the other spies or have access to the information the others have.[9] Each spy has been assigned a code name and a secret phone with which to get in touch with the others. They have an assignment to complete where Aja knows the target, Katya the method, and Shea the time and the place. The person who set up the mission was involved in a car crash and is lying in a coma in hospital somewhere. Shea has been instructed to invite the other two to come to the designated place at the designated time, Katya to bring the means, and Aja to put them to use against the target. Between them, they have all the information necessary to successfully complete the assignment. However, can the spy ring as a collective be said to have knowledge about what the assignment is before it is carried out?

8 Hormio 2018.
9 I use the same example in Hormio 2018.

I believe that the spy ring does have operating knowledge about the assignment precisely because it is able to carry it out. If the spy ring is part of some organised espionage group, it is the institution rather than the spy ring per se that knows what the assignment is. However, if the person who is now in a coma is some rogue agent, then the spy ring per se has the knowledge. That said, this knowledge is highly fragmented and not robust at all: if one link was missing, they would not be able to achieve their goal. Recall the lone researcher in the earlier example. The knowledge that the university has on these obscure frogs is highly fragmented and dependent on one person (at least until the researcher writes their knowledge down in a research paper, or teaches students a course on the frogs, and so on).

Coming back to the spies, the spy ring knows *how* to perform the assignment, but not *that* the assignment is to *X*, i.e. what it entails. After they have carried it out, the spy ring will ostensibly also know more about the assignment – who the target was, where, and by what means it was achieved – as the knowledge of the individual group members will have merged through action. Knowing both how to do something and the details of what you are doing constitutes more robust knowledge than knowing just the former.

I refer to knowing how to do something as *operating knowledge*, and the knowledge that allows the individual members to pool what they know and reflect upon it as *shared knowledge*. The people directing the institution have to decide what type of knowledge can be fragmented or compartmentalised operating knowledge, and what type of knowledge needs to be shared knowledge, that is, more robust knowledge within the institution. With knowledge about obscure frogs, for instance, it seems acceptable that the institutional knowledge is not robust, and that operating knowledge is sufficient and economical. Sometimes institutional knowledge should also be fragmented, for example when there are concerns about privacy. With other types of knowledge, it might be the case that steps need to be taken to make the institutional knowledge more robust, so that it is widely shared among members.

For operating knowledge to be ascribed to an institution, it must fall in line with the institution's structure regarding institutional roles and lines of communication. Institutional statements, such as principles, codes of conduct or mission statements will help to distinguish rogue behaviour from institutional behaviour within roles. Below, I will provide an example that illustrates these differences in a group setting before applying it to the institutional setting.

A small mobile phone repair company is operated and owned by the five engineers who fix the phones. One of the engineers installs malware in some of the phones. The installation is intentional and all five engineers know about it, although it has never been discussed by them as a group. The engineers as a group have knowledge about the malware. Even without an explicit plan to install the malware, the company can also be said to know about it in the shared knowledge sense, as the five engineers are the only owners and employees of the company. If the company was owned and operated by a sixth person, who did not know about the malware, then the information within the company would be fragmented (on purpose in this case), and the knowledge that the experts had would not be available to the rest of the company. Note that in this case the repair company does not have operating knowledge about the malware, even though the company's engineers knew, because the information was not shared along the company lines.

The same would apply if the five engineers were part of a large institution and did not inform others along the lines of communication about what they knew. The experts within the institution knew, so there was fragmented knowledge within the institution about the malware, but the institution did not have operating knowledge in the relevant sense. They could not have warned their customers about the malware, for example, as the institution did not know it was being installed. One could argue that the institution should seek to establish policies and procedures to try to prevent blockages of this sort along its knowledge lines from happening again. This leads us to the parameters of institutional knowledge: what should institutions know? This is the question that I will address next.

4 Parameters of Institutional Knowledge

Institutions have fewer excuses for ignorance than individuals do. Simply hiding behind ignorance rarely works for institutions, as their collective capacity to process information far exceeds any individual's capacities. Institutions can rarely say that they did not know and be done with it. Often, they *did* have knowledge in the relevant sense, or at least they *should* have. They can pool knowledge and skills, fund research or have a group of experts dedicate their working hours to thinking through an issue from the institution's point of view. If the required expertise cannot be found among their existing members, they can hire new staff or employ consultants. They can and should do this when new issues arise that affect their operating environment and future operations. As Steve Vanderheiden puts it:

> While cognitive limits on the ability to know must allow for some excusable ignorance in the case of persons, states and other large-scale organizations have a much greater ability

to process information than do individual persons, and are as a result more circumscribed in their claims to excusable ignorance.[10]

For an institution to be in a position to know *X*, it has to bring enough people together to *find out about X*, to have knowledge that was previously outside the institution. Knowledge flows can of course be interrupted in many ways within institutions, but these are cases where the institution should amend its practices for the better. The institution can draw resources together to *find that X* when it comes to information that is already within the institution, but too fragmented to count as institutional knowledge. In other words, there is a dysfunction of some kind in pooling these resources, and the institution wants to address this.

In general, it is the responsibility of the institution to make sure that when it comes to important issues, the information that it has is not too fragmented across departments, and that members are aware of the issue at least to the degree relevant for their roles. In other words, the institution has to carefully determine which knowledge should be shared within the institution.

In theory, the parameters of institutional knowledge are set by the executive levels of the institution, laying out what knowledge the institution should have or obtain in the future, and in which areas it can remain ignorant. In practice, the picture is not this simple, however. Much institutional knowledge is acquired without top-down directives and incentives, based purely on the interests and dislikes of its members. The frog researcher is a case in point. Institutions can also have information that leads to only partial knowledge, or the information it has is misleading. The more complex an institution is, the more it is prone to errors. There might even be a system failure due to a design fault in the institution, resulting in ignorance. Systemic errors should be addressed at the earliest opportunity once they become apparent. They should be actively looked for and tested for at least in core areas of the institution, although there will always be surprises.

Along with errors and systematic failures, a major challenge for institutional knowledge is so-called tacit knowledge. This kind of institutional memory is difficult, almost impossible, to document in writing and in guidelines. Rather, it gets passed on from one employee to another and is retained in the memory of long-serving members of staff. Retaining this institutional memory is a major practical challenge for all institutions, and it also raises interesting questions about who needs and should have knowledge in times of large-scale restructuring and institutional change.

10 Vanderheiden 2016: 306.

Lack of institutional knowledge can also be rooted in ignorance about knowledge and facts. What I call *knowable recognised unknowns* are issues that could be addressed, given the right resources and motivation.[11] There is no science or technology lacking when it comes to obtaining knowledge about these facts, rather they are either outside the focus of the institution, or the benefits derived do not warrant the expenditure in terms of resources. If something is clearly outside the focus of the institution, leading to a lack of motivation in acquiring the knowledge in question, the resulting ignorance is justified. A library does not have to know about the intricacies of mortgage lending, but a bank involved in such lending should.[12]

I would argue that institutions with the capacity to process a lot of information have greater obligations to know about complicated large-scale social issues than individuals, as long as the issue falls within their scope of interest. After all, institutions have fewer excuses for being ignorant about facts than individuals do, as argued above. Some institutions should also know how certain issues affect their members. For example, states should know how climate change is likely to affect their citizens, as protecting their interests is one of the reasons for the continued existence of states as institutions.

What an institution should know depends on its focus, its *ethos*, namely the reason(s) for the continued existence of the institution. Ethos consists of the central questions and practical matters that are vital to the purpose of the group (*the group's realm of concern*) and the answers it has collectively accepted as its view (*intentional horizon*).[13] The ethos thus covers the central goals and commitments of an institution. However, it is not set in stone, as elements may change (and almost always do, even in very conservative institutions). The institutional ethos is thus in a state of flux to a degree. Examples abound: political parties amalgamate new goals, the jurisdiction of local authorities changes, a university begins to offer courses in a new subject, financial institutions come up with a new product, and so on.

To simply state that some knowledge is currently outside the realm of concern of an institution does not, in itself, settle much in terms of the normative

---

11 Hormio 2018.

12 Fragmentation of knowledge could also be described in terms of knowable recognised unknowns, as the process of specialization and coordination allows them to be confined to or sustained within parts of the institution. With institutional operating knowledge, the fact that some members of the institution have the knowledge is often widely known, so for the other members expert knowledge on a given issue is a knowable recognised unknown at the individual level.

13 Laitinen 2014; Tuomela 2007.

question pertaining to the responsibility of institutions. As institutions are responsive to their environments and must regularly review their realm of concerns as well their intentional horizons, knowable recognised unknowns are always a normative matter. This applies to universities and corporations, libraries and banks alike. To give just one example, the intentional horizon of a state government often changes after an election, resulting in new answers to central questions vital to the institution. This is reflected as changes in policy: the new answers can and often do conflict with the previous answers (e.g. tax rates go up or down, money is allocated differently).

When the intentional horizon of an institution changes, from the viewpoint of institutional knowledge there should still be consistency despite the changes. I do not refer to policy changes here, as there is no inconsistency from the viewpoint of institutional knowledge (although a state's policies could be inconsistent in other ways). Policy changes are a normal feature of institutional politics. Rather, what I have in mind is consistency in knowledge claims. For example, can the U.S. federal government really claim at this point in time that climate change is not a priority and cast doubt on science previously endorsed by their own agencies? Of course they can – and do – but the claim is inconsistent with the knowledge that the government has previously admitted to be privy to. I will discuss this in the next section, where I return to my case study concerning institutional knowledge of climate change.

5 Climate Change Knowledge Revisited

Climate change offers fertile ground for discussing institutional knowledge claims. It is a common misconception that climate science, or even climate policy, is something new. In 1895, Svante Arrhenius presented a paper to the Stockholm Physical Society on the influence of carbon in the atmosphere on the surface temperature of the Earth.[14] Charles David Keeling, a researcher at the Scripps Institution of Oceanography, began measuring carbon dioxide concentration in the atmosphere in 1958. His research showed that the concentration was rising steadily roughly relative to the amount of fossil fuel burned. The data gathered would later become known as the Keeling Curve. The measurement has been taken at the Mauna Loa Observatory in Hawaii ever since, providing the longest continuous data on CO_2 concentration.[15]

14 Fleming 1998.
15 Monroe 2013.

Scientists were quick to alert the policymakers and the U.S. Federal Government has known about climate change for many decades as an institution. Knowledge about climate change can thus be attributed to the USA as a nation state in the operative knowledge sense (the knowledge of U.S. citizens and denizens is a different question). President Lyndon Johnson mentioned the effect that carbon dioxide and fossil fuels have had on the global atmosphere in a speech to the United States Congress as early as 1965. As global warming began to gain wider scientific interest and was noticed at the top levels of the administration in the U.S. during the latter half of the 1970s, it prompted an increasingly organised and determined response from groups and individuals with either vested interests in the fossil fuel industry, or ideological distaste for any environmental concerns that could bring with them added regulation and government involvement in the market.[16]

I have argued that what matters for institutional operating knowledge is whether the relevant people knew, usually the experts and the executives. Apart from cases like Juliana et al., which are directed towards governments, there are currently several legal cases underway in the USA and elsewhere concerning the knowledge that certain oil companies had about climate change back in the early 1980s. One question concerns whether or not these institutions misled their shareholders by not making their operating knowledge available to them, namely by making it shared knowledge among the stakeholders of the institution.

For example, there is a discrepancy between the way in which ExxonMobil saw climate change internally, and the message it communicated externally through paid advertisements and other PR efforts.[17] Internal documents show that ExxonMobil's scientists and managers were able to identify climate change as a potential threat to its business interests even by the early 1980s. They also acknowledged its anthropogenic nature (i.e. that it is caused by humans). These documents "consistently tracked evolving climate science" and acknowledged that climate change "is real, human-caused, serious, and solvable".[18] However, the corporation's message in its advertorials was different and concentrated on emphasising the uncertainties in the science. Their external communications thus promoted a narrative that was inconsistent with the operating knowledge that the institution held about the science.

16 Oreskes and Conway 2010: 170–71.

17 Supran and Oreskes 2017.

18 Supran and Oreskes 2017: 15.

Although Exxon has possibly been the most persistent lobbyist, it was not the only corporation to adopt a public stance on climate change that contrasted with their internal documents on the issue. Another example is Royal Dutch Shell, which understood the gravity of climate change as early as the 1980s, some ten or twenty years before the severity of the threat entered the public consciousness. This operating knowledge is demonstrated in the quote below from their confidential 1988 report *The Greenhouse Effect*:

> It is estimated that any climatic change relatable to CO_2 would not be detectable before the end of the century. With the very long time scales involved, it would be tempting for society to wait until then before doing anything. The potential implications for the world are, however, so large that policy options need to be considered much earlier. And the energy industry needs to consider how it should play its part.[19]

Shell had set up a Greenhouse Effect Working Group, who warned in that same confidential report that by the time the effects were detectable around the turn of the century, it might already "be too late to take effective countermeasures to reduce the effects or even stabilise the situation". However, despite this operating knowledge, Shell lobbied against regulation and effective measures to tackle the problem early on through the Global Climate Coalition (GCC), which was formed in 1989 to act as a counterforce to the Intergovernmental Panel on Climate Change (IPCC). The GCC counted among its members big oil companies, car manufacturers, and industry associations, spreading misleading information to discredit climate science and foster scepticism about it in order to keep legislation at bay to protect profits in the short-term. It seems that Shell had a strong operating knowledge about climate change science, but this knowledge was not shared knowledge among its shareholders, let alone among other stakeholders. Its own experts had recommended that the industry should consider how to play its part in finding a solution to the emerging problem, but maybe this knowledge was too painful for the industry to properly process at the time. Be that as it may, the end result was a cynical delaying of action and buying more time.

I argued at the end of the last section that even with changes to its intentional horizon, an institution should not be making inconsistent knowledge claims. What I have in mind are claims such as climate change not being the top environmental priority, made by the new head of the U.S. Environmental

19 The confidential report *The Greenhouse Effect* has been deposited in Climate files, and is available at www.climatefiles.com/shell/1988-shell-report-greenhouse.

Protection Agency (EPA) in 2019.[20] Even with a new intentional horizon, such claims are inconsistent with the knowledge that the institution has.

While such a statement is clearly a statement by an official appointed to represent the institution, and therefore a claim made by the EPA, it is also an inconsistent statement in the light of previous statements and reports by the institution. As the science that the previous position was based on has not changed (i.e. no new scientific evidence has emerged that would make climate change less of a threat), this means either that the claim is in contrast to what the institution in fact knows, or that the institution is no longer able to draw together the necessary resources to have knowledge on the issue.

In either case, it could prove embarrassing to the institution if the plaintiffs in Juliana et al. were allowed discovery, that is to obtain evidence from the other party. It could be that they would obtain evidence showing that what EPA scientists and other experts within the institution know about climate change is indeed inconsistent with what the EPA now states publicly. It is possible that the public statements by the institution are inconsistent with its operating knowledge, which seems to have been the case with the oil companies. It is even possible that the statements are inconsistent with the shared knowledge of the institution.

The case shows how institutional knowledge can be awkward to deal with when there is a change in the administration of an institution. When the current U.S. government took charge, it purged a great deal of information from government websites. To give an example, the section on the EPA website that used to be dedicated to climate change (www.epa.gov/climatechange) can now only be found in the archived version and is no longer updated.[21] Some material on climate change disappeared altogether and words have been adjusted throughout the website.[22] While climate change was listed as one of the popular topics on the frontpage of the EPA website in January 2017, the frontpage no longer even includes climate change in its list of "Key Topics", focusing instead on other issues such as mould.[23] In addition, the EPA set new rules to prevent certain data from entering its regulatory decision processes, and also to get rid of some of its experts, as leading scientists who have received EPA research grants were replaced by industry-funded scientists.[24] This effectively changes

20 Hook and Stacey 2019.
21 The archived January 2017 website can be found at https://19january2017snapshot.epa.gov.
22 Barron 2018.
23 The EPA website (www.epa.gov) was accessed on 30 September 2019.
24 Cornwall 2017.

who is allowed an expert status and say within the institution. Actions like these could be construed as waging war on the EPA's institutional knowledge.

6 Closing Remarks

Although attributions of institutional knowledge are for the most part context-specific, we can still say that institutions have knowledge about something when the members tasked with dealing with knowledge in this area possess it, and the knowledge is attached to the appropriate lines of communication. This knowledge comes in degrees, depending not only on how well the lines of communication work and how fragmented the information is, but also on what the knowledge is used for. Sometimes operative knowledge is preferable to shared knowledge. What is clear is that ignorance on its own rarely excuses institutions.[25]

References

Barron, Laignee (2018) "Here's What the EPA's Website Looks Like After a Year of Climate Change Censorship". *Time.com*, 1 March 2018, available at https://time.com/5075265/epa-website-climate-change-censorship.

Blumm, Michael C. and Mary C. Wood (2017) "'No Ordinary Lawsuit': Climate Change, Due Process, and the Public Trust Doctrine". *American University Law Review* 67(1),1–87.

Cornwall, Warren (2017) "Trump's EPA has blocked agency grantees from serving on science advisory panels. Here is what it means". *ScienceMag.org*, 31 October 2017, available at https://www.sciencemag.org/news/2017/10/trump-s-epa-has-blocked-agency-grantees-serving-science-advisory-panels-here-what-it.

Fleming, James Rodger (1998) *Historical Perspectives on Climate Change*. Oxford: Oxford University Press.

Hook, Leslie and Kiran Stacey (2019) "Climate change not top environment priority, says new EPA chief". *Financial Times*, 30 April 2019.

Hormio, Säde (2018) "Culpable ignorance in a collective setting", in Jaakko Kuorikoski and Teemu Toppinen (eds.) *Action, Value and Metaphysics – Acta Philosophica Fennica*. Helsinki: Philosophical Society of Finland, 94 (XCIV), 7–34.

Juliana v. U.S. (2015) *First Amended Complaint for Declaratory and Injunctive Relief* 6:15-cv-01517-TC.

25 I would like to thank the participants at the Glasgow workshop for their comments and feedback, especially Jessica Brown and Kirk Ludwig, who pressed me on key points. Special thanks are due to Miguel and Rachael for putting together such an engaging workshop and following it up with this book.

Juliana v. U.S. (2017) *Federal Defendants' Answer to First Amended Complaint for Declaratory and Injunctive Relief* 6:15-cv-01517-TC.

Laitinen, Arto (2014) "Collective Intentionality and Recognition from Others", in Anita Konzelmann Ziv and Hans Bernhard Schmid (eds.) *Institutions, Emotions, and Group Agents: Contributions to Social Ontology*. Dordrecht: Springer Science+Business Media, 213–227.

Monroe, Rob (2013) "The History of the Keeling Curve", Scripps Institution of Oceanography, 3 April 2013, available at https://scripps.ucsd.edu/programs/keelingcurve/2013/04/03/the-history-of-the-keeling-curve.

Oreskes, Naomi and Erik M. Conway (2010) *Merchants of Doubt: How a Handful of Scientists Obscured the Truth on Issues from Tobacco Smoke to Global Warming*. New York: Bloomsbury Press.

Rubinton, David S. (2017) "Save Yourselves, Kids: The Atmospheric Trust Litigation". *Natural Resources & Environment*, 32(2): 11–14.

Supran, Geoffrey and Naomi Oreskes (2017) Assessing ExxonMobil's climate change communications (1977–2014). *Environmental Research Letters* 12.

Tuomela, Raimo (2007) *The Philosophy of Sociality: The Shared Point of View*. New York: Oxford University Press.

Vanderheiden, Steve (2016) "The Obligation to Know: Information and the Burdens of Citizenship". *Ethical Theory and Moral Practice* 19(2): 297–311.

Wood, Mary Christina (2013) *Nature's Trust: Environmental Law for a New Ecological Age*. New York: Cambridge University Press.

Leonie Smith

The Right to Press Freedom of Expression vs the Rights of Marginalised Groups: An Answer Grounded in Personhood Rights

1 Introduction

No case in which a member of the UK print press media ('PPM') uses pejorative language against a group of people as a class in print can *ever* fall foul of the *Editors' Code* (the industry's main code of conduct) anti-discrimination guidelines. Discrimination claims can be made against members of the PPM for reporting which contains 'prejudicial or pejorative' language with regard to features such as the race and gender of identifiable individuals. But the guidelines specifically prohibit consideration of any similar complaint against *groups* of individuals. This results in the main regulatory body for the national press, IPSO, concluding that news articles with content describing, e.g., asylum seekers, as "spreading like a norovirus" and "a plague of feral humans", are not even *investigable* on the grounds of discrimination (IPSO, 02741-15 *Greer v The Sun*).

Opponents and proponents of the above approach typically frame this as a classic 'free speech' vs 'harm principle' dilemma. Specifically, that we need to balance:

(A) The need for a free press within a functioning democracy; and
(B) The harms caused to marginalised groups by derogatory and prejudicial language about them.

Those in favour of press freedom argue that the PPM's right to freedom of expression beats any perceived or actual harm caused, and those against argue the opposite. Predictably, little progress is made in either party convincing the other. We ought therefore to try a different approach.

I therefore propose that we assess the PPM's freedom to print prejudicial language against groups of individuals purely on the basis of the fundamental value from which that freedom is derived. This approach has one major benefit over the free speech vs freedom from harm perspective in which different rights are weighed up: if we cannot uphold that fundamental value at the same time as permitting discriminatory reporting against collectives of individuals, then this would indicate a problem which all parties would have to recognise, on

https://doi.org/10.1515/9783110663617-006

pain of irrationality. This would then be a strong basis from which to argue for a change in PPM policy.

There are, I think, at least two strong contenders for the value of press freedom. First, that the PPM's role as a democratic institution might grant them special testimonial rights to freedom of expression. And second, that regardless of any special role held, the PPM, individual news agents, journalists and editors have the same right to agential epistemic participation as all other agents have. Provided that the PPM do not incite or cause identifiable harm to individuals, then the right to participate in relevant epistemic spheres over-rides worries about distasteful or unpleasant language used in exercising that epistemic agency.

In this chapter I focus on that right to epistemic participation.[1] Taking the example of reporting on UK welfare-claimants I argue that, first, the actions of the PPM may restrict the free speech of groups through increasing the likelihood of *epistemic injustice* against them in ways which undermine their right to agential epistemic participation. For groups who are already marginalised, background conditions of prejudicial beliefs entail that any contribution to those beliefs effectively maintains or worsens the likelihood of *testimonial injustice* and *epistemic exclusion*. At the very least, this indicates the need to weigh up damage to *practical* agential epistemic participation on either side in any debate around the freedom of expression of the PPM. And second, when we examine the basis of the right to epistemic agency as a part of performative personhood, we may have strong grounds for erring *against* the PPM in favour of marginalised groups at the outset of assessing discrimination claims.

I proceed as follows: In §2, I outline the current regulatory landscape of the UK PPM and present some surprising figures relating to the outcome of complaints made against the PPM. I outline a basic plausible case for *restricting* discrimination claims to individual claimants. In §3, I give reason to undermine one of the premises of that case by demonstrating that, with epistemic participation as the grounds of the right, free speech concerns are relevant to both the PPM and marginalised groups. In §4, drawing on my earlier work Smith (2018), I introduce the question of why the right to epistemic participation matters, and argue that, along with other agential rights, it at least matters to being able to perform as a person within the social communicative sphere. I consider who the relevant persons amongst the PPM might be and conclude that there are some particularly powerful agents involved. I surmise that this means that the exercise of freedom of pejorative expression by the PPM against marginalised persons has the power to undermine the latter's personhood

1 See (Smith nd) for analysis of the rights of the press as a special democratic institution.

status altogether. As such, we have good reason to consider cases of group discrimination on the same grounds as individual cases. §5 concludes.

2 Print Press Discrimination Against Groups

2.1 The PPM, IPSO and the Editors' Code

The UK national print press media (PPM), including their online output, are predominantly regulated by the self-funded and self-regulatory body, the Independent Press Standards Organisation (IPSO). A handful of members of the national PPM self-regulate without being members of IPSO – *The Guardian*, *Financial Times* and *The Independent* – however, for the purposes of understanding press regulation in the UK, most major news groups *are* members and this provides us with a rich source of data on what the PPM take their responsibilities to be with regard to the rights of those they report on.

IPSO's main sources of guidance with regard to press complaints are the *Editors' Code of Practice* (a list of sixteen recognised grounds for complaint) and the *Editors' Codebook* which is a weightier 130-page (non-binding) handbook. Clause 12 of the *Code* outlines how members should avoid complaints on grounds of 'Discrimination'. Specifically:

i) The press must avoid prejudicial or pejorative reference to an individual's, race, colour, religion, sex, gender identity, sexual orientation or to any physical or mental illness or disability.
ii) Details of an individual's race, colour, religion, gender identity, sexual orientation, physical or mental illness or disability must be avoided unless genuinely relevant to the story (ECPC, 2019a).

Note that not *all* discriminatory language is included above. As written, derogatory reporting against some potentially vulnerable groups on the basis of that characteristic, such as homeless people, people who are considered to be overweight or unattractive, and people living in poverty and on welfare support, would not be covered at all. But let's assume for now that the class of protected characteristics might, in principle, be extended (§3 below might provide good reason to include at least one of these categories). What actually happens to claims made under 'Discrimination'?

Between October 2014 and August 2019, 16,337 complaints were made to IPSO, which included claims on the grounds of 'Discrimination'. Of these, only *two* were apparently ultimately found to be breaches of the code (IPSO).[2] 776 were not pursued; 70 were resolved through mediation with either IPSO or the publication; and 64 were found not to be in breach. The vast majority were rejected for investigation or were determined to be outside of the regulator's remit (15,423).[3]

As there are no records for the cases not actually heard by IPSO it is difficult to identify exactly why the committee refuses to hear cases. Nevertheless, it is evident from those complaints which include discrimination claims but which are either rejected or upheld on other grounds (typically item 1, 'Accuracy'), that – in addition to claims rejected as the language is not deemed derogatory against a protected characteristic – many are rejected due to their involving claims against *groups* of people, as opposed to individuals. This comment in a case upheld on the grounds of accuracy, is typical and common:

> The terms of Clause 12 are designed to protect identified individuals mentioned by the press against discrimination on the basis of their race, colour, religion, gender, sexual orientation or any physical or mental illness or disability, and do not apply to groups or categories of people. The complainant's general concern that the article was discriminatory against refugees did not engage the terms of this Clause. (IPSO, *06593–15 Clarke v Daily Express*)

The Editors' *Code* and *Codebook* guidelines specifically prohibit hearing a complaint on the basis of discrimination against a group of individuals. This means that no case in which a member uses discriminatory language, phrasing or framing against a group of people as a class can ever fall foul of IPSO guidelines, on the grounds of that language.

2.2 Why Do IPSO Not Consider Collective Discrimination Claims?

This is not an oversight. The Leveson inquiry was established in 2011 as a judicial public investigation into the ethics, role and practices of the British press,

2 Figures accurate to 30 November 2019. Discrepancies between the summarised totals available and the detail of actual claims means that the summary figure reports *four* cases. However, on investigation into each case found in breach, I can only find two in which the discrimination claim was upheld: *00572–15 Trans Media Watch v The Sun*; and *18685–17 Evans v The Argus (Brighton)*.

3 There is a (very) minor discrepancy on IPSO's website in reporting the total number of claims rejected. I have taken the lower of two figures provided.

following the *News International* phone hacking scandal.[4] The *Code's* policy is in explicit contravention of the inquiry's recommendations which argue that:

> the power to require a correction and an apology must apply equally in relation to individual standards breaches [. . .] and to groups of people (or matters of fact) where there is no single identifiable individual who has been affected.
>
> (Leveson 2012: Vol.4; part L; recommendation 15: 1803)

And the pressure group Hacked Off have challenged IPSO on this exact point (Hacked Off, 2019).[5] The guidelines are explicitly written to continue to exclude collective discrimination.

Charitably, the guide offers three reasons for excluding these kinds of claims. Doing so would:

(i) "inhibit debate on important matters" (ECPC, 2019b: 84)
(ii) "involve subjective views" (*ibid.*)
(iii) "be difficult to adjudicate upon without infringing the freedom of expression of others" (*ibid.*)

It is not obvious why collective discrimination claims would "involve subjective views" in a way that discrimination against individuals does not, nor why "debate on important matters" ought to require discriminatory language, and the *Codebook* offers no more in defence of these claims. But I believe the key to understanding both is in item (iii). The foreword to the latest version of the *Codebook* references ongoing pressure to amend item 12 (without explicitly saying that this is a demand to include collective discrimination) and offers the following additional information in support of their decision not to do so:

> The suggested amendments we have received regarding Clause 12 are both thoughtful and heartfelt. Nevertheless, it is vitally important that the committee also takes into account the *potentially chilling effect that changes might have on the ability of the press to report on and debate major issues of the day.* (ECPC, 2019b: 5, my emphasis)

The worries seem to be that allowing for collective discrimination claims would inhibit the freedom of expression of the PPM, and that this would in turn, be harmful in some way. Let's assume then that the principle being upheld is that of the importance of, and possibly right to, freedom of expression. The worry

4 *News of the World* reporters were found to have hacked the voicemail of a murdered child and of numerous other individuals.

5 Quote: "Is IPSO suggesting that journalists and newspapers are somehow incapable of writing stories or opinion without offending a group?" (Hacked Off Executive Director Kyle Taylor).

might be that the PPM need to be able to speak freely in order to either fulfil some democratic duty, or simply because all agents have the right to free expression, including agential individual and corporate members of the PPM. As this free expression is limited by the *Code* when it involves discrimination against individuals, then we can also assume that this freedom only extends as far as the boundaries of the rights of others. And, that IPSO and the *Code* either believe that this cannot apply in the case of discrimination against groups, or that the harm faced by the PPM in not being able to speak freely is greater in a qualitatively distinct way, such that these cases do not even warrant a hearing.

What might undermine this claim, as it stands? A number of arguments might be made, but in §3, I will argue for one that most ought to find compelling: that the actions of the PPM in exercising freedom of expression to write pejorative reports about groups of individuals may result in undermining the value which is intended to ground that freedom.

3 The Fundamental Value of Press Freedom

The argument of this section runs as follows:

P1. *The non-contradiction principle*: one non-controversial basis for *not* protecting the freedom of the PPM to report pejoratively on groups without those groups having a right to redress would be that doing so would undermine the same value which grants the PPM this freedom.

P2. *The underlying value thesis*: a key motivation for protecting the freedom of the PPM to report pejoratively on groups without those groups having a right to redress is that doing so preserves the PPM's agential right to epistemic participation. This right is something which ought to be protected for *all* agents.

P3. Epistemic injustice undermines agential epistemic participation for marginalised groups.

P4. Pejorative reporting adds to, or maintains, conditions for epistemic injustice for marginalised groups.[6]

C1. The freedom of the PPM to report pejoratively on groups may result in undermining the value which grants the PPM this freedom (*from P2, P3 and P4*).

6 At least for groups who already experience this.

C2. The freedom of the PPM is not grounds for a blanket prohibition on hearing cases of discrimination against groups who experience epistemic injustice *(from P1 and C1).*

I take it that the *Non-contradiction* principle in P1 can be granted. There may be other grounds for arguing against the freedom of the press to report pejoratively on groups, but these are always open to being contested on the basis of competing values (the right to free speech vs harm to human dignity, the wrongness of making discriminatory comments, risk of harm or incitement to violence etc.). In contrast, if the PPM's freedom of expression when it comes to reporting on groups is grounded in a value which their own behaviour undermines, then there is a case for the legitimacy of complaints with regard to that reporting.

We now need to examine the remaining premises.

3.1 P2: The Underlying Value Thesis

The claim here is that we ought to be concerned with automatically prioritising the freedom of the PPM to report pejoratively about marginalised groups, specifically because that freedom is grounded in it being necessary to preserve the members' rights to agential epistemic participation. Regardless of any *special* role that the PPM might have, as a democratic institution, for example, which might motivate increased protection of freedom of expression, the PPM is also comprised of individual and collective agents. And at least one reason for granting freedom of expression or speech to all agents in a democratic society, is that we value epistemic participation for *all* agents.

This right to epistemic participation does not entail that all agents have the same right to epistemic involvement in *all* possible contexts. Rather, to know if I have a right to epistemic participation it is enough to ask: is this what similar agents ought to all have access to, all else being equal, within this context? I will return to the question of who exactly the agential members of the PPM are that ought to be respected by this value (§4). But provided that those agential members of the PPM do not fall foul of some other over-riding competing important social value or law, then their right to participate in relevant epistemic spheres over-rides worries about distasteful or unpleasant language used, to the same extent that it does for all other agents in society.

3.2 P3: Epistemic Injustice Undermines Agential Epistemic Participation

Epistemic injustice involves a harm done to someone in their capacity as a knower (Fricker, 2007). Epistemic injustice undermines epistemic participation in multiple ways. Given space constraints, I will focus here on just one of Fricker's classic forms of epistemic injustice: testimonial injustice.

Testimonial injustice occurs when an individual speaker is not accorded due credibility by the person she is speaking with, resulting in the hearer failing to believe the speaker (in full or in part), when she otherwise ought to (Fricker, 2007: 28). To count as an injustice rather than only as a misfortune or mistake, this reduced credibility deficit must take place within – and result from – an environment of systematically prejudicial false beliefs about individuals who share aspects of the speaker's identity. The credibility deficit must be "identity-prejudicial" (*ibid.*). The primary harm is epistemic because a downgrading of credibility entails that the speaker fails to be treated appropriately as one who is capable of having and transmitting knowledge. As a result, she is prevented from exercising her right to full epistemic participation within certain scenarios or on given topics.

Consider, for example, the case of UK welfare claimants. The primary cause of benefit 'sanctions' (cancelled funding) in the UK is 'a failure to look for work' (Jitendra, 2017). Within the context of a job centre interview, being believed or not can make the difference between physical survival versus starvation, homelessness, or even death. Do benefit claimants experience testimonial injustice in these types of situation? It is at least evident that they experience standing conditions of disbelief. Consider Sophie, a young woman and a benefit claimant, reporting her experience of being interviewed by job centre employees in Ruth Patrick's longitudinal study:

> [Job Centre staff] do look down at you [. . .] last week when I went down, she went, 'Have you applied for any jobs?' I went 'Yeah, 23.' And she looked at me as if to say 'Right okay, whatever'. (Sophie, a single parent cited in Patrick, 2016: 248)

Here, Sophie is disbelieved when she reports on her experience of job hunting. Her experience is not uncommon for welfare claimants. We can't be certain that this is testimonial injustice, but evidence of background conditions of prejudice would indicate that it might be. And these conditions do appear to exist. DeVries, for example, reports that in tests used to determine implicit bias:

> Participants found it much easier to group words relating to benefit claimants together with negative words like "bad", "useless", and "dirty" than they did to group them together with positive words like "friendly", "clean", or "wonderful". This was true even for people who, when asked directly, did not report having any negative opinions about people on benefits. (DeVries, 2017)

Background conditions of prejudice against welfare claimants make it likely that the disbelief Sophie, and many like her, face in these and other scenarios is likely, on many occasions, to demonstrate testimonial injustice. If this is the case, then welfare claimants' ability to epistemically participate in an effective way (for their testimony to be heard without hindrance when it ought to be) is unjustly at risk due to background conditions of prejudice.

3.3 P4: Pejorative Reporting Adds to or Maintains Conditions for Epistemic Injustice

In the case of recent reporting on welfare claimants, Laura Basu presents a strong case for the actions of the media having 're-written' the timeline of the 2008 financial crisis, by 2009, so as to shift blame away from the banks and onto those who were alleged to have driven the UK into debt (welfare claimants) (Basu, 2018).

This corresponds with research findings in 2012 that, "[w]hile fraud remains very important in negative coverage, articles are much more likely now to refer to lack of reciprocity and effort on the part of claimants than they were previously" (Baumberg et al, 2012: 3). The narrative of waste and blame for public spending becomes something with which to target the 'laziness' of those viewed as costing the state money. And ultimately, this shows up in the implicit biases of others, as we saw in DeVries', above. As Baumberg et al report in their investigation into UK benefits stigma:

> [...] we found that people who read more stigmatising newspapers perceived higher levels of fraud and reported more personal stigma [and] taking into account other factors that are associated with newspaper readership, we still found a link between newspaper coverage and perceived deservingness [...] All of this suggests that there is a genuine link between negative media coverage and stigma. (Baumberg et al, 2012: 8)

It is not a novel claim to suggest that beliefs in general, and the existence of prejudicial beliefs more specifically, are influenced and even established by reporting in the mainstream print and online press. The role of the media as public agenda-setters has been well-established since McCombs and Shaw's analysis of media reporting and public opinion on important issues (1972), with subsequent work demonstrating the media's power to shift public opinion on specific issues, as in the case of the Watergate scandal (Lang and Lang, 1981).

Headlines such as *The Daily Express*', 'Party is over for benefit skivers' (Hall, 2013), and *The Sun*'s 'Welfies' awards (The Sun, 2015), both of which use pejorative language against the class of welfare claimants are therefore likely to add to, or worsen, social prejudicial views of that group. Testimonial – and other forms of epistemic – injustice are the result. And epistemic injustice harms the ability of individuals within that group to participate epistemically in relevant spheres. As such, when the PPM reports in a pejorative way about this class, they undermine individual members of that group's right to agential epistemic participation.

I have used welfare claimants as an example. But this model, in which pejorative reporting adds to prejudicial beliefs which allow for epistemic injustice and restricted epistemic participation, will apply to many marginalised groups of individuals. As such, they ought not to be ruled out from discrimination complaints as a matter of regulatory policy.

3.4 Summing Up

The first conclusion, C1, now follows from P2, P3 and P4. The freedom of the PPM to report pejoratively on groups of individuals without risk of discrimination claims risks undermining the chance for epistemic participation of those groups. As epistemic participation is an important underlying value which grants the PPM their freedom of expression, this in turn leads to the second conclusion, C2: the PPM cannot refuse to engage with complaints of discrimination against groups of individuals, but instead must hear them and weigh up the impact of the discriminatory reporting just as it would in individual cases.[7]

The claim is not that the PPM should not be allowed to report on groups of individuals in a negative way. Rather, it is that they must allow for the legitimacy of discrimination complaints against groups of individuals. In §4 however, I will argue that we might have good reason for expecting that claims ought to generally find in favour of the group rather than of the PPM, where that group is a marginalised one (one which faces a high risk of epistemic injustice).

7 In one sense this is still a free speech vs harm point; clearly the harm to one's ability to epistemically participate is a harm. However, it is not the fact that it is a harm that does the work. It is the fact that one of the values underpinning free speech itself is at stake when we report pejoratively against already-marginalised groups.

4 Powerful Persons and the Limits of Personhood Rights

4.1 Weighing Up Rights

So far, this then pits the right to epistemic participation of the PPM against the right to epistemic participation of groups and argues that we have grounds to allow complaints against the PPM to be heard, if this is one important value which supports the PPM's right to freedom of speech. But how should we actually adjudicate in discrimination cases raised?

One argument is that the press simply needs the freedom to report as they see fit more than any agent needs the freedom from discrimination which might impact on their own individual epistemic participation. That speaking truth to power as a democratic institution takes precedence over the risk of epistemic injustice elsewhere. This would not entail that the PPM might permissibly use discriminatory language carte blanche: the epistemic participation risk argued for is still a factor and complaints could be legitimately made. But it might mean that it would be rare for discrimination complaints against groups to be actually found in the groups' favour. However, I will assume here that we can deal with this claim, an argument which stems from the presumed special democratic role of the press (Smith nd). If that is the case, then we enter into a weighing up of the impact on epistemic participation for the agents involved in the PPM, versus the impact on epistemic participation of the agents who make up a discriminated-against group.

It still seems initially plausible that this might mean that, although now heard as complaints, few cases are actually found in *favour* of the group in question. It is easy for a member of the PPM to express the impact on their freedom of expression if they are not able to print claims about groups of individuals as they see fit: the very clear impact is that they cannot express their full opinion on the group in question. And in the case of discrimination against identifiable individual agents, it is arguably relatively easy to quantify the impact on the epistemic participation of those individual agents. Someone who is discriminated against in the national press is likely to face the risk of direct rejection or downgrading by others as a credible source in ways that they can quantify in a formal complaint. It is far more difficult for anyone bringing a case on behalf of a discriminated-against group to quantify exactly what the specific impact of any given report, series of reports, or editorial stance is on a group of non-identifiable individuals. As such, it may be that the majority of cases will be found against groups of individuals, in favour of the PPM.

I believe that this is not the case. But to demonstrate this, we first need to understand why epistemic participation matters at all.

4.2 Performative Personhood And Rights: Why Does Epistemic Participation Matter?

We might want to make various arguments for the *intrinsic* moral value of agential epistemic participation. We might think that agential epistemic participation is involved in an agent being able to develop or demonstrate epistemic virtue, whether this is on a reliabilist or responsibilist account for example; or that it is essential to being able to act on a deontological 'epistemic imperative' (Elgin, 2013). But all of these types of accounts of the value of epistemic participation will depend on acceptance of some quite heavy ethical baggage: first signing up to a given general ethical view, and then arguing that agential epistemic participation is in some way a part of being able to be ethical in those terms.

One very straightforward response, however, is the instrumentalist one. And this is simply that in order to perform as an agent in relevant social spheres (however these are defined), one needs to have the practical ability to reciprocally epistemically participate, to the same extent that other agents can. Restrictions on this ability simply prevent an agent from performing as a 'person'. On this account, in which "the mark of personhood is the ability to play a certain role" (List and Pettit, 2011: 171), epistemic participation is simply a relevant part of that role.

And to the extent that we value agents being able to perform as persons, then we must value and protect that which allows them to do so. One cannot enter into *reciprocal* obligations and entitlements without being able to epistemically participate. I present and defend this account in earlier work (Smith, 2018), as an ontologically-grounded source of personhood rights. Agents have the right to do that which is necessary to perform as a person in relevant social spheres. If we are not willing to grant these rights, then we cannot preserve the agential ability to perform as persons. The idea is that:

> [. . .] a person can be held to account for promises made, but equally, a person has to be provided with the opportunity to freely enter into promises, else she cannot be said to be a person at all [. . .] this reciprocity is the source of her personhood rights. The only thing that might ground rights, without requiring further normative or metaphysical commitment, can be that a person must have those rights in order to count as a person fulfilling the criteria for [performative personhood] itself. The rights this suggests include the right to free speech, to free association, and to be able to enter into legal contracts, amongst others. (Smith, 2018)

If we do not grant rights to do the things needed to interact with other agential persons, then we cannot demand that they be persons at all, whether corporate or individual agent.

I will not defend this account further here. But I will suggest that, while our own ethical theories might generate additional sources of the intrinsic (or additional instrumental) value of epistemic participation, this is a plausible account of one reason that we do value epistemic participation, not only for individual agents but also for corporate ones. For the PPM to be able to perform its role as a source of information, we need to grant it (its members) the ability to fully epistemically participate; to have freedom of expression. Else, we cannot hold those PPM agents accountable for their epistemic assertions. And for individuals to be able to simply engage with other persons, as we see when this is obstructed by epistemic injustice, they require the same. As such, all agents from whom we demand or expect accurate information and / or opinion, must have the right to the level / extent of epistemic participation which allows them to proffer that.

So, both PPM and individuals have a performative personhood-grounded right to epistemic participation, of some kind. What are the limits of that right, for each type of agent? To answer this, we need to know which agents we are actually discussing when we talk about the PPM.

4.3 Which Persons And What Rights?

Not all persons are created equal in the realm of performative personhood. My account, building on Pettit's account of non-domination freedom (1996; 2006; 2007) argues that rights grounded in our status as persons are determined not according to a single list ('all persons have right X'), but on having that which allows us not to be dominated by others persons, in a given sphere. Those who have a lack of dominative power are likely to have more rights than those who have the ability to dominate simply because these are necessary in order for them to perform as a person in a way that they are not for more dominant persons (Smith, 2018: 19).

Therefore, to understand the extent of the rights of the PPM to print pejorative commentary about groups of individuals, and the extent to which discrimination complaints ought to be found in favour of those groups under their right to epistemic participation, we need to know who the dominant and non-dominant parties are in the exchange.

Both the wording and spirit of the *Editors' Code* appear to see the PPM as the plucky underdog, prepared to hold itself to account, fighting to exercise its epistemic participation rights and be heard amongst a sea of fake news. Its complaints process is designed to ensure that it can be held accountable for the claims it makes, even while other parties shirk the duties that accompany a right to epistemic participation:

> it has become even more difficult for the public to separate the truth from a murky maelstrom of fake news, propaganda and manipulation [. . .] Where others seek to duck accountability, the press is, through a binding contractual agreement, prepared to be held to account and to offer redress to people it has wronged. (ECPC, 2019b: 5)

Against this backdrop, in which it is in others' interests to silence and disrupt the work of disseminating truth, the press has a strong claim to the right to freedom of speech. Without this, it will be prevented from performing as a set of epistemic agents or persons able to be relied upon to speak the truth. And arguably, this right might require the freedom to use derogatory language without fear of censorship or recrimination. Restrictions on this right might otherwise easily be used against the otherwise non-powerful journalistic agents of the PPM to silence or coerce. We do, after all, want the press to be able to speak in critical, even damning and derogatory terms, about political parties, powerful corporations and interest groups, and collections of terrorists, without being worried that they will face silencing or punishment from the state or elsewhere for doing so. This suggests that members of the PPM have very robust epistemic participation rights which are likely to be more important to defend than those of random groups of individuals in society, in cases of pejorative discrimination.

The reality, however, is a bit more complicated. First, try to identify which persons are actually involved in the modern PPM. Some suggestions are:

(a) The individual journalist(s) responsible for the story.
(b) The editor (and division editor) who approved the piece for publication.
(c) The newspaper as a corporate person.

These persons become increasingly more powerful as we move down the list. And we can also make one other suggestion within the framework of the UK:

(d) The conglomerate corporate (or even individual) person who owns multiple newspapers.

The UK media landscape is dominated by a handful of very powerful corporate persons, owning multiple news outlets and, potentially, directing editorial policy. The Media Reform coalition summarises the current situation:

> [. . .] just three companies (News UK, DMG and Reach) dominate 83% of the national newspaper market [. . .]. When online readers are included, just five companies (News UK, DMG, Reach, Guardian and Telegraph) dominate some 80% of market share. (MRC, 2019: 2)

This is set to increase further with DMG's recent acquisition of another national newspaper, *the i* and its online news website, *inews.co.uk*. (Nilsson, 2019). More specifically, when it comes to the PPM agents who have had the most complaints raised against them on discrimination grounds, it is only *two* powerful persons we need to consider:

- *News UK* (owned by Rupert Murdoch), which owns *The Sun*, *Sun on Sunday*, *The Times* and the *Sunday Times*.
- The *Daily Mail and General Trust* (*DMG*), controlled by Lord Rothermere, which owns the *Daily Mail*, the *Mail on Sunday*, the *Metro*, and (as of late 2019) *the i*.

Whilst an individual journalist might have robust epistemic participation rights against their own newspaper, or as an independent writer,[8] the persons whose epistemic right to print pejorative commentary that we are actually discussing are extremely powerful ones. Pejorative reporting is very rarely the province of a single journalist speaking out against a group of others, but is something written in line with, at the very least, the editorial policy of the newspaper corporate person, and perhaps often, of the conglomerate owner. Murdoch, in particular, is widely believed to be actively engaged in controlling the editorial and journalistic voice of his publications (e.g., Hosenball and Holton, 2011).

On the other side of the equation, we have the groups of individuals that are being pejoratively discussed. Some of these groups are also, perhaps, persons in their own right (political parties, for example). But many are simply 'welfare claimants', 'refugees' or groups of individuals identified by gender, race or religion. In these cases, as we saw in §3.2, the individuals being discussed are the type whose ability to enact the epistemic participation needed to perform as a person is already under threat. When faced with pejorative reporting by powerful corporate persons these individuals may, in the general case, have far stronger claim to epistemic participation rights protection vs the freedom of the press, precisely because it is a one-way street: the powerful persons of the PPM have the ability to dominate through multiple media outlets such that groups of individuals see their personhood status damaged (through not being able to perform as persons in a relevant way). The same can hardly be said the other way around.

8 And these may well not be protected within newsrooms right now; when journalists are silenced on important matters by the need to comply with the editorial direction, they are arguably having their personhood status undermined.

It will not *always* be the case that complaints should find in favour of groups of individuals. The benefit of a personhood-grounded account of rights is that we need to know the dominative status of parties involved before determining what rights each party has, and what ought therefore to be protected. But it is, I suggest, highly likely that most cases in which the complaint is made on behalf of a marginalised social group, such as welfare claimants, that the finding ought to be in their favour. No persons, PPM or otherwise, have the unchecked right to that which would prevent another from operating as a person, which pejorative reporting against marginalised groups has the potential to do.

If the PPM is unwilling to fulfil their duty to ensure this, through documenting this principle in the *Editors' Code* and upholding it in regulatory complaints, then there is a case to be made for taking this aspect of regulation out of their current self-regulating hands, and into those of the courts.

5 Conclusion

I have argued here that epistemic participation is an important value and one underpinning of the media's claim to freedom of expression, which grounds their claim to be able to report in pejorative ways against groups of individuals. Respect for this value requires that we also consider the extent to which pejorative reporting undermines the ability of marginalised groups of persons to epistemically participate. Marginalised groups are those against whom epistemic injustice is regularly committed, and whose epistemic participation is already restricted. Additional pejorative reporting shores this up or worsens that epistemic participation status. This gives grounds for allowing that cases of discrimination against groups of individuals ought to at least be heard by print regulatory bodies.

But further, we might also have grounds for believing that in weighing up competing claims around the impact on epistemic participation (of printing or not printing the pejorative and prejudicial claims), this weighing up will generally come out in favour of the groups discriminated against, rather than the PPM agents involved. This is because, in many cases, the agent of the PPM is a powerful corporate person whilst those being pejoratively reported against are dominated persons in society. If we recognise that epistemic participation is an important right in being able to perform as a person, then no person has the right to arbitrarily damage that personhood status in another by undermining that right. Dominant agential members of the PPM do exactly that when they report pejoratively, in many cases. Thus, the epistemic participation rights of conglomerate media powers to print freely are limited when it comes to reporting on those groups who already experience prejudice and risks to their ability to epistemically participate. And we ought to expect that complaints will find against the PPM, far more often than they will find in their favour.

References

Basu, L. (2018). *Media Amnesia: Rewriting the Economic Crisis*, London: Pluto Press.
Baumberg, B. et al (2012). 'Benefits stigma in Britain'. Produced by The University of Kent, for Turn2us. Available at https://www.turn2us.org.uk/About-Us/Research-and-Insights/Benefits-Stigma-in-Britain. (Accessed 21 Nov 2019).
DeVries, H. (2017). 'How our unconscious minds are prejudiced against benefit claimants'. The Conversation. Available at: https://theconversation.com/how-our-unconscious-minds-are-prejudiced-against-benefit-claimants-83926. (Accessed 10 Nov 2019).
ECPC, Editors Code of Practice Committee (2019a). The Editors' Code. Available at: https://www.editorscode.org.uk/the_code.php. (Accessed 10 Oct 2019).
ECPC, Editors Code of Practice Committee (2019b). *The Editors' Codebook*. Available at: https://www.editorscode.org.uk/downloads/codebook/codebook-2019.pdf. (Accessed 10 Oct 2019).
Elgin, C. (2013). 'Epistemic Agency'. Theory and Research in Education 11(2): 135–52.
Fricker, M. (2007). Epistemic Injustice. Oxford: oxford University Press.
Hacked Off (2019). 'IPSO responds to open letter signed by John Barnes MBE, Baroness Warsi, David Lammy MP and 49 other prominent voices demanding they do more to tackle racism in the press'. Available at: https://hackinginquiry.org/ipso-responds-to-open-letter-racism-in-the-press/. (Accessed 15 Nov 2019).
Hall, M. (2013). 'Party is over for benefit skivers'. Available at: https://www.express.co.uk/news/uk/369554/Party-is-over-for-benefit-skivers. (Accessed 15 Nov 2019).
Hosenball, M. and Holton, K. (2011). 'Special report – Rupert Murdoch, a hands-on newspaperman'. *Reuters*. Available at: https://uk.reuters.com/article/uk-newscorp-murdoch-papers/special-report-rupert-murdoch-a-hands-on-newspaperman-idUKTRE76I1J920110719. (Accessed 15 Nov 2019).
IPSO. Case outcomes. Available at: https://www.ipso.co.uk/rulings-and-resolution-statements/. (Accessed 20 Jan 2020).
Jitendra, A. et al (2017). 'Early Warnings: Universal Credit and Foodbanks', produced by *The Trussell Trust*. Available at: https://www.trusselltrust.org/wp-content/uploads/sites/2/2017/04/Early-Warnings-Universal-Credit-and-Foodbanks.pdf. (Accessed 28 Nov 2019).
Lang, G. E. and Lang, K. (1981). 'Watergate: An exploration of the agenda-building process'. G. C. Wilhoit and H. de Bock (Eds.). *Mass Communication Review Yearbook 2*. Newbury Park, CA: Sage: 447–468.
Leveson, L. J. (2012). 'An inquiry into the culture, practices and ethics of the press'. London: The Stationery Office Limited.
List, C. and Pettit, P. (2011). *Group Agency*. Oxford: Oxford University Press.
McCombs, M. E. and Shaw, D. L. (1972). 'The Agenda-Setting Function of Mass Media'. *Public Opinion Quarterly*, 36(2): 176–187.

MRC, Media Reform Coalition (2019). 'Who Owns the UK Media?'. *MediaReform.org*. Available at: https://www.mediareform.org.uk/media-ownership/who-owns-the-uk-media. (Accessed 19 Nov 2019).

Nilsson, P. (2019). 'Daily Mail owner buys UK daily i newspaper for £50m'. *Financial Times*. Available at: https://www.ft.com/content/a3abf1c6-129a-11ea-a225-db2f231cfeae. (Accessed 30 November 2019).

Patrick, R. (2016). 'Living with and responding to the 'scrounger' narrative in the UK: exploring everyday strategies of acceptance, resistance and deflection', in *Journal of Poverty and Social Justice, vol.24, no.3*: 245–59.

Pettit, P. (1996). *The Common Mind: An Essay on Psychology, Society, and Politics.* Oxford: OUP.

Pettit, P. (2006). 'The Republican Ideal of Freedom'. D. Miller (Ed.). *The Liberty Reader.* Edinburgh: Edinburgh University Press: 223–242.

Pettit, P. (2007). 'Joining the dots'. G. Brennan, G (Eds.). *Common minds: Themes from the philosophy of Philip Pettit.* Oxford: OUP: 215–344.

Smith, L. (2018). 'The Curious Case of Ronald McDonald's Claim to Rights: An Ontological Account of Differences in Group and Individual Person Rights'. *Journal of Social Ontology 4*(1): 1–28.

Smith, L. (nd). 'The Print Press Media and Welfare Claimants: Collective Responsibility for a Breach of Democratic Duty'.

The Sun (2015). "The Welfies: Brits with talent for playing the benefits system". *The Sun*. Available at: https://www.thesun.co.uk/archives/news/11453/the-welfies/. (Accessed 10 December 2019).

Kent Hurtig

Consent and Normativity

1 Introduction

It is nearly universally accepted, by philosophers and common opinion alike, that the giving and receiving of valid consent is *normatively transformative*: A's validly consenting to B's φ-ing changes the normative situation from its being impermissible for B to φ before A consents to its being permissible for B to φ after A has consented. The idea that consent has this normatively transformative power is prominent in bioethics and in the ethics of health-care more generally (including biomedical and psychological research) and it also plays a central role in discussions of sexual ethics and in various areas of political and legal theory.

I have two independent but related aims in this paper. The first, which is a fairly modest aim, is to present some considerations that provide at least a presumptive case in favour of what I will call *Mental State Views of Consent*. The second, more ambitious aim, is to challenge the idea that consent has, or indeed can have, the normatively transformative power that most people assume it has. At first glance it may seem obvious that an agent's consenting to the performance of an action by another agent can, and does, alter the normative status of that action, but on reflection it is philosophically puzzling how this can be. First, those who endorse the idea that consent is normatively transformative must identify a range of possible actions which is such that actions in that range are impermissible before consent and permissible after consent. I will argue that is no easy task. Second, how is it that, simply by consenting to the performance of an action, φ, an agent can reshape the balance of reasons for or against the performance of φ? In general, for any action, φ, to which consent may be granted or withheld, there are antecedent, consent-independent, reasons for and/or against the performance of φ; i.e. there are reasons that obtain prior to, and independently of, an agent's consenting to someone's performance of φ. It is puzzling how an agent's consenting can add or subtract to those antecedent reasons. The second aim of this paper is to articulate and defend these objections

Note: Thanks to the audience and participants at the *Social Ontology, Normativity and Philosophy of Law* workshop at University of Glasgow, with special thanks to Rachael Mellin and Miguel Garcia for organising the workshop and for inviting me. Thanks also to Rowan Cruft, David Macdonald, Peter Milne, and Sarah Payne for very useful comments and criticisms. Funding for the writing of the paper was provided by the Arts and Humanities Research Council (GB) (AH/G009252/1).

https://doi.org/10.1515/9783110663617-007

to the assumed normatively transformative power of consent. I will also explore various responses to them. As far as I can tell, even if I fail to achieve the more modest aim (to show that there is good reason to believe that a Mental State view of consent is correct), that failure has no obvious bearing on the success or failure of the more ambitious aim since it is perfectly coherent to agree with everything I say in the second part whilst strongly disagreeing with what I say in the first part. In the first half of this paper I will use John Kleinig's theory of consent as a foil for arguing for a Mental State view of consent and for setting the stage for part two where I argue that consent is not necessarily normatively transformative; that, on the contrary, *consent is necessarily not normatively transformative.*

2 What is Consent?

What is it to consent? Throughout this paper, for simplicity, I will make a number of assumptions. First, I will assume that the standard *consent relation* is [A consents to B's φ-ing]. Second, I will assume that A and B are separate persons – indeed that A and B are agents: they have a general capacity to form and act on what they believe to be normative considerations. Third, I will assume that A and B are individuals – i.e. that A and B are not corporate entities. Finally, I will assume that 'φ' stands for actions only.

With these assumptions in place we can say that there are, broadly, two kinds of views about what consent is:

1. *Mental State Views of Consent*: To consent is to be in a certain state of mind.

One such view is represented by Peter Westen who says that to consent is to be in '. . . a state of mind of acquiescence . . . a felt willingness to agree with – or to choose – what another person seeks or proposes.'[1] Other Mental State theorists may disagree and argue that being in some other specific state of mind should be identified with consenting. Yet other theorists may hold that there is a range of mental states that are such that being in any one of them constitutes consenting.[2] These kinds of views should be distinguished from

1 Peter Westen, *The Logic of Consent: The Diversity and Deceptiveness of Consent as a Defense to Criminal Conduct* (Aldershot: Ashgate, 2003), p. 5.

2 There is of course a big difference between believing that to consent *is* to φ (where this is the 'is' of identity) and believing that to consent is *constituted* by φ-ing. Nonetheless, for simplicity, I will use the two expressions interchangeably unless I explicitly say different.

2. *Communicative Act Views of Consent*: To consent is to engage in a particular communicative act.

A strong version of this view is represented by John Kleinig who says that 'Consent is centrally and most appropriately a communicative act that serves to alter the moral relations in which A and B stand – and that for the moral relations to have been altered for B, a communicative act must have occurred.'[3] Communicative Act theorists may of course also have different views about which particular communicative act one has to perform in order to consent. They may also deny the claim that acts of consent are necessarily normatively transformative. As with Mental State views one could also, as Kleinig does, hold the view that there's a range of communicative acts that are such that performing any one of them constitutes consent: 'The form taken by the act of consent may vary considerably, though it will commonly be constituted by some gesture, word, or other recordable behavior that conventionally and contextually expresses it.'[4] In this paper I will assume that these kinds of theories of consent are mutually exclusive and jointly exhaustive. If this assumption is correct, and given the assumption that there really are instances of consent, an argument against either kind of view will *ipso facto* be an argument in favour of the other kind of view.

Before I go on to present my argument against Communicative Act views – and thus, given the assumption above, in favour of a Mental State view – I need to point out an important distinction that cuts across the Mental State/ Communicative Act distinction and which complicates things. This is the distinction between *conceptual/semantic* views about what 'consent' means and metaphysical views about what consent *is*. Consider the following passage from Kleinig:

> Consent is not a neutral act that is then separately justified as having normative force, but is normative through and through even though it also has a descriptive content. *To say that* A consented to φ is not *to report* some evaluatively neutral doing, such as A's saying 'yes,' which is then to be followed by further discussion about the significance of saying 'yes.' Instead, it is intended to convey that whatever it was that A did to consent (including, perhaps, saying 'yes'), it also possessed a certain normative force.'[5]
>
> (My italics.)

3 John Kleinig, 'The Nature of Consent' in Franklin Miller and Alan Wertheimer (eds), *The Ethics of Consent: Theory and Practice* (Oxford: Oxford University Press, 2010), p. 4.
4 *Ibid.*, p. 11.
5 *Ibid.*, p. 5.

Contrast this with the following passage from Tom Beauchamp:

> 'Consent,' 'the obligation to obtain consent,' and 'the right to consent' are strikingly different notions. . . . 'The obligation to obtain consent' and 'the right to consent' . . . are moral notions, but . . . 'consent' [is] not obviously [a] moral [notion]. It seems a matter of fact (or perhaps of metaphysics or the philosophy of mind), not a matter of ethics or value, whether one . . . consents.'[6]

These views differ in at least three respects; the most important for present purposes is that, on Kleinig's view, it is *conceptually* necessary – i.e. true in virtue of meaning – that if A consents to B's φ-ing, then A has performed a communicative act that transforms the shape of the normative situation. This view, then, essentially contains the following three claims:
(i) To consent is to perform a communicative act
(ii) Consent is necessarily normatively transformative
(iii) (i) and (ii) are conceptual truths.

If I've understood him correctly, Beauchamp denies all three of these claims. I think he is right in doing so. Let us start with claim (iii).

According to this claim, it is analytically true that consent consists in performing a communicative act which is such that when performed it necessarily transforms the normative situation. Of course, it is perfectly possibly to agree with (i) and (ii) and reject (iii). In other words, it is perfectly coherent to think that to consent is to perform a communicative act which is necessarily normatively transformative and deny that this is guaranteed by semantic fiat. So what's wrong with (iii)? Taking our lead from G. E. Moore and his Open Question Argument we can argue that if we endorse a view like Kleinig's we commit ourselves to holding that someone who sincerely asks questions like

> *A consented to B's φ-ing, but did A communicate this (to B)?*
> and
> *A consented to B's φ-ing, but did this change the normative shape of the situation?*

is not a competent user of 'consent'. However, there seems to be no conceptual confusion involved in asking these questions – these questions appear to be, in Moore's words 'open questions'.[7] If someone can ask questions like these without

6 Tom Beauchamp, 'Autonomy and Consent', in Franklin Miller and Alan Wertheimer (eds), *The Ethics of Consent: Theory and Practice* (Oxford: Oxford University Press, 2010), p. 56.
7 See G.E. Moore, *Principia Ethica*, T. Baldwin (ed.), Cambridge: Cambridge University Press, 1993, pp 62–69.

conceptual confusion ‘consent’ does not conceptually entail either (i) or (ii). The soundness of the Open Question Argument as a test for synonymy or conceptual entailment has of course been challenged[8] but even if the argument above fails to demonstrate conclusively that ‘consent’ does not entail (i) and (ii) at the very least it forces those who endorse a conceptual entailment view to explain why questions like the ones above appear open. Without such an explanation there is good reason to be suspicious of views according to which ‘consent’ conceptually entails things like (i) and (ii) – i.e. without such an explanation there is good reason to reject (iii).

A more plausible Communicative Act theory denies the conceptual entailment claim and runs the story via metaphysical necessity instead.[9] On such a view, it is metaphysically, but not conceptually, necessary that A’s consenting entails that (i) A has performed a communicative act and (ii) A’s consenting transforms the shape of the normative situation.[10] I will argue that a correct view of consent entails neither of these things since consent is not constituted by a communicative act and consent is not necessarily normatively transformative – in fact, it is *necessarily not* normatively transformative. I will end this section by arguing against the idea that consenting is performing a communicative act. The claim that consent is necessarily normatively transformative will be the focus of the next section.

What reason is there to believe that to consent is to perform a communicative act? Recall that Kleinig says: ‘ . . . consent is centrally and most appropriately a communicative act that serves to alter the moral relations in which A and B stand – and that for the moral relations to have been altered for B, a communicative act must have occurred.’ I will assume that thoughts like these provide the main motivation behind Communicative Act views. The general line of reasoning seems to be that

1. If A consents to B’s φ-ing then the moral relations between A and B have changed for B (and A) in virtue of A’s consenting.

---

8 See W.K. Frankena, ‘The Naturalistic Fallacy’, *Mind*, Vol. 48, No. 192 (Oct., 1939), pp. 464–477

9 Issues are further complicated by the fact that it is possible to hold views according to which one of the elements is entailed by conceptual necessity and the other element isn’t. Setting this complication to the side, we should note that if conceptual necessity entails metaphysical necessity, any argument that has force against views which connect consent and normatively transformative communicative actions via metaphysical necessity will *ipso facto* have force against views which attempt to do it via conceptual necessity.

10 A familiar parallel here is the view that although ‘Water’ does not *mean* ‘H_2O’, water *is* H_2O.

2. The moral relations between A and B have changed for B in virtue of A's consenting only if B is aware of A's consent.
3. B is aware of A's consent only if A communicates A's consent to B.
   So,
4. A consents to B's φ-ing only if A communicates A's consent to B.
5. A communicates A's consent to B only if A performs a communicative act.
   So,
6. A consents to B's φ-ing only if A performs a communicative act.[11]

If this is correct, then to the extent that Communicative Act views are motivated by an argument of this kind, such views are not well-motivated since the argument is unsound. Premise 1 will be the focus of the next section. Although premise 3 is certainly questionable,[12] I shall focus my attention on premise 2.

Premise 2 says that the moral relations between A and B change for B in virtue of A's consenting only if B is aware of A's consent. As a general view about the nature of moral relations this is patently false. Changes in moral relations is one thing and people being aware of those changes is another. If B becomes aware of the fact that the moral relations between him and A have changed, then what B becomes aware of (*that the moral relations between him and A have changed*) is something that occurred *prior to*, and *independently of*, his becoming aware of it. If this were not the case, then *what* is it that B becomes aware of? So moral relations between A and B can change without A and B being aware of this. To illustrate: Suppose, plausibly enough, that we are morally obliged to have a special concern for the wellbeing of our close friends. A and B are best friends. For some reason A does something that constitutes a serious breach of that friendship. The breach is so serious that it constitutes a

11 Support for the idea that something like this argument lies behind Communicative Act views (and certainly behind Kleinig's view) is provided by Kleinig himself who says: 'The position that I articulate and defend . . . is that there is always an expressive dimension to consent – that consent must be signified – and that only if consent takes the form of a communicative act can the moral relations between *A* and *B* be transformed. Absent such communication, *B* has no business doing that for which *A*'s consent is needed even if *A* condones or would acquiesce to it. Consent is a social act in which *A* conveys something to *B* – something that, once communicated . . . now gives B a moral right or entitlement that B previously lacked.' *Op. Cit.*, p. 10.

12 Why suppose that B is aware of A's consent only if A communicates A's consent to B? To do so is arguably question-begging against Mental State views. Suppose consent consists in being in a particular mental state. For some states of mind, it seems possible to know that a person is in that state of mind without them having communicated that state of mind to us. But if this is so, why couldn't the state of mind which constitutes consent be such a state of mind?

betrayal of their friendship. In addition A is also completely unrepentant about this betrayal. Unfortunately for B, in addition to A's betrayal, B is unaware of it. A has violated a serious moral obligation he had to B, and on any sensible view of friendship A is no longer B's friend – let alone best friend (although B will no doubt still believe that A is). As a result B is no longer bound by the obligations of friendship and is no longer obliged to have a special concern for A's well-being. In light of this Premise 2 looks highly implausible.

But perhaps, although it's true in general that moral relations can change without people normatively affected by that change realising it, consent is different in this respect? Perhaps consent is such that it can work its 'moral magic' (to use Heidi Hurd's phrase[13]) only if it is communicated? Kleinig says:

> What is critical [for consent] is that A communicates with B such that B knows that A has authorized B to φ. Consent requires signification – not in the sense that a state of mind is reported but in the sense that a right or entitlement is created or permission given or obligation assumed. Consent is not about agreeing with but to, and the latter, as a morally transformative act, requires signification.[14]

But this again prompts the question: why can't A create a right or entitlement or give permission to B without B knowing that such a right or entitlement has been created, or that such a permission has been given? After all, a legislative body can create legal rights and entitlements *for me* without my knowing that it has done so. If and when I become aware of the fact that such a legal right or entitlement has been created (and that I now have such a right or entitlement) what I become aware of is something that is true independently of me being aware of it. The same is true for moral rights and entitlements.

Let us relate this back to consent. Consider the following case. The only means you and I have of communicating is by writing handwritten letters and posting them. You write me a letter asking for permission to come and stay at my house in two weeks' time. I receive the letter and read it on Monday. The same day I write a response saying you are more than welcome to stay at my place. I post the letter on Monday evening. You receive the letter on Wednesday and you read it then, finding out that I'm happy for you to stay at my place. Everyone can agree that I have consented to your staying at my house, but *when* did I so consent? On the Monday or the Wednesday? It seems obvious that I consented on Monday and that you *found out* about my consenting on the

---

13 See her 'The Moral Magic of Consent' in *Legal Theory*, 2 (1996), pp 121–146.
14 *Op. Cit.*, p. 11.

Wednesday. Kleinig, it seems to me, would have to say that I consented on the Wednesday. This rings false. Insofar as Communicative Act views are motivated by the idea that the essence of consent is to create, *and impart knowledge of*, permissions (etc.), then to this extent such views should be rejected. We need to ask ourselves what is lost if we draw a distinction between consenting on the one hand, and communicating that consent on the other? My contention is that the answer is 'nothing'. The central problem for Communicate Act views as I see it is that they cannot allow for cases of uncommunicated consent. It seems a patient can consent to an operation but be unable to communicate this to the surgeon – perhaps her cognitive faculties are in full working order, but she is paralysed and cannot speak. Another scenario is where a potential research subject fills out a consent form but the form is lost before it reaches the researcher or the relevant ethics committee. These seem like genuine possibilities, but it's very difficult to see how a Communicate Act view can allow for such cases. I think that in the end we do better to reject Communicative Act views of consent.

3 Why Consent is Not Normatively Transformative

As we saw earlier, Kleinig's view has three central elements to it: (i) To consent is to perform a communicative act; (ii) Consent is necessarily normatively transformative, and (iii) The two previous claims are conceptual truths. So far, I have argued against (i) and (iii). In the remainder of this paper I will argue against (ii). Before I do this I need to say something about the distinction between consent and *valid* consent. Just what valid consent is thought to amount to will emerge presently, but for now we need to recognise that in order for this distinction to be of any use, there must be clear possible (at least) cases of non-valid, or invalid, consent. Most people when they talk about valid consent have in mind instances where someone consents and that person satisfies certain conditions, call them C. Conversely, invalid consent is consent that is given without C having been satisfied. Importantly, on such views, consent is normatively transformative if and only if it is valid. Others, like Kleinig, have a different view. On this view, if someone fails to satisfy C, they simply fail to consent. On this view all consent is valid consent and there is no such thing as invalid consent. As Kleinig puts it: ' . . . invalid consent no more counts as consent than an invalid vote counts as a vote.'[15] This remark helps us understand why

15 *Ibid.*, p. 15.

Kleinig thinks that consent is necessarily normatively transformative. Since there is no such thing as invalid consent, if some (communicative) act fails to be normatively transformative, that act is simply not an act of consent *full stop*. We should reject this view. Consider again the analogy with the invalid vote. A more accurate analogy is provided by the distinction between valid and invalid arguments. Both kinds of arguments are genuine instances of arguments (at least up to a limit), but only the former has any chance of being imbued with normative force. If one endorses a 'normativised' theory of consent, like Kleinig's, the normatively transformative power of consent comes for free, but it does so at the price of having a seriously extensionally inadequate theory of consent. This is not a price worth paying.

We can put this debate to the side and focus on the fact that there is near universal agreement that certain conditions ('C' as I referred to them above) have to be met in order for someone's consent to be valid (or, in Kleinig's terminology, for someone's act to be an instance of consent) and thus for it to be normatively transformative. Although theorists disagree about the details of these conditions – about how many conditions there are and what exactly their content is – there seems to be a consensus that A is in a position to validly consent to B's φ-ing if and only if A satisfies the following three conditions:

1. *The competence condition*
   A's general cognitive and emotional abilities at the time of consenting are 'sufficiently mature' and they are not at the time of consenting impaired by conditions like being depressed, seriously intoxicated, in excruciating pain, agitated, and irritable, etc.
2. *The knowledge condition*
   A has sufficient knowledge of all the facts that are relevant to B's φ-ing. (What is the purpose of B's φ-ing? How is B's φ-ing related to that purpose? What are the potential payoffs and risks of B's φ-ing?)[16]
3. *The voluntariness condition*
   A is not being coerced, unduly persuaded, or manipulated. (A's assenting to B's φ-ing must be above the threshold of voluntariness.)

---

16 I take the knowledge condition to subsume what is sometimes called 'The intention condition' – roughly, the condition that A assents to B's φ-ing under a certain description of B's φ-ing. When I let you borrow my hammer, I'm not letting you borrow an offensive weapon. I also take the knowledge condition to subsume what is sometimes called 'The disclosure condition' – roughly, that B discloses to A all relevant information he is in possession of.

So A is in a position to validly consent to B's φ-ing if and only if these conditions obtain, and if A is in this position and does consent, it is argued, his so doing transforms the normative situation. In the rest of this paper I will drop 'valid' and only use it when context requires it. So what, then, is supposed to happen, normatively speaking, when A consents? Those who believe that consent is normatively transformative will endorse what I will call

> *The Transformation Thesis* (**T**):
> Necessarily, A's validly consenting to B's φ-ing changes the situation from there being decisive reason for B not to φ before A consents to its not being the case that there is decisive reason for B not to φ after A consents.[17] (There is decisive reason for someone to φ just in case the balance of total reasons for and/or against φ-ing favours φ-ing.)

Everyone agrees that in order for **T** to be plausible the acts that 'φ' ranges over must be restricted in certain ways. For example, it can never be the case that there is decisive reason for B to make A his slave, or to kill A for some trivial reason. So A cannot validly consent to becoming B's slave or to allow B to kill him for some trivial reason. If B's φ-ing is consent-independently impermissible, then A's consenting to B's φ-ing cannot make it permissible.[18] Are further restrictions necessary? To answer this, consider the following case

> *Tattoo*
> B approaches A and asks if A is interested in getting a large facial tattoo. A is made aware of all the following salient facts about the procedure and outcome: 1. The procedure will be very expensive. 2 It will be very painful. 3. The tattoo will be ugly and permanent. 4. The tattoo will cause friends and family serious discomfort. 5. A will enjoy wearing it for only a very short period. 6. B will be slightly better off financially by tattooing A. A consents.

---

17 This idea is frequently spelled out in terms of moral permissibility:

> A's consenting to B's φ-ing changes the situation from its being morally impermissible for B to φ before A consents to its being morally permissible for B to φ after A consents.

From this idea, we can derive **T** via the two very plausible principles

> Necessarily, if it is morally impermissible for B to φ then there is decisive reason for B not to φ
> Necessarily, if it is morally permissible for B to φ then it is not the case that there is decisive reason for B not to φ

18 In a legal context A's (validly) consenting to B's φ-ing can change the legal permissibility of B's φ-ing. And just like in the moral case, if B's φ-ing is consent-independently legally impermissible, A's consenting to B's φ-ing cannot make B's φ-ing legally permissible (at least in all recognisable, and minimally sensible legal systems). It is plausible that consent can be 'legally transformative' without being morally transformative just as it is plausible that consent can be morally transformative without being legally transformative. The law is after all, at least sometimes and in some places, an ass.

What are we to make of this case? Recall the knowledge condition: 'A has sufficient knowledge of all the facts that are relevant to B's φ-ing.' In addition to the relevant facts listed in the example, here are some more relevant facts: First, 1–4 are very strong reasons in favour of A's not having the tattoo. Second, 5 and 6 are comparatively very weak reasons in favour of A's having it. Third, the combined weight of 1–4 is far greater than the combined weight of 5 and 6. So, fourth, the balance of reasons favours A's not getting the tattoo. So, fifth, there is decisive reason against A's getting the tattoo. Now, either A knows that there is decisive reason against having the tattoo or he doesn't. If A doesn't know this then, since this fact is highly relevant to the case, A plausibly fails to satisfy the knowledge condition and his consenting is not valid. If, on the other hand, he does know that there is decisive reason against getting the tattoo, but he consents nonetheless, then he suffers from a form of practical irrationality, he is weak-willed. But if A is weak-willed, then he does not satisfy the competence condition.[19] So either way, A cannot validly consent to having the tattoo.

Since there is nothing special about *Tattoo* the point generalises. This suggests, perhaps somewhat surprisingly, that A's consenting to B's φ-ing is valid just in case A's consenting to B's φ-ing is in accordance with the balance of reasons for or against B's φ-ing. But if A can validly consent to B's φ-ing just in case A's consenting is in accordance with the balance of reasons for or against B's φ-ing, how can A's consenting to B's φ-ing change the normative situation? It's very difficult to see what the range of 'validly consentable' actions could be. In what range of cases can **T** be applied and actually work its moral magic? For simplicity, let us assume that there are no cases where the reasons for and against B's φ-ing are exactly balanced. On this assumption, the balance of reasons will either favour B's φ-ing or it will favour B's not-φ-ing. This means that there is either decisive reason for B's φ-ing or there is decisive reason against B's φ-ing. If there is decisive reason for B's φ-ing then it is not the case that there is decisive reason against B's φ-ing. Let us also assume, again for simplicity, that A either consents or withholds consent. We have four possibilities here:

(a) There is decisive reason for B's φ-ing and A withholds consent to B's φ-ing.
(b) There is decisive reason for B's φ-ing and A consents to B's φ-ing.
(c) There is decisive reason against B's φ-ing and A withholds consent to B's φ-ing.
(d) There is decisive reason against B's φ-ing and A consents to B's φ-ing.

---

19 It's not entirely implausible to suggest that A fails the voluntariness condition as well: when we act against our better judgment we are manipulating and unduly influencing ourselves. Even if this manipulation and undue influence is something that is experienced as alien and unbidden, we are nonetheless being manipulated and unduly influenced.

So what are the cases in which **T** can actually be applied? Well, the only cases that are relevant for **T**'s application are those in which, prior to A's valid consent, there is decisive reason against B's φ-ing (i.e. cases where the balance of reasons favours B's not-φ-ing). That means that **T** has no application in (a) and (b) – these are cases in which there are decisive consent-independent reasons for B's φ-ing. **T** has no application in (c) either since, although there is decisive reason against B's φ-ing, A withholds his consent. This leaves (d), but as we have already seen A's consent in cases like (d) is invalid (because of ignorance or irrationality, or both). We can call this *the application problem*. What this problem shows, I think, is that at best, the range of actions to which A can validly consent is vanishingly small; at worst it shows that there is no such thing as valid consent as the range of actions to which A can validly consent is empty.

In reply to the argument that **T** cannot be applied to cases like (d) it might be argued that the knowledge referred to in the knowledge condition of voluntary consent does not include the kind of normative knowledge I have been talking about. All that's needed in order to meet this condition is that one knows all the relevant non-normative facts – like the fact that the tattoo will be expensive and that it will be permanent, etc. Even if it's a fact that what is to count as relevant knowledge is determined by what facts are reasons for or against consenting, the agent need not have knowledge of *this* fact. If salient normative knowledge is unnecessary the charge of irrationality loses all its traction: one is practically irrational only if one acts contrary to what one believes the balance of reasons dictates. This is not a plausible response. To start with, it is unacceptably *ad hoc*. We need some principled reason why knowledge of this kind should be excluded from the knowledge condition. Even if some such reason can be provided, this response seems to assume that irrationality is possible only where there is *normative ascent*: where one has explicitly formed a belief about what there is decisive reason to do. So if one does not have such a belief a charge of irrationality loses all its traction. This is highly dubious. Normative ascent is not necessary for irrationality. Someone who knows that getting a facial tattoo will be very expensive, that it will be very painful, ugly, and permanent and still consents to it *is* practically irrational. Such a person either has the *tacit* belief that these considerations provide decisive reason against having the tattoo, or he doesn't. If he does have such a tacit belief the charge of irrationality remains in full force. If he doesn't have such a belief, then whatever we want to say about this person, he or she is certainly not sufficiently competent.

Another response to the application problem would be to argue that the kind of practical irrationality I am accusing A of in cases where he knowingly acts contrary to the balance of reasons should be excluded from the competence condition on the grounds that it's not a severe enough condition to render him incompetent. But if practical irrationality of this kind is to be excluded what reason could there be for including things like being depressed, seriously intoxicated, in excruciating pain, agitated, and irritable etc.? These are included in the competence condition precisely *because* they are likely to cause an agent to become, among other things, practically irrational.

There may be better responses to the application problem, but since I don't know what these are I can't consider them here. Instead I want to shift focus on to a bread-and-butter case in the consent literature: the Jehovah's Witness who refuses to receive a blood transfusion:

> *Blood transfusion*
> Unless A gets a blood transfusion he will die. B is well-placed to administer a quick, safe, and near enough cost-free transfusion, and A knows this. A refuses to consent on account of, as he believes, God's disapproval of blood transfusions.

Many people consider the administering of the blood transfusion impermissible until the patient consents to the procedure and the transfusion thereby becomes permissible. For the reasons canvassed above, this is puzzling. But I am going to put this puzzling feature to the side and focus on a slightly different aspect of consent: the reasons for and against consenting.

In *Blood Transfusion* let us suppose that the reasons in favour of B's administering the transfusion include the following: A will not experience any of the pain that he would experience were he not to have the transfusion; A will live and continue to lead a life that's well worth living, having many wonderful experiences and accomplishing many worthwhile things; A's friends and family will be delighted. These are all very powerful reasons in favour of B's administering the transfusion. Again, let us call B's administering the transfusion 'φ'. If, as we are supposing, it is impermissible for B not to φ there must be reasons against B's φ-ing that are strong enough to outweigh the normative force of the considerations that favour B's φ-ing. What provides this extraordinarily powerful reason or reasons? As I see it, there are only two options here. Either this reason is a consent-independent reason, or the reason is simply the fact that A withholds his consent. If A's consent really does change the normative situation, it's very difficult to see how a consent-independent reason (or a set of consent-independent reasons) against B's φ-ing could be a decisive reason against B's φ-ing. If the decisive reason against B's φ-ing really were a consent-independent reason, then presumably this reason would still obtain after A consents and A's consent would not change the balance of reasons. In light of this, if A's consent really does change the balance of reasons it must be the fact that he withholds his consent that provides the decisive reason against B's φ-ing.

But now we must ask, how is it possible that *this* could be a reason with sufficient weight to make it a decisive reason against B's φ-ing? The fact that A withholds his consent does not seem to be the right sort of consideration to play the role of a reason – let alone a decisive reason. Regardless of whether consenting consists in being in a particular mental state or in performing a communicative act, consenting and withholding consent are themselves the sorts of things for which reasons can sensibly be asked and offered. Either there is reason for A to withhold consent or there isn't. If there is no reason for A to withhold consent it's difficult to see how A's withholding consent can *create* a decisive reason for B not to φ. Such a creation of a decisive reason would involve an objectionable kind of voluntarism about the normative: it would involve bootstrapping a decisive reason into existence *ex nihilo*. If, on the other hand, there is reason to withhold consent, this reason would have to be a consent-independent reason since A's withholding consent can't be a reason for itself. But if there is consent-independent reason for A to withhold consent it is equally difficult to see how the fact that A withholds consent *adds* to the stock of reasons that obtain independently of his doing so. Supposing then, that there is a consent-independent reason for A to withhold consent in *Blood Transfusion*, what could this reason be?

Again, there seem to be only two alternatives. Either the reason is the fact that A believes that God disapproves of blood transfusions, or the reason is provided by the content of A's belief (that God disapproves of blood transfusions). It's implausible that both could be reasons since this would again involve an objectionable double counting of reasons. Let's take the second option first. Once more, there are two options: Either A's belief is true or it is not. If A's belief is false (i.e. his belief has a false proposition as its content) then, aside from the obvious suspicion that A fails the knowledge condition necessary for valid consent, how can a false proposition provide the relevant reason? There is a robust consensus among philosophers of normativity that only facts (or fact-like things, like the obtaining states of affairs perhaps?) provide reasons. So on this option, there is no reason for A to withhold consent and since this is so his withholding consent does not provide a decisive reason against B's φ-ing. The other option then is that A's belief is true (i.e. God forbids blood transfusions). But if it is this consideration that gives A reason to withhold consent, then surely it is *this* consideration that provides the (decisive) reason against B's φ-ing.[20] A's withholding of consent seems entirely redundant – A's withholding of consent is merely *normatively epiphenomenal.*

But what about the first option? Recall that on this option, it is the fact that A believes that God forbids blood transfusions that is the decisive reason for A's withholding consent. Those who endorse this general line of thought are no doubt more likely to express this by saying that A's having this belief is part of A's deep commitments and forms an essential part of his life plan, and there is considerable normative pressure on us to respect others' deep commitments and life plans. This line of reasoning is not very plausible; it's certainly implausible if we understand the claim as being content-independently true. We can easily imagine gangsters and others who have wicked commitments and abhorrent life plans. It would be a serious mistake to think that there is a normative pressure on us to respect such commitments and plans. Nonetheless, for the sake of argument, let's grant that we have very powerful reasons to respect people's deep commitments and life plans. Suppose then that A is deeply committed to his religion and its tenets shape his long term plans, his ambitions, and the general ways in which he relates to and interacts with other people. The thought is that administering the blood transfusion is incompatible with showing due respect for A's deep commitments. But, if we are to respect A's deep commitments and such respect can be shown only by not administering the blood transfusion, then this (presumably decisive) reason obtains *independently* of whether A consents or not. However, like we have seen before, if A consents to the transfusion, then A has either forgotten about his deep commitments or he is irrational. So A's consent to the transfusion is not valid and therefore cannot change the balance of reasons. If on the other hand A withholds his consent, his so doing is, again, at best an acknowledgement of the reasons that obtain independently of his consenting or withholding consent. Either way, A's withholding of consent makes no normative difference, and nor does his consenting.

One line of thought that has not been explored yet appeals to the bad consequences of ignoring consent. Suppose A refuses the transfusion. Imagine what would happen if B knowingly went ahead and began to administer the transfusion anyway. Presumably, A would resist in some way and the situation

20 Of course, as Socrates taught us, since there must be an explanation for why God forbids blood transfusions, it will be the normative reason that will figure in this explanation that provides A with the *real* reason for withholding consent and which counts decisively against B's φ-ing.

would turn very ugly. In addition, if, as is very likely, consent is *legally* transformative (in the way briefly discussed on p.12 n19) B would no doubt have to face various legal sanctions, including imprisonment. If B's job involves performing blood transfusions he will very likely be fired from his job. It's very easy to imagine all sorts of bad things happening to B if he were to attempt to administer the transfusion without A's consent. All these bad things that would happen to B were he to initiate the procedure without A's consent are all powerful reasons against (trying to) administer the blood transfusion. But given all this, does this mean that A's not consenting provides a powerful reason against B's administering the transfusion? No, it doesn't. A's not consenting is at best an *enabling condition* for the obtaining of reasons against administering the transfusion. What counts against B's φ-ing is the fact that bad things will happen to him if he φs. Of course, those bad things would not happen if A consents (i.e. those reasons would not obtain were A to consent), but this does in no way show that A's withholding of consent itself provide reasons against B's φ-ing. If B φs without obtaining A's consent A may well feel violated in various ways by this and the explanation for his so feeling will of course be that B φs without obtaining his consent. But this does not show that A's withholding of consent is a reason against B's φ-ing either. Rather, B's φ-ing without A's consent is what enables there to be reasons against B's φ-ing.

I'll end this paper by briefly discussing two ways in which consent might be normative after all. The first is that A's withholding of consent may provide B with reason to *believe* that there is reason against his φ-ing. I say 'may' because it seems likely that the epistemic status of A's withholding consent needs to be settled by considerations that arise in the epistemology of testimony. A's withholding of consent may, in many contexts, reasonably be thought of as A's testifying that there are strong reasons against B's φ-ing. This line of thought naturally inherits all the complexities of the epistemology of testimony, so I will not say anything more about this line of thought – save one thing: Even if A's withholding of consent is good reason to believe that there is reason against φ-ing, since the fact that there is reason to believe that p does not entail p, A's withholding consent does not entail that there is reason against φ-ing.

The second way in which consent may be normative emerges when we reflect on the fact that there are many things we have reason to care about and to protect. We all have good reason to care about ourselves and others and to protect ourselves and others from being exploited, manipulated, coerced, deceived, and in other ways used as mere means. However, given our limited altruism, our less than perfect knowledge, and our general moral fallibility, there is excellent reason for us to create and maintain legal and social institutions that protect the dignity and interests of all against our own moral and epistemic shortcomings. That we should require people's consent before we can permissibly – in a legal and social sense – act in various ways with respect to one another is one of the best ways we have to ensure that people's dignity and interests are to the greatest feasible extent protected. This is an unashamedly *instrumental* approach to consent: creating and maintaining legal and social institutions of this kind arguably serves that very worthwhile goal better than any other feasible alternative. So there is excellent reason to create and maintain institutions that place consent at the centre of many of our interactions with each other. This *still* doesn't show that consent itself is normatively transformative.

References

Beauchamp, Tom. 'Autonomy and Consent', in Franklin Miller and Alan Wertheimer (eds), *The Ethics of Consent: Theory and Practice*. Oxford: Oxford University Press, 2010, pp. 55–78.
Frankena, William K. 'The Naturalistic Fallacy', *Mind*, Vol. 48, No. 192, (1939), pp. 464–477.
Hurd, Heidi. 'The Moral Magic of Consent', *Legal Theory* Vol. 2, No. 2, (1996), pp. 121–146.
Kleinig, John. 'The Nature of Consent' in Franklin Miller and Alan Wertheimer (eds), *The Ethics of Consent: Theory and Practice*. Oxford: Oxford University Press, 2010, pp. 3–24.
Moore, George E. *Principia Ethica* (2nd. edition). Baldwin, T. (ed.). Cambridge: Cambridge University Press, 1993.
Westen, Peter. *The Logic of Consent: The Diversity and Deceptiveness of Consent as a Defense to Criminal Conduct*. Aldershot: Ashgate, 2003.

Olof Leffler

Reasons Internalism, Cooperation, and Law

I shall paint a surprising picture. First, I shall present a reasons internalist argument for thinking that many moral norms depend on agreements between agents, as agents all have a fundamental reason to cooperate.[1] Then I shall argue that if one construes some of the moral norms that depend on agreement as laws, slotting them into the theoretical framework natural law theorists usually defend, a natural law theory looks surprisingly attractive. The cooperation-based norms can solve some fundamental theoretical problems for natural law theories. I shall not, however, endeavour to conclusively defend natural law theory, for I am not certain about whether we should prefer a natural law framework to some other one, such as a legal positivist framework. My fundamental aim is, instead, to paint the picture.

To do so, in section 1, I introduce my preferred interpretation of reasons internalism. In the lengthy section 2, I present an argument which suggests that a desire to cooperate with other cooperative agents is partially constitutive of ideal agency. By reasons internalism, this desire can explain moral norms. In section 3, I transpose these norms into a natural law framework and show how the emerging framework is attractive. I conclude in section 4.

1 Reasons Internalism

Reasons internalists take there to be a necessary relation between a reason for action and a person's psychology, whereas externalists deny that this is always the case. I think internalism is correct, but I do not have the space to defend it, so I shall just assume it and my favourite formulation of the view.[2] This formulation is:

> (*REASONS INTERNALISM*) For all $r(F,A,\alpha,C)$, $r(F,A,\alpha,C)$ is a reason relation holding between a fact F and an agent A's action a in circumstances C iff (and because) $r(F,A,\alpha,C)$ holds in virtue of the desires that feature in P's idealized psychology.[3]

1 This argument is developed in greater depth in Leffler (2019).
2 See, however, Leffler (2019) for that too.
3 $r(F,A,a,C)$ may hold between more *relata*, e.g. times, as well. But I stick with this formulation for simplicity.

https://doi.org/10.1515/9783110663617-008

To clarify: when I mention a fact *F*, I am indifferent between talking about a (true) proposition, an instantiated property, or whatever else one may take a fact to be (cf. Peter, 2019, for discussion). Furthermore, I shall not make any commitments about how an action *a* works, but I shall discuss *A* and *C* in more depth below.

Moreover, I shall not discuss the 'in virtue of'-relation that holds between idealized desires and reasons in much depth. There are many theoretical options about what this relation might be – e.g. constitution, or even identity – but for the sake of convenience, I shall usually say that agents' reasons have their sources in, or are grounded in, ideal desires (cf. Chang, 2009; 2013). For present purposes, nothing turns on what one thinks here.

But what does 'the desires that feature in *P*'s idealized psychology' mean? I shall explicate this aspect of *REASONS INTERNALISM* at some length, for it will be important in my argument below. First of all, *REASONS INTERNALISM* is a particular type of desire-based reasons internalism. While not all forms of internalism must look like it, let alone be desire-based, this is still probably the most common version of reasons internalism in general (cf. Williams, 1981; Joyce, 2001; Smith, 1994; 1995; 2012*a*). On this view, the agent *A* whose desires explain reasons has desires, beliefs, and is otherwise suitably rational – not least instrumentally rational. I shall also assume that this psychology should be given a functionalistic interpretation; in particular, the function of beliefs is to represent the world accurately, the function of desires is to motivate the agent to act, and (instrumental) rationality functions to make the agent take the best means (that she believes there are) to her ends (set by her desires). From here and on, I shall follow convention and call fully idealized agents of this kind '*A+*', while non-idealized ones still will be called '*A*'.

It is the desires of *A+*-style agents, suitably idealized, that explain reasons for *A*. As *A+* has beliefs, desires, and is rational, and desires do the key explanatory work here, the core idea behind *REASONS INTERNALISM* is that if *A+* desires to φ, then *A* has a reason to φ. And the idealization of *A*'s psychology, i.e. that which turns *A* into *A+*, plays a supporting role in ensuring that *A+* has the *right* desires to explain *A*'s reasons. Perhaps some of our desires are short-sighted and incompatible with some of our other, deeper, desires. Or perhaps some of our desires are based on faulty information. But in better conditions, our desires might explain our reasons better.

How may we reach better conditions? As *REASONS INTERNALISM* explains reasons by appealing to the desires that feature in an idealized psychology, and that psychology is functionalistic, I shall take an ideal agent to be a fully functional agent, in the sense that all the psychological states and capacities she has *qua* agent function fully, and that she manifests these capacities fully insofar as she acts. I shall also assume that, *qua* ideal agent, she has or is in the right background conditions to be able to exercise those well-functioning psychological states and capacities. Here, a 'background condition' is any fact about the agent or the context she is in which may affect her psychology, decisions, or actions.

To be idealized, then, *A+* is supposed to feature all the properties of *A* just mentioned, fully functioning or fully manifested when acting. So, for example, the idealized agent does not just have the capacities for believing, desiring, or instrumental rationality, but actually is instrumentally rational insofar as she acts (cf. Smith, 2012*b*). This idealization condition rules out the possibility that the mental states involved in idealization are blocked so the agent is unable to make use of them, e.g. by accidie (cf. Hurtig, 2006).

Furthermore, full idealization requires that *A+* has or is in the background conditions that allow her to have the states or capacities of her psychology fully functioning or manifested when acting. The point here is that the agent cannot be in background conditions that hinder her psychology from living up to its functions. For example, insofar as having capacities to deliberate requires ways of applying the instrumental principle in deliberation, and deliberation is something that an ideal agent may do, having the ability to apply the instrumental principle in those ways is an idealizing condition of the agent. As (Williams 1981) famously noted, instrumental rationality need not just involve the taking of already known means to given ends, but can also involve deliberation about how to do so by finding constitutive solutions in cases where desires conflict, using one's imagination to find new possible solutions, etc.

This kind of background conditions idealization can also explain why *A+* ought to be epistemically refined. Epistemic refinement does not just mean that *A+*'s beliefs are fully functional or manifested so that she satisfies the aim of belief, viz. represents the world accurately. Just by assuming the full functioning of beliefs, I shall assume that, insofar as the ideal agent has beliefs, these live up to their aim. However, many authors have also tended to assume that the agent must have some particular set of beliefs, e.g. all relevant true beliefs and no false ones (Smith, 1994, ch. 5). I am not sure exactly what set of beliefs matters here, but it is plausible that there is a set like that, for it is plausible that *A+* needs fairly many true beliefs to manifest her agential capacities fully insofar as she acts – without them, she might take the wrong means to her ends. And if there is such a set, *A+* has it.

Summing up, then, idealization involves fully functioning or manifested capacities *as well as* relevant background conditions. The latter is also what explains why *A+* is able to apply the instrumental principle in complex ways and is epistemically refined.

2 Cooperation

Assume, then, the version of reasons internalism that I have formulated. It will allow us to sketch an *argument from idealization* for a certain conception of morality. Though I do not have the space to develop the argument fully or to respond to all potential objections here, I do consider it promising. The argument goes like this:

(1) If *A+*'s psychology is able to explain the reasons of an agent *A* in our world, then *A+* is suitably idealized.

(2) If *A+* is suitably idealized, then *A+* has a set of idealized desires (based on *A*'s desires) for what to do in a range of situations or circumstances, many of which feature the circumstances of justice.

(3) If *A+*'s psychology is able to explain the reasons of an agent *A* in our world, then *A+* has a set of idealized desires (based on *A*'s desires) for what to do in a range of situations or circumstances, many of which feature the circumstances of justice.

(4) If *A+* has a set of idealized desires (based on *A*'s desires) for what to do in a range of situations or circumstances, many of which feature the circumstances of justice, *A+* must have a desire to cooperate with other cooperative agents as a matter of being suitably idealized.

(5) If *A+* must have a desire to cooperate with other cooperative agents as a matter of being suitably idealized, *A+* has a desire to cooperate with other cooperative agents.

(6) If *A+* has a desire to cooperate with other cooperative agents, her desire to cooperate and its presuppositions and implications can explain some central moral norms in terms of cooperation.

(C) If *A+*'s psychology is able to explain the reasons of an agent *A* in our world, her desire to cooperate and its presuppositions and implications can explain some central moral norms in terms of cooperation.

How does the argument work? To start off, premise (1) might seem fairly obvious already. I have already presented the work I think idealization should do to explain reasons; I claimed that it makes sure that the agent has the right desires to explain reasons. This is because it ensures us that the ideal agent is fully functional or fully manifests her capacities insofar as she acts, and that she is in the relevant background conditions for doing so. So premise (1) seems safe.

Nevertheless, suitable idealization has some important implications that I shall introduce here. They, in turn, have surprising normative upshots.

I wrote above that I would discuss the circumstances *C* an agent may be in in more depth later, and it is now time for that. By 'circumstances', I mean the natural, social, physiological or psychological background conditions that an agent faces or could face, viz. the conditions of those kinds that may affect her psychology, decisions, or actions. Examples of what I have in mind are what species she belongs to, what planet she inhabits, and what society she lives in.

To introduce some more terminology, I shall call a particular set of circumstances that an agent may be in a *situation*. As an ideal agent can plausibly be in or have desires for what to do in many situations, situations may sometimes be understood as possible worlds, however they should be interpreted if they are to be compatible with interpretations that do not have any controversial ontological implications about what they or the ideal agent must be like.[4] For the same reason, a situation may sometimes be a subset of the circumstances inside some world – an ideal agent can be in or have desires about what to do in many possible subsets of circumstances there too. However, if you do not like possible worlds-talk, feel free to reinterpret what a situation is using your preferred interpretation of 'sets of circumstances' – fundamentally, what matters here is that the ideal agent may inhabit or have desires about what to do in different natural, social, physiological and psychological circumstances. This has important ramifications.

Why? I have presumed that the desires of ideal agents explain the reasons of non-ideal agents. But *REASONS INTERNALISM* does not, by itself, say which circumstances ideal agents must be in or have desires about what to do in, only that their desires explain the reasons *actual* agents have in their circumstances *C*. This seems to make it possible that an *A+*'s situation (or the situations she has desires for what to do in) may differ from an *A*'s.

But too great a divergence between *A+*'s situation or desires and *A*'s circumstances could, in turn, give *A+* different kinds of desires than those *A* plausibly has – and therefore give *A* different reasons than those she plausibly has. This risks generating several explanatory worries for *REASONS INTERNALISM*. For example, how do we know our reasons if *A+* may be in very different circumstances from us? How can the desires *A+* has in such cases be related to us and our actions? And might such a view get the extension of our reasons wrong?

4 Of course, if the reader prefers more ontologically heavy-duty possible worlds, she should feel free to go with them instead.

Fortunately, these worries can be handled by resources internal to *REASONS INTERNALISM* as I understand it. Idealization is supposed to have two main dimensions: *A+* should be fully functional (or a fully capacity-manifesting agent when she acts) in background conditions relevant for maintaining her full functionality. Hence, *A+*'s psychology (or circumstances, which might alter her psychology) should not plausibly be altered in more ways than by idealization in these two dimensions, for further changes are irrelevant. So something like the following constrains any *A+*:

> (*CLOSE*) *A+*'s idealized desires explain *A*'s reasons only if *A+*'s desires and other psychological states range over circumstances that are similar enough to those *A* may be in.

This means that at least some circumstances that *A+* inhabits or has desires for what to do in must be similar to those *A* is in.[5] There are hard questions to ask about how we should understand this kind of similarity (e.g. in terms of possible worlds in some technical sense?), but while such questions are interesting, taking positions on them would risk making controversial commitments that do not matter for present purposes.

Instead, here, it is enough to have an intuitive grasp on the limits *CLOSE* sets: *A+*'s desires must range over circumstances that are similar enough to those *A* is in if they are to explain *A*'s reasons. Hence, for example, if *A* is a human, we can safely rule out cases such as when *A+* is Cthulhu from explaining *A*'s reasons. Cthulhu's desires, let alone background natural, social, physiological or psychological conditions, are plausibly very different from those of any human. Understood like that, a condition like *CLOSE* seems extremely plausible.

There is also another, similar, property of *A+*'s that does very important work when it comes to explaining *A*'s reasons. This property is:

> (*ROBUST*) *A+* must have psychological dispositions and capacities that remain the same over minor changes in the circumstances she may inhabit or otherwise have desires for what to do in.

ROBUST, too, can be explained by idealization. Idealization involves making an agent fully functional or fully capacity-manifesting insofar as she acts, as well as making sure that she is in the right background conditions. *ROBUST* is such

---

5 Is *A+* not a *hypothetical* agent, and hence unable to 'inhabit' situations where her desires might change? Well, if we can think of hypothetical agents, we may also think of the habitation hypothetically.

a background condition. This is because *A+* hardly can manifest her psychological states to act if they were to change capriciously with various more or less randomly occurring events – and this would soon also undermine their functionality. If *A+*'s desire to drink when thirsty, for example, were to turn into a desire to wear a red jumper when thirsty because her neighbours have acquired a cat, she would not be able to act on the desire to drink if her neighbour indeed did acquire a cat. Then she would soon die of thirst, completely undermining the functionality of her psychology. A 'minor' change, then, is a change in *A+*'s circumstances which is such that, if *A+* had been sensitive to it, it would undermine her being ideal. *A+*'s psychology must be *ROBUST* in the face of such changes.

On to premise (2). I assume that the circumstances of justice include the sort of things that Rawls (1971, pp. 126–130), following Hume (1978, pp. 473–534), took for granted to apply in ordinary human circumstances. The most significant one is that people's desires usually cannot all be easily satisfied given the constraints that their social circumstances put on them. Moreover, in the circumstances of justice, there is a moderate scarcity of resources, moderate generosity on part of others (or moderate ideological agreement between agents), and it is within others' power to – either individually or together – thwart any given individual's attempts to satisfy her desires by overpowering her. (To be clear, this use of power need not be moral or nice; the point is that agents are able to use their power to use force to stop each other.) Under these circumstances, living in cooperative societies usually benefits individual agents, but participating in them does not always lead to the best results for any individual agent, given what they desire.

CLOSE ensures that ideal agents must have desires about what to do in an extensive set of situations that feature these circumstances of justice. To recapitulate, *CLOSE* says that *A+*'s idealized desires explain *A*'s reasons only if *A+*'s desires and other psychological states range over circumstances that are similar enough to those *A* may be in. But our situation contains the circumstances of justice, and situations that do not would be very different from ours, and they would be so *just because* they would not feature the circumstances of justice. Moreover, there may be all kinds of differences between different versions of the circumstances of justice that we inhabit. There are already many such versions in the actual world, and there may be further ones still. So if *A+* had lacked desires for what to do in an extensive set of such circumstances that we may inhabit, *A+*'s desires would not range over circumstances that are similar enough to ours to explain our reasons.

True, it is also possible that some agents do not inhabit these circumstances, or if they presently inhabit them, they may come to leave them. Hence, ideal agents should also have desires about what to do in at least some *other* circumstances. But any even remotely humanlike creature is also likely to risk being in the circumstances of justice, so their ideal counterparts should have desires about what to do in situations that feature them, too. This means that premise (2) is in place. And premise (3) follows.

Premise (4) says that if *A+* has a set of idealized desires (based on *A*'s desires) for what to do in a range of situations or circumstances, many of which feature the circumstances of justice, *A+* must have a desire to cooperate with other cooperative agents as a matter of being suitably idealized.[6] This conclusion follows from the nature of idealization and *ROBUST*.

How? I shall argue that because the ideal agent has desires for what to do in an extensive range of situations featuring the circumstances of justice, to be able to exercise her instrumental rationality in a *ROBUST* way, she must have that cooperative desire (in all such situations), for that desire is what allows her to be instrumentally rational in a *ROBUST* way. And *ROBUST*, I have argued, follows from *REASONS INTERNALISM*, so the 'must' here is not normative. It is explained by the features of idealization.

Now, it is well known that, *prima facie*, it need not always be better for individually self-interested agents to abide by the rules of justice. Gyges, Fooles, and Sensible Knaves populate the history of philosophy. These characters are sometimes better at satisfying their desires than the virtuous are. Nevertheless, having desires for what to do in the circumstances of justice, *A+* benefits from participating in human societies, including benefiting just from living in a society in general.

In fact, being able to enjoy the good of cooperation is a matter of *A+*'s idealized instrumental rationality. Whatever else instrumental rationality requires, it requires taking the best means one believes there are to one's ends, where 'best' should be understood weakly, as whichever means is the one to take in one's circumstances. And the two main idealizing conditions of the ideal agents are that they, first, are supposed to have the features constitutive of agency fully functional or manifested when acting, and, second, that their background conditions are the right ones for their functionality.

But to be able to be fully functional or manifest her capacity for instrumental rationality in actions, an ideal agent must be able to take the best means she believes there are to her ends. Similarly, the ideal agent must be able to take

6 What is 'cooperation'? Good question. I shall only assume that cooperation involves several agents trying to achieve some end together (cf. Regan, 1980, p. 129). The reader is free to fill in with more.

the relevant means to satisfy some different desires, since the agent can have multiple, conflicting or changing, desires. This means that insofar as the ideal agent has desires for what to do in the circumstances of justice, the goods of social interaction are necessary background conditions to ensure that her psychology is functional or possible to manifest when acting. And this is because, in situations featuring the circumstances of justice, social interaction generates more and better means both relative to the ideal agent's existing desires and relative to other possible desires she may have. The former is usually the case, and the latter is always the case, for even if agents do not have desires that are better satisfied using means available in social interaction, they can always acquire such desires. So in the circumstances of justice, social interaction is a background condition for the ideal agent's instrumental rationality.

Then we may draw a distinction. Either the ideal agent has a final desire to engage in cooperative schemes, at least given that other agents also do so, or not. If she does, all is well with her when she participates in social interaction. She will happily do so. But assume instead that she lacks such a desire. She need not necessarily be a disinterested maximizer like Gyges, the Foole, or the Knave; she can be anyone who doubts the value of any kind of cooperative arrangements but still benefits from them. What matters is that she lacks the final desire for cooperation.

If *A+* lacks that desire to cooperate, however, but still benefits – again *ex hypothesi* – from those schemes with respect to her instrumental rationality, then she is essentially a free rider.[7] Free riders will, in many situations, be punished by the other participants in the cooperative schemes. In the extensive range of situations featuring the circumstances of justice for which *A+* must have desires, there are no doubt some where that happens – other agents would not, usually, punish an agent with a desire to cooperate. However, in situations where free riders would be punished, an agent with a final desire to cooperate would be able to be more fully instrumentally rational, whereas an otherwise ideal agent who lacks that desire would not.

But then comes the magic trick. An ideal agent who lacks the desire to cooperate is not able to be fully instrumentally rational with respect to taking the best means to satisfy her desires in a *ROBUST* way. *ROBUST*, I wrote, says that

7 Note that the ideal agent here would be a free rider with respect to the means she can take to her ends. That should be enough to run the argument, for I presume that making use of possibilities that other agents' work give her is enough to annoy some others. But it should also be possible to run the argument, *mutatis mutandis*, with the agent free-riding with respect to her desire satisfaction.

A+ must have psychological dispositions and capacities that remain the same over minor changes in the circumstances she may inhabit or otherwise have desires for what to do in, where a 'minor' change is a change in *A+*'s circumstances which is such that, if *A+* had been sensitive to it, it would undermine her being ideal.

Assume, then, that *A+* inhabits some situation featuring the circumstances of justice. If *A+* were to lack a desire to cooperate, in many such situations, she would be punished as a free rider so that she no longer would be able to be instrumentally rational – she might even become literally incapacitated, for example by being killed. Clearly, that would undermine her ideal rationality. So *A+* will only be *ROBUST*-ly disposed to be instrumentally rational if she has a desire to cooperate with other agents in situations where she may be punished. But her psychology should be *ROBUST*, and if she has the pro-cooperative desire, she will be able to maintain her ideal rationality. And as she may be punished in this way in all situations featuring the circumstances of justice – *ex hypothesi*, as she always may be overpowered – it follows that her psychology is *ROBUST* only if she has a desire to cooperate in *all* situations featuring the circumstances of justice.

To be clear, this is not to say that the ideal agent would be *more* instrumentally rational if she were to have a desire to cooperate. It is possible that she would be able to be instrumentally rational in at least some situations even without the desire to cooperate. Rather, with it, she is able be robustly instrumentally rational, which is needed for the manifestation of her capacities and dispositions to the extent which makes her ideal. It is *ROBUST* which does the magic trick here.

How should we characterize the desire that *A+* must have to be ideal? For a start, the desire cannot allow her to cooperate when that seems instrumentally best and free ride when that seems instrumentally best. As the agents in the circumstances of justice are of roughly equal power, she would be able to be punished when attempting to trick others by free riding whenever she would be found out.

Would an *ideal A+* always be potentially found out and punished? Yes. *A+* cannot be smart enough to always be able to trick others. If we were to idealize her to that extent, to ensure a balance of power between agents in the circumstances of justice, we would have to idealize the other agents too. And we must do so, because that balance of power is an aspect of the circumstances of justice. This means that it will, in principle, always be possible for others to find out and punish even an ideal agent.

Furthermore, the desire to cooperate plausibly has to be final, and not merely instrumental, or else it would not be very robust. A merely instrumental desire to cooperate is unreliable and will likely end up punished, since whether or not it is rational to enact will often be up for grabs, given the agent's other desires. *A+* could, possibly, completely lack desires that would benefit from social cooperation, and in such cases, a merely instrumental desire to cooperate would not matter for her at all. For the same reason, the final desire must be strong enough for *A+* to act on it, or else she would not be taken seriously by other agents.

With these considerations in mind, I take it that, to be fully ideal, *A+* must have a fairly strong final cooperative desire with a content which suggests that *A+* cooperates with others to satisfy *A+*'s other important desires. Moreover, as an enabling condition for the successful and robust exercise of that desire, *A+*'s psychology must be *sensitive* to her situation. Sensitivity, in turn, imposes two conditions on her psychology. First, (*i*) *A+*'s desire to cooperate must be in one sense disjunctive; it recommends cooperation if others cooperate *or* acting on *A+*'s other desires if they do not. Second, (*ii*) *A+* must not (otherwise) have important anti-social desires that would impede the exercise of the pro-cooperative desire.[8]

A+ is subject to these two extra sensitivity conditions because the desire to cooperate would not be possible to exercise successfully or robustly without them. First, cooperating with all agents, independently of their motives, would put the agent at risk of either being harmed by cooperation or a sucker's pay-off. On many occasions, this would undermine the rest of her psychology. But her psychology is supposed to be *ROBUST*. Hence, the desire to cooperate must be disjunctive.

Second, we could ask what would happen if *A+* were to cooperate on anti-social desires. By 'anti-social desires', I mean (final) desires for goals the satisfaction of which would significantly impede others' abilities to satisfy their own desires. For example, they might be desires to hurt others so that they cannot satisfy their other desires. If *A+*'s desires to hurt others so that they cannot satisfy their other personal desires are satisfied, then those who are hurt cannot satisfy their own desires when cooperating. But then, the other agent(s) would not desire to cooperate with *A+*, given (*i*). It is obvious that if such desires are known among potential co-operators – which they will be by at least some co-operators in the circumstances of justice – aiming to cooperate on the desires will not have others wanting to cooperate with the agent who has them. So for the desire to cooperate not to be self-undermining, condition (*ii*) puts limits on *A+*'s other desires.

---

8 I write 'important desires' rather than 'desires' here because it is possible that we still can have some weak anti-social desires that do not matter for our actions or reasons. Such desires need not be ruled out.

It seems plausible to think, then, that a desire to cooperate must feature in *A+*'s idealized psychology. But how exactly does the desire to cooperate feature there? This takes us to a discussion of (5). Premise (5) says that if *A+* must have a desire to cooperate with other cooperative agents, *A+* possesses a desire to cooperate with other cooperative agents.

There are two possibilities here. Either the desire to cooperate is ('just') an extra desire of *A+*'s, or the desire is part of *A+*'s instrumental rationality. I prefer the former view. Building such a condition into instrumental rationality would be very clunky, for then instrumental rationality would require coherence between desires and means-beliefs *and* a particular desire, making it much less theoretically elegant than adding the desire to *A+*'s psychology. Nevertheless, the desire should still be added to the ideal agent.[9]

Then we arrive at premise (6). How can we go from a desire to cooperate to moral norms? Following (Smith 1994, ch. 5), I suspect that there are two properties that are the strongest marks of the moral – universal prescriptivity and conventional recognizability.[10] The former means that a moral norm must have prescriptive force for all, and the latter that it should be able to be recognized as moral via some moral convention. Using the desire to cooperate, we can explain two fundamental moral norms with these properties. They lie at the heart of a full account of moral norms.

First, according to *REASONS INTERNALISM*, reasons have their sources in the desires of ideal agents. With their desires to cooperate, idealized agents all have a reason-explaining desire to sensitively cooperate to satisfy their other important (and respective) desires. So they all have a reason which suggests that they cooperate with other cooperating agents. Moreover, they also lack anti-social desires via the second condition, (*ii*), on the cooperative desire. Because reasons internalism says that the desires of an ideal agent explain our reasons, it follows that we all have a reason to cooperate to satisfy our other

9 Moreover, it is plausible that ideal agents are *constituted* by their psychologies (cf. Leffler, 2019). If that is so, it follows that the desire is partially constitutive of the ideal agent. This assumption is, however, not necessary for my argument here.

10 Based on a comprehensive literature review, (Forcehimes and Semrau 2018) list four potential moral/non-moral distinctions: (*i*) moral reasons are not merely social but have stronger force than that, (*ii*) moral reasons do not depend on individual commitments (but are categorical), (*iii*) moral reasons are responsibility-implying, and (*iv*) moral reasons are altruistic. Here, (*i*) and (*ii*) look like ways to try to spell out the intuition of universal prescriptivity, whereas (*iii*) and (*iv*) are ways to spell out conventional recognizability.

respective important desires – except important anti-social desires, which ideal agents are ruled out from having.[11]

Since reasons are prescriptive, and all ideal agents have this pro-cooperative desire, guaranteeing that we all have the same reason to cooperate, it follows that we all have the same universally prescriptive reason. Anyone whose reasons can be explained by *REASONS INTERNALISM* has a reason to cooperate with other cooperative agents.

Moreover, the reason is recognizably moral, for a fundamental pro-cooperative reason seems like the kind of thing we want to count as moral. We have a reason to cooperate in our social interactions so that we can act on our other important desires, which means that we have a reason to simultaneously *benefit* each other – we can act on reasons set by our respective desires – *recognize* each other's ends – since those are what we have reason to cooperate on – and *respect* each other as setting ends – for that is what important desires set. Moreover, since the desire to cooperate extends to all other cooperating agents, beneficence, recognition, and respect are mutual between all cooperating agents, so one may well argue that it is *fair*. These are familiar moral themes. Hence, the reason to cooperate explains a fundamental moral norm.

Second, there is also another moral norm that can be explained by the conditions that enable the cooperative desire. This norm stems from condition (*ii*). Condition (*ii*) rules out cooperating on anti-social desires, for it rules out (important) anti-social desires on part of the ideal agent. Given reasons internalism, it follows that it rules out some potential reasons. Moreover, it does so universally, since all ideal agents have it, and it is clearly recognizably moral, because it seems to explain a norm against anti-sociality in its own right. Hence, it explains a moral norm – but not a moral norm based on a reason; rather, it *rules out* some potential reasons.

To exemplify this, consider Bernard Williams' (1995) case of a husband who abuses his wife but lacks any motivation to stop (even after being idealized). Assume that the husband has a final desire to abuse her and lacks desires not to do so.[12] On Williams' view, the husband lacks an internal reason to stop because he cannot be so motivated. On my view, however, he would not have a reason to start in the first place, because his desire is anti-social. On any

11 I just wrote: 'reason to cooperate to satisfy (. . .)'. Does this mean that agents have a reason to cooperate to *actually* satisfy each other's respective desires, or to cooperate in a way which *allows* them to satisfy their other respective desires? I think this is an issue in first-order ethics that my theory does not answer. Here it is enough to say that we have a reason to cooperate.

12 This is, of course, not a very realistic interpretation of all cases of abuse. But I am not after realism here, I am just after illustrating my point.

plausible interpretation of what 'abuse' is, the abuse limits his wife's abilities to satisfy her own desires when this desire is satisfied – perhaps out of physical pain, but more likely out of the psychological impact of such actions. This means that the idealized counterpart of the husband, whose desires give him reasons, will lack that desire. So he cannot have a reason to abuse his wife grounded in the desire to do so.

Can we say even more about the moral norms we have on this theory, beyond the two fundamental ones? Yes. In virtue of the structure of the theory, we can also explain an additional type of moral norms. This type is based on reasons that are necessary means to cooperate, and hence for acting on our fundamental reason to cooperate, insofar as we are involved in social interactions. Given the reason-grounding desire to cooperate so we can satisfy our other, respective, desires, a necessary means for cooperating is to cooperate to satisfy those other desires. Insofar as we are involved in cooperation-inducing situations, then, cooperating to satisfy them is a necessary means for living up to the central cooperative norm, for there is no other way to do it than through these desires (cf. Strandberg, 2019). These necessary means are *secondary moral norms*. Secondary moral norms are universally prescriptive because everyone has them (in the right situations) and are (at least usually) recognizably moral, but they are more contingent than other norms, for people's desires may, of course, vary.

There can, therefore, be all kinds of moral norms, depending on what people in various social settings desire to do. But regardless of our distance to others, we have reason to cooperate with them, *qua* cooperating agents. This gives a basis for a conception of society as a system of mutual cooperation. And, importantly, it gives us the conclusion (C) in the argument from idealization.

3 Law

I have now presented and briefly defended an argument from idealization which suggests something about the nature of morality. What does it have to do with the nature of law? The two main competing theories about the nature of law in philosophy of law are natural law theories and legal positivism. It is sometimes thought that one key difference between them is that natural law theories feature the idea that there is a theoretically important necessary connection between moral norms and legal norms, whereas legal positivists deny this claim.[13] But natural law

13 I add the 'theoretically important' qualifier here as positivists may accept that there are several necessary connections between law and morality. Even arch-positivist H.L.A. Hart thought there

theorists tend to believe that law has its basis – perhaps its source or ground – in morality.

The connection between law and morality gives natural law theories, at least, two fundamental and well-known problems just on their face. One is to explain which moral norms there are that plausibly can play their role as being necessarily connected to, and even be the bases of, law. Call this the *problem of moral foundations*. To be sure, natural law theorists have tried to solve it. Perhaps most famously, John Finnis (2011) is the paradigmatic defender of such norms, and he defends an Aristotelian-*cum*-Thomist conception of the morality that underlies law. But whether that framework does any important explanatory work well is very much an open question.

Another major problem is the *problem of bad law*. Perhaps it is the case that laws, in many societies, indeed are moral. But that cannot always be the case. What do we make of, for example, Nazi law if law is supposed to be necessarily connected to, and indeed based on, morality?

It is here that the cooperation-based conception of morality just defended comes in helpful. To see why, we need to explore the theoretical structure of natural law theories further. At least one significant strand of natural law theories is, to use Jonathan Dancy's (2018) term, *focalist* in structure.[14] This means that the theories are structured so that one takes a certain class of cases or instances of the phenomenon one is trying to analyze to be focal (or 'central', or 'paradigmatic', or 'ideal') and other instances of the phenomenon one is analyzing to be less focal (or 'central', or 'paradigmatic', or 'ideal'). Despite being similar to the focal case, and in some sense belonging to the same kind of phenomenon, they deviate from it in some interesting way.[15]

There are several distinct kinds of focalist theories, and their structures are the same regardless of what they are supposed to be theories of. Perhaps most notably, one may either take the focal case(s) to be the function of the phenomenon one is discussing or hold a disjunctivist view. On the former type of theory, the phenomenon one discusses has a function, but various instances may live up to it to greater or lesser extents. If the function of the eye is to see, seeing eyes may be focal cases, but blind ones are not. On the latter type of

were two: law often depends on morality in interpretations, and moral and legal principles are similarly public (Hart, 1961, ch. 9). But these connections are not explanatorily important.

14 Dancy does, in fact, refer back to natural law theorist Finnis when outlining this type of theory (Dancy, 2018, pp. 105–106).

15 I formulate focalism slightly differently from Dancy: he does not like the term 'paradigmatic', and prefers to say that the non-focalist cases depend on the main one rather than deviate from it. For present purposes, nothing of interest turns on these changes.

theory, the phenomenon one discusses comes in distinct kinds, one of which is more fundamental than the others. The non-fundamental kinds may then also deviate from the fundamental kind. The fundamental kind of perception may, perhaps, be veridical, whereas hallucinatory perception is a non-fundamental kind of perception (cf. Martin, 2004).

Natural law theorists need not, for present purposes, decide which type of focalist theory is preferable. For regardless of which type of theory is better, the cooperation-based moral norms from the last section can contribute. In particular, the secondary moral norms I have discussed seem like excellent candidates for sometimes *being* laws. They are socially recognized, and if they are also formally recognized, for example by being codified by being written, they look a lot like actual laws. Indeed, I hypothesize that if some moral norms of that kind are instantiated, it is very likely that at least some of them actually are laws.

If that is right, we can provide fairly easy solutions to the problems of moral foundations and bad law. The former problem can be solved by counting at least some moral norms – usually, the codified or written ones – as the moral foundations of a natural law theory. If the argument from section (2) is correct, we can see how a particular kind of norms seems likely to play the role in the theory.

Moreover, the problem of bad law can be solved by a manoeuvre that natural law theorists often make anyway, namely, by appealing to the focalist structure of the theory (cf. Finnis, 2011, pp. 351–366). For regardless of whether one goes for a functionalist or a disjunctivist focalist theory, one can count laws that are not secondary moral norms as not living up to the function of law – which one may construe as 'instituting secondary moral norms in a society' or suchlike – or the fundamental kind of law – when that in itself is a certain subset of the secondary moral norms there are.

Admittedly, this manoeuvre is only as plausible as what one posits the function or fundamental kind of law to be. But that is a point that speaks in favour of the agreement-based conception of morality as a basis for law that I have defended here. On more traditional natural law theories, the relation between the norms that lie at the basis of law and how we usually understand law can be murky. Why would human social institutions have a lot to do with mind-independent or even God-given moral facts, for example? By contrast, the interpersonal elements of the reasons internalist picture I have presented clearly shows how secondary moral norms have a social element from the start, which, as I have stressed, makes them very intuitive candidates for lawhood.

4 Conclusion

In this chapter, I have presented some surprising developments of a natural law theory. In section 1, I introduced reasons internalism. Then, in section 2, I sketched an argument from idealization for a cooperation-based theory of moral norms. In section 3, I indicated how these socially accepted norms, in the right circumstances, might be slotted into a natural law account of laws and yield unexpectedly plausible results.

Does that mean I have defended a natural law theory? Sort of. I am attracted to the picture I have presented, but I am not sure about why one should prefer a theory with a focalist structure to one which is more straightforward, or, more generally, why one should prefer a natural law framework to some other one. So I recommend the reader to treat this paper as exploratory. It fundamentally aims to paint a picture and show why it has some attractions. But whether or not that picture is accurate will have to be determined elsewhere.

References

Chang, R. 2009. Voluntarist Reasons and the Sources of Normativity. In: Sobel, D. and Wall, S. eds. *Reasons for Action*, New York, NY: Cambridge University Press, pp. 243–271.

Chang, R. 2013. Grounding Practical Normativity: Going Hybrid. *Philosophical Studies*. 164(1), pp. 163–187.

Dancy, J. 2018. *Practical Shape: A Theory of Practical Reasoning*. Oxford, UK: Oxford University Press.

Forcehimes, A. and Semrau, L. 2018. Are There Distinctively Moral Reasons? *Ethical Theory and Moral Practice*. 21(3), pp. 699–717.

Finnis, J. 2011. *Natural Law and Natural Rights*. 2nd Edition. Oxford, UK: Oxford University Press.

Hart, H.L.A. 1961. *The Concept of Law*. Oxford, UK: Oxford University Press.

Hume, D. 1978. A Treatise of Human Nature. In: Selby-Bigge, L.A. and Nidditch, P.H. eds. *A Treatise of Human Nature*. 2nd edition. Oxford, UK: Oxford University Press.

Hurtig, K.I. 2006. Internalism and Accidie. *Philosophical Studies*. 129(3), pp. 517–543.

Joyce, R. 2001. *The Myth of Morality*. Oxford, UK: Oxford University Press.

Leffler, O. 2019. *The Constitution of Constitutivism*. PhD Dissertation, University of Leeds, UK.

Martin, M.G.F. 2004. The Limits of Self-Awareness. *Philosophical Studies*. 120(1–3), pp. 37–89.

Peter, F. 2019. Normative Facts and Reasons. *Proceedings of the Aristotelian Society*. 119(1), pp. 53–75.

Rawls, J. 1971. *A Theory of Justice*. Cambridge, MA: Harvard University Press.

Regan, D. 1980. *Utilitarianism and Cooperation*. Oxford, UK: Clarendon Press.

Smith, M. 1994. *The Moral Problem*, Oxford, UK: Blackwell Publishing.

Smith, M. 1995. Internal Reasons. *Philosophy and Phenomenological Research*. 55(1), pp. 109–131.

Smith, M. 2012*a*. Agents and Patients: Or, What We Learn about Reasons for Action by Reflecting on Our Choices in Process-of-Thought Cases. *Proceedings of the Aristotelian Society*. 112(3), pp. 309–331.

Smith, M. 2012*b*. A Puzzle about Internal Reasons. In Heuer, U. and Lang, G. eds. *Luck, Value and Commitment: Themes from the Philosophy of Bernard Williams*. Oxford, UK: Oxford University Press, pp. 195–218.

Strandberg, C.S. 2019. An Ecumenical Account of Categorical Moral Reasons. *Journal of Moral Philosophy*. 16(2), pp. 160–188.

Williams, B.A.O. 1981. Internal and External Reasons. In: Williams, B.A.O. *Moral Luck: Philosophical Papers 1973–1980*. Cambridge, UK: Cambridge University Press, pp. 101–13.

Williams, B.A.O. 1995. Internal Reasons and the Obscurity of Blame. In: Williams, B.A.O. *Making Sense of Humanity and Other Philosophical Papers 1982–1993*. Cambridge, UK: Cambridge University Press.

Arto Laitinen

Varieties of Normativity: Reasons, Expectations, Wide-Scope Oughts, and Ought-to-be's

1 Introduction

This chapter distinguishes between several senses of "normativity". For example, that we ought to abstain from causing unnecessary suffering is a normative, not descriptive, claim. And so is the claim that we have good reason, and ought to drive on the right, or left, side of the road because the law requires us to do that. Reasons and oughts are normative, by definition.[1] Indeed, it may be that "[t]he normativity of all that is normative consists in the way it is, or provides, or is otherwise related to reasons" (Raz 1999, 67).[2] That is what the "reasons-first" view holds, but there are also other views, and what is by definition a normative statement, or a normative fact if you like, depends on how we define normativity.

It may seem that requirements are also by definition normative.[3] But it seems that there can also be requirements that one has no reason to meet: it is less clear whether such requirements are normative in the same sense that reasons and oughts are normative. This paper will go through various further phenomena, which are candidates for being normative in some other sense than normative reasons and oughts, defending however the view that not all of them are. But arguably four or so different senses of normativity can be distinguished.

The paper will accept the view that the normativity of reasons and oughts, which is here called *normativity*$_1$, is central.[4] It is an open question whether all requirements or expectations or socially constructed norms are normative in that sense. Arguably it depends on the contents and content-independent authority of the legislators, whether we have good reasons, or ought, to meet the

1 A valid argument can lead to a conclusion about reasons or oughts only if there is a premise that includes reasons or oughts.

2 See e.g. Fabianne Peter (2019), Simon Robertson (2012) and Daniel Star, ed (2018) for discussions of this "reasons first" view, defended e.g. by Parfit (2011), Scanlon (2014) and Raz (2010).

3 Chisholm (1964).

4 This is defended by a number of authors, Broome (2013), Dancy (2000), Kolodny (2005), Parfit (1997), (2001), (2011), Raz (1999), for example. They disagree on the relationship between oughts and reasons, but agree that these are the central normative concepts.

https://doi.org/10.1515/9783110663617-009

requirements, obey the law, or to follow the etiquette, or to conform to others' interpersonal expectations, requests, demands or prescriptions. Whether and when we do have such reasons is a difficult and important substantive question, which concerns the *normativity*$_1$ of requirements of law.[5]

In another sense, norms (intended to guide behavior) are trivially or by definition normative, and constitute normativity: some forms of behavior are ruled as acceptable (e.g. driving on the right) and others as unacceptable (e.g. driving on the left) in light of the norm. Even in the case of a bad norm (that we have no reason to follow, and which ought to be changed, and ought not prevail) classifies behaviours as acceptable or unacceptable in light of the norm.[6] Surely norms are by definition normative? Call this conformity to social norms and actual expectations *normativity*$_2$. It is *not* an open question whether social norms are normative in *that* sense – they are by definition normative$_2$. But importantly, it is an open question whether one has good reasons, or sufficient reason, or ought, to follow any social norm – that is, whether the norm in question is normative$_1$.

The first section of the article characterizes further the difference between these two senses of normativity, and additionally introduces various other candidate senses of "normativity". These possible senses of "normativity" may be at stake in the debates about normative requirements of rationality,[7] about so called ought-to-be -rules,[8] about normativity of linguistic meaning,[9] about "directions of fit" of beliefs and desires,[10] about subjective authority of intentions and decisions[11] and interpersonal authority or co-authority of concrete others.[12]

In later sections these cases are discussed. Do they constitute separate senses of normativity? And are the later phenomena such that they give agents good reasons: do they include normativity$_1$ – the core sense? A "normative

---

5 See Raz (1999), Christiano (2008), also Searle (1995) for whom institutional statuses can generate desire-independent reasons for action. Raz (1999, 67) writes that "The normativity of rules, or of authority, or of morality, for example, consists in the fact that rules are reasons of a special kind, the fact that directives issued by legitimate authorities are reasons, and in the fact that moral considerations are valid reasons. So ultimately the explanation of normativity is the explanation of what it is to be a reason, and of related puzzles about reasons."

6 Bicchieri (2006), Brennan et al. (2013).

7 Broome (1999), Kolodny (2005), Sellars (1991).

8 Chisholm (1964), Sellars (1968), Tuomela (2007), Wedgwood (2007).

9 Kripke (1982), Boghossian (2003), Glüer and Wikforss (2018), Kusch (2006), Millar (2004), Hattiangadi (2007), Whiting (2013).

10 Anscombe (1957), Humberstone (1992), Platts (1979), Zangwill (1998).

11 O'Brien (2019).

12 Ikäheimo & Laitinen (2007).

power -model" is suggested as a framework for examining whether actual social norms, laws, expectations provide good reasons and oughts or not. Once we understand the relation between the first two senses of normativity, do the later phenomena follow the same pattern – is the "normative powers – model" relevant for them as well?

2 Different Senses of Normativity

Sometimes talk of normativity (we will call this normativity$_2$) has a negative connotation, related to the external *pressure to conform* with *factual demands* and *behavioural expectations* that others pose, or that result from *actually accepted social norms,* whether justified or not.

The term "heteronormativity", for example, is often used for a kind of insensitive expectation that everyone be heterosexual: deviation from this norm is held to be somehow shameful, and it is perhaps tolerated in some contexts, say, military service or football teams, only on the condition that it is not made public. Our everyday practices indeed often have such in–built assumptions even when not explicitly acknowledged, and by participating in the practices we collectively uphold such norms.

As this example shows, the factual social norms and actual expectations can be quite unjustified, and criticisable. But the claims that such expectations or norms are "unjustified", "criticisable", or that people "ought" to resist such insensitive pressures, or that there are in fact "no good reasons" behind such intolerant demands, are *normative* claims in what I take to be the central sense – not in the sense of conformity to prevailing norms, but in the sense of what one really ought to do or believe, or has good reason to do or feel. This we call *normativity$_1$*.

The mere fact that something *is* demanded or expected by someone does not show that it *ought to* be demanded or expected, or that people ought to behave accordingly.[13] And the core sense of normativity concerns precisely how agents ought to respond to the reality; what people have reason to do, believe

13 "I do not use 'requires' as a normative term. For instance, I might say that freemasonry requires you to roll up one trouser-leg, without suggesting you ought to do that. However, it seems plausible that the requirements of rationality are indeed normative. This paper investigates whether that is so. What would it mean, exactly? It might mean that, necessarily, if rationality requires you to F then you ought to F, and moreover you ought to F because rationality requires you to F." (Broome 2005, 324).

or feel; what expectations and demands are justified; and what is criticisable. Arguably, making some kind of normative claims or assumptions in this sense is inescapable in human life: human mind and action, as well as institutional reality and possibly language are thoroughly "fraught with ought" (Sellars 1991). So, what we mean by "normativity" comes out different when we start from social norms, or from reasons and oughts.

The central question concerning the authority of law is whether and when and why we ought to obey the law. Two approaches give very different answers: one starting from practical reality which is already normatively structured, and seeing social constructions like law as modifications of such reality, and the other starting from a normative vacuum and seeing social constructions (from informal to institutional, with law as a special case) as the origin of normativity. Both approaches must conceptually distinguish between good reasons and requirements of social and institutional norms, to be able to ask whether the norms ought to be followed. The answer to that question turns out to depend on a number of variables, to be discussed in the next sections. The crude answer is that if the norms and expectations are justified exercises of normative power, they do result in reasons for action.

A third paradigmatic starting point for approaching normativity is *formal* rationality, stressing the consistency and logical impeccability of one's beliefs, intentions or commitments – but formal consistency is not by itself any reason to believe or intend anything: it may be consistent to believe that the moon is made of cheese and the moon is a dairy product, but such consistency alone gives us no reason to believe either of these. Thus, although formal rationality may by definition be "normative" in some sense of normativity$_3$, this sense must be distinguished from the core sense of normativity$_1$ related to reasons and oughts. (see Broome 1999). Such requirements of rationality need not be socially constructed, but are something that for example theorists of logic find. Rules of logic may be both constitutive of "inferring" and normativity$_3$: one feels normative pressure to accept the conclusion, if one accepts the premises.

So, we can distinguish normativity in the sense of good reasons and oughts (normativity$_1$), normativity in the sense of meeting any norms or standards (normativity$_2$), and normativity in the sense of meeting the logical demands of formal rationality (normativity$_3$). It is naturally an interesting question to ask under what conditions one ought to obey social norms and expectations (see e.g. Raz 1990), and whether there are reasons to be formally rational, consistent (see e.g. Kolodny 2005, Broome 1999, 2007).

Concerning the normativity of formal rationality, we can again distinguish an open and a closed question: it is an open question whether rationality is normative$_1$, but there may be a sense of normativity$_3$ where requirements of

Table 1: Four senses of normativity.

Normativity 1	Normativity 2	Normativity 3	Normativity 4
Reasons and oughts: what one really *ought to (has good reason to, is justified to)* do, believe, intend, judge etc.	Meeting a given social norm, standard or expectation (whether or not the norm, expectation or standard itself is justified)	Meeting the formal requirements of logic and consistency. One "ought" to accept the conclusion if one accepts the premises. It does not follow that one ought to accept the conclusion, period. The "ought" has a wide scope.	Ought-to-be's: what ought to be the case

rationality are by definition normative. (Instrumental rationality may be some case in point: "in order to get to Hamburg, one should take the A train" – but what if one has no reason to get to Hamburg? Should one take the A train?). This indirectly strengthens the idea that normativity$_1$ and normativity$_2$ should be distinguished, by showing that there may be further forms of normativity that should be distinguished from the core sense of normativity$_1$, and which are not reducible to normativity$_2$.

> An important fact about statements of the form "If *X* wants *A*, he ought to do B" is that they do not permit what we might call unconditional detachment. Suppose "If Harry wants his inheritance now, he ought to kill his father" and suppose "Harry wants his inheritance now." We do not draw the unalloyed conclusion "Harry ought to kill his father." The reasonableness of killing his father remains strictly relative to Harry's desire and does not achieve the objective status signaled by unconditional detachment.
> (de Vries 2016, 7.2)

John Broome has suggested about such cases, that the "ought" has a wide scope: one ought to (if one accepts the premises, accept the conclusion). One cannot detach a narrow scope ought to accept the conclusion: after all, perhaps one ought accept the premises. This seems different from the oughts that substantive reasons generate, and from the (putative) normativity$_2$ involved even in unjustified norms. Here are some of Broome's examples:

> *First requirement.* Rationality requires of you that you do not both believe p and believe not-p.
> *Second requirement.* Rationality requires of you that, if you believe p and you believe (if p then q), and if it matters to you whether q, then you believe q.

> *Third requirement.* Rationality requires of you that, if you intend to G, and if you believe your Fing is a necessary means to your Ging, and if you believe you will not F unless you intend to F, then you intend to F.
> *Fourth requirement.* Rationality requires of you that, if you believe you ought to F, and if you believe you will not F unless you intend to F, then you intend to F.
> (Broome 2005, 322)

These are genuine requirements, but you can typically satisfy them in two ways: by dropping one of the beliefs that causes a contradiction, and by either forming the intention or dropping the belief. The requirements do not tell which one should do; they have wide scope. These requirements seem to be constitutive of rationality, and thus unlike contingent social norms and expectations.

A fourth case whose reducibility to the previous forms of normativity is worth considering, are the so called "Ought-to-be -norms", which differ from ought-to-do -norms (see e.g. Sellars 1968).[14] What does it mean that legal systems "ought to be" morally just? Does it mean merely that it is good that they are just? Or does it mean that the responsible agents or communities in charge ought to see to it, that they are just? A separate "agentless" form of normativity of artefacts and biological entities is discussed e.g. by J.J. Thomson (2007), so we can take it into consideration that this is a separate idea from ought-to-do – norms (or better, ought-to-do – principles, if we reserve the term "norms" for social norms).[15] We can reserve the term normativity$_4$ for it. DeVries, in his article on Sellars, explains this notion as follows:

> Sellars's other 'ought' is the *ought-to-be*, aka rules of criticism. For example, it ought to be the case that dogs come when their masters call. Such a rule speaks to no agent in particular, and it is certainly not a rule that dogs *obey* in the paradigmatic sense. It simply endorses a particular state of affairs without regard for any mode of achieving it. Still, dogs can exhibit a pattern of behavior that accords with the rule, and they can do so *because* of the rule, if their masters train them to come when called because the masters have reasoned along the following lines: 'It ought to be the case that dogs come when their masters call. Therefore, it ought to be the case that my dog comes when I call. My dog will come when called only if I train it to do so. Therefore, I ought to train my dog to come when called.' This reasoning moves from an ought-to-be to a relevant ought-to-do

14 Glüer and Wikforss (2018) characterize *norms for action* and *norms of being as follows:* "Norms of being are often associated with evaluations; they tell us that a certain state of affairs *ought to obtain*, i.e., is valuable or good in a certain sense. Norms for action, on the other hand, tell us *what to do*." They refer to von Wright (1963), 14; Schnädelbach (1990, 83ff); Hartmann (1925), and Moore (1922).
15 See also Ikäheimo (2011).

> and comes to full fruition not in a belief about one's obligations, but in a set of actions that result in one's dog learning to come when called. Ought-to-be's imply ought-to-do's; and ought-to-do's typically lead to action. (DeVries 2016, sec. 7.3)

This notion of norms of being, or ought-to-be's seems a distinct normative phenomenon from action-guiding normativity of reasons and norms (See Table 1).

We can think of four other phenomena, where either the term "normativity" is used, or normative considerations are at stake, but which seem irreducible to the question of reasons and oughts, that is, $normativity_1$. They may, however, be reducible to the previous kinds of normativity or not be normative at all (See Table 2).

Table 2: Further putative senses of normativity.

Normativity 5?	**Normativity 6?**	**Normativity 7?**	**Normativity 8?**
"Normativity" of linguistic meaning: correctness of use?	The direction of fit of desires: the world ought to match the desire?	The subjective authority of intentions and motivations?	Interpersonal normativity of requests and demands?

One context is the debates on normativity of linguistic meaning:

> To say that meaning . . . is essentially *normative* is to say that meaning . . . is essentially such that *certain norms are valid, or in force*, whenever something has meaning/content. (Glüer and Wikforss 2018, 1.2)[16]

Kripke's (1982) book on rule-following made the point that a satisfactory theory of linguistic meaning must be able to distinguish between correct and incorrect use of terms (e.g. applying "cow" to cows and not horses). That came to be called "normativity" of meaning, as there is a natural sense in which one should use language correctly. But in the debates that ensued, these two senses of normativity have been distinguished, correctness and prescriptivity.[17] The latter seems reducible to either oughts ($normativity_1$) or norms ($normativity_2$).

---

16 Note that for them, the normative concept is "norm" ($normativity_2$), not "reason" or "ought" ($normativity_1$). They seem to think that normativity has to do with (constructed) norms in force for some individuals or communities. (It may of course be that they think oughts are also involved as normativity is action-guiding, I thank Aleksi Honkasalo for the comment). They mention, but put aside, the possibility that normativity of meaning is related to norms of being ($normativity_4$).

17 See e.g. Fennell (2013).

It has been pointed out that no reasons for action or belief follow from meanings alone. If that is correct, then the normativity of meaning is not normativity_1 but something else. Early on in the debate, these were not so clearly distinguished. It may be that the correctness of linguistic usage is normative in the same sense that different norms or rules (such as rules of etiquette) are by definition normative – what is at stake is a match between a token case and a rule.[18] So it is worth examining whether there is an irreducibly new sense of normativity at play at all; we can call the candidate normativity_5.

The debates on "directions of fit" of desires and beliefs suggests another, possibly different usage of normative terms.[19] The idea is that states such as desires and beliefs may have the same propositional content, e.g. "that it rains". I may believe that it rains and I may desire that it rains. What is the difference? It has been suggested, that one's beliefs ought to conform to the world, whereas the world ought to conform to one's desires (see e.g. Gregory 2012). It has been pointed out that in the case of a mismatch between reality and the mental state, desires and beliefs are constitutively different: if one perceives that it does not rain, one ought to (or has epistemic reasons to) alter one's belief to fit the state of the world. But in the case of desires there is no normative pressure to change one's mind to fit the world – rather, the world ought to change to match the desire.

Elizabeth Anscombe's (1957, §32) example of a shopping list with various items in it, and a shopping basket which ultimately ought to have all the same items as the shopping list, has been widely and rightly regarded as a nice illustration of the difference between two directions of fit, although Anscombe does not use the phrase "direction of fit". It may help to think of this in terms of a boss (the shopper's wife in Anscombe's text) having first made the list, and then sent a personal assistant to the shop – the assistant's task is to obey the shopping list and regard it as fixed, and collect the mentioned items.

Such a shopping list contrasts with the record of a detective spying on what the shopper puts in the shopping basket: The detective's record ought to have all the same items as the shopping basket. The detective obviously should not regard his or her list or record as fixed in advance. When both the shopper and the detective have been successful, the shopping list, the basket, and the detective's record have the same items in them. The difference with the shopping list and the detective's record concerns the unsuccessful case: What happens if the list in

18 For Millar (2004), the normativity of meaning derives from social practices (normativity_2 in our terms); and it is an open question, whether one ought to (normatively_1) participate in such practices. (But if one does participate, and violates the norms of the practice, one may act against what one ought to do; I thank Aleksi Honkasalo for the comment).
19 Anscombe (1957), Humberstone (1992), Platts (1979), Zangwill (1998).

question contains, say, "bananas" when there are no bananas in the basket. The shopper should not delete "bananas" from the list but add bananas to the basket. And the detective in turn should not add anything to the basket but delete such unfit items from the detective's record. Anscombe asks what distinguishes the shopping list from the detective's list, and answers: "It is precisely this: if the list and the things that the man actually buys do not agree, and if this and this alone constitutes a mistake, then the mistake is not in the list but in the man's performance (. . .) whereas if the detective's record and what the man actually buys do not agree, then the mistake is in the record." (Anscombe 1957, p. 56)

The point is that the detective's record functions like beliefs or assertions about the contents of the basket, the shopping list functions like desires, intentions, or orders about the contents of the basket. The direction of fit of theoretical representations (record, belief, assertion) is such that their contents should fit the world, whereas the direction of fit of practical representations (shopping list, desire, intention, order) is such that their contents should be kept fixed, while the world should come to fit them.

This is fine as such for illustrating one difference between desires and beliefs, but in the context of this chapter it is interesting to ask what it possibly could mean to say that the world ought to change? It could be that we deal with "ought-to-be's" of the sort discussed above. Or are we dealing with (desire-based) practical reasons such that the agent has reasons to fulfil the desires? That is no doubt often the case, but it is a different issue (that concerns ought-to-do-norms), and not always the case (some desires we have no reason to fulfil). Or perhaps what is at stake is a wide scope -ought: in order for the world to match the desire, it ought to be thus-and-so. This cannot be reduced to mere statement that if the world is thus-and-so it matches the state of mind, because that is true both of desires and beliefs, and loses the direction of fit.[20]

Once we already have a variety of senses of normativity, it is harder to see clearly whether a new suggestion is irreducible to all the previous suggestions. It is clear that descriptions of the world (it rains), and "orectic" characterizations (I want that it rains) differ, but it is unclear whether the latter is normative at all. Normativity will in any case differ not only from descriptions of the world, but also from evaluations, explanations, causal relations, constitutive relations, modality etc. So again, it seems to me there is not a new form or sense of normativity at play. But of course there could be – it could be that on closer scrutiny we

20 Thus, the direction of fit – debate is not merely about the normativity of the intentional (Wedgwood 2009), but the difference between beliefs and desires, and the special sense in which desires make demands on the world, and not merely the agent.

come to appreciate that desiring is in some sense a normative relationship to the world, a matter of implicitly demanding something from the world, or prescribing something to it.

Finally, even though normative and motivating reasons are typically distinguished, sometimes "normativity" is used for what the agent is motivated by, moved by (see Parfit 2011 on Korsgaard). The idea may be that something, like intentions, has "subjective authority" and is experienced as binding. (see e.g. O'Brien 2019). Similarly, interpersonal prescriptions or demands (or threats or appeals, for that matter) are positive attempts to make a normative difference – analogously to law. Indeed, I will below suggest that the subjective and interpersonal cases can be understood on the same model as law, it is just that the holder of the normative power is different in these cases: in case of personal motivations, expectations, decisions and intentions it is oneself, in interpersonal cases it is the other (who asks for a favour or makes a demand), and in social and institutional cases it is the larger collective. So I will suggest that at least these forms of normativity turn out to be extensions of normativity$_2$.

In this section we have seen that different definitions of what normativity is give different answers to what is by definition normative. Let us now turn to the core sense of normativity: reasons and oughts, and after that, the exercises of normative powers that result in a variety of demands and expectations.

3 Normativity$_1$: Reasons and Oughts

A reason to do something is a consideration that favours doing it (Dancy 2000, Scanlon 1998, 2014).[21] That the trash can is full is a reason to take it out. That she is in pain is a reason to give her a painkiller. That resources are unevenly allocated is a reason to redistribute resources more justly. That something is humiliating is a reason not to do it.

When there are overall stronger considerations to do X than to do Y, then one has more reason to do X. This can be the result of several more minor considerations favouring X-ing, even though the strongest individual consideration would favour Y-ing. Suppose you are deciding which apartment to live in: there may be one major reason to choose Y, but the combined weight of considerations favouring choosing X may nonetheless override them.

---

21 For Scanlon (2014, 31), the reason-relation is "a four-place relation, R(p, x, c, a) holding between a fact, p, an agent x, a set of conditions c, and an action or attitude a. This is the relation that holds just in case p is a reason for a person x in situation c to do or hold a."

This suggests that one reason is a consideration that does what it does, favours some course of action, on its own, and can do it even if there is some other reason that favours the opposite action (Dancy 2004a). In that sense, reasons may seem "atomistic". There may, however, be contextual features which make a difference to whether the reason is a reason, and how strong the reason is. These contextual features may be called disablers and enablers, and intensifiers and attenuators (Dancy 2004a). That a band's gig tonight promises to be great is a reason to go to the gig, but the fact that it has been sold out disables that consideration from having relevance in one's practical deliberation about what to do tonight. That something was done in full awareness of the suffering it causes intensifies the reason others have to condemn the action. And so on. According to Jonathan Dancy (1993, 2004a), there may even be contextual features that change the polarity of the reason: while typically the fact that something would be a lie is a reason not to say it, in the context of playing a game of "Contraband" one is, however, supposed to lie, so the same consideration ("that it would be a lie") is a reason for, not against, saying it. That something looks to me red is normally a reason to believe it is red, but if I have taken a pill that makes red things look green, it is a reason to believe it is not red. Such contextual features suggest "holism" about reasons: while reasons can function individually, the way they function depends on the context (Dancy 2004a).

Typically, what one overall ought to do in a situation is the same as what one has most reason to do, or has conclusive reason to do, in a situation. Overall "oughts" are determined by the balance of reasons for and against all alternative courses of action in a situation.[22] In a different situation of course one ought to do a different thing, but in each situation what one ought to do, depends on the strengths of the normatively significant considerations in that situation. If holism is right, those strengths in turn already depend on the presence and absence of enablers, disablers, intensifiers, attenuators and reversers.

Oughts are requirements on what one is to do, and so it is often rationally impermissible or criticizable to omit doing it. In some cases, the reasons do not add up to a requirement on what to do, but merely a recommendation. The reasons may merely "entice" one to do something, without any normative pressure against not doing it. For clarity, I will not use "ought" for such overall recommendations, but only for overall requirements.[23]

What one ought not do, or has conclusive reason against doing can be called rationally impermissible. It need not be morally impermissible, if the reasons

22 Raz (1990).
23 Dancy (2004b).

that speak against the course of action are not moral reasons.[24] Whatever view we have about how to distinguish moral considerations from other considerations, it is clear there are other types of reasons. These may include prudential reasons to do what is good for oneself, one's well-being but also value-based reasons of many other sorts: if ecological diversity is a good thing, one has reason to promote it independently of its role in promoting one's own well-being. If something is against the democratically set law, one has reason not to do it. That something is requested by a friend is a reason to do it. That it would be slightly more convenient is a (small) reason to close the door, and so on.[25] All in all, there are many kinds of reasons, of varying strength and nature.

Some features of the world are arguably objectively reason-giving independently of any social or subjective decision that they are (Raz 1999). Suppose suffering is always, or at least in almost all contexts, bad. That something causes suffering is (in those contexts) a reason against doing it, even when there is no socially accepted norm of avoiding suffering. One does not need a law, or social practice to confer normative significance to suffering, it is normatively significant independently.[26]

It is helpful to distinguish normatively significant claims or facts from normative claims or facts (cf. Parfit 2011, McNaughton and Rawling 2004):
1) X-ing causes suffering
2) Fact 1 is a reason against X-ing

Fact 1 is normatively significant or relevant, because it figures in a normative claim (or fact). A claim (or a fact) is normative, if it features the terms "reason" or "ought" in the normative sense. (Or so at least for normativity$_1$).

The characterization of normativity in terms of reasons or oughts can only be circular, because both terms are used also in non-normative senses.[27] *Motivating* reasons are the reasons for which an agent acted, and sometimes the agents act for considerations they should not have acted on. By contrast, *normative* reasons are good reasons, for which the agents should act on. They are considerations that speak in favour of the action. In happy cases, the agents act on good reasons, and then normative and motivating reasons coincide. Further, there are *explanatory* usages of "reason", as in talking about the reason the snowman melted, where "reason" really refers to a cause.[28] Similarly, there are non-

24 Parfit (1997).
25 Raz (1999).
26 Shafer-Landau (2003).
27 Broome (1999).
28 Dancy (2000).

normative usages of "ought" as in "it ought to rain by 12". I take it that intuitively it is easy to grasp the difference between clear normative and non-normative usages (while there may also be hard cases).

Note that all normative "facts" (Fact 2: fact 1 is a reason against X-ing) can be generalized to be conditional principles (Principle: if fact 1 obtains, it is a reason against X-ing).[29] I will reserve the term "norm" for socially constructed expectations, and use "principle" in ways which is neutral between socially constructed and independent normative features.

The question about the normativity of law can be put as: is the fact that law tells us to drive on the left side a normatively significant fact? Ought I to drive on the left *because* the law tells me to? Do I have reason to drive on the left merely because to law says so. The answer to such questions is often positive: the law gives us valid reasons for action.

Consider the following claims:

1) As such, there are no independent reasons to favour driving on the left or driving on the right
2) The law demands me to drive on the right
3) I have stronger reason to drive on the right
4) I drive on the right

Of these claims, the last one is descriptive claim. The first and third are normative$_1$ claims, claims about reasons. What about the claim (2)? It is less clear whether it is a descriptive claim (as it is about demands, and not about events in the world), but it does have a descriptive aspect: it can be mistaken about the contents of the law. And yet it seems normative, as it poses a demand, a normative pressure to act in some way. But contrast it with the following scenario:

1′) There are strong reasons against killing humans
2′) The law demands me to kill humans if they engage in blasphemous activity
3′) I have strong reason to oppose the law publicly, in acts of civil disobedience

This shows that the generalization that I always have a good reason to obey the law is not true. But here as well, the law is normatively significant. It is just that thanks to the morally abhorrent nature of the law, the citizens have a reason to protest publicly against it. It may be that the law is in this case disabled, silenced, prevented from having the intended normative effect, because the content is morally unacceptable – if so, it would be wrong to think that it gives

29 Shafer-Landau (2003).

me *some* reason for killing the blasphemous humans. It is rather that I have *no* such reason, as the law fails to provide me a reason. It is null and void, when normatively disabled, like counterfeit money, or javelin throws that are out-of-bounds.

The story may continue that

4′) I will be punished and labelled a criminal unless I act in accordance with (2′)

5′) I have reason to avoid punishment and reason to avoid being labelled a criminal, so I have some reason to kill the blasphemous humans (even if those reasons are outweighed by the moral considerations).

This may be true in many cases. Here (4′) is either true or false descriptively, and it can be reformulated as high risk of being later punished, so that it can be true even if one happens not to be punished. Claim 5′ is again a claim about normativity$_1$ and it shows that law generates several kinds of reasons.

We have seen three ways in which some norm, namely a law, can be normatively significant: I may have a direct reason to do as the law demands (drive on the right), and I may have a moral reason to act in an opposite way to what the law demands (kill people), and I may have prudential or social reasons to avoid breaking the law, as that comes with punishments and labelling.[30]

What, then, explains that one sometimes has such a *direct* reason to obey the law, and sometimes not? Why is it that one has a direct reason to drive on the right, or pay one's taxes, but no reason to engage in the killing required by the unjustified law? This is a contested substantive question, but the basics suffice here.

One central concept is the *authority* of law (Raz 1990). Law differs from other social rules and norms in that it is collectively intended to be binding and reason-giving. The point of making laws is to affect the reasons for action that people have. If the law-maker has authority, it can confer normative force to actions, that one need not have independent reasons to pursue. The authority of law can derive from democracy: democratically legislated laws derive their reason-giving force from being democratically legislated, expressions of collective autonomy (Christiano 2008). Just like exercises of individual autonomy can

30 Can a norm or a law ever be normatively$_1$ insignificant – and give neither reasons for nor against the prescribed activity? Arguably it can. Suppose the law of the country has some remnants from four centuries ago, but these laws are mere dead letters. Or suppose there are some rule-collections, perhaps rules of etiquette, or rules of secret brotherhoods which make no difference to one's life. See Foot (2001), Broome (1999).

generate reasons, exercises of collective autonomy can generate reasons. If I promise you something, I generate a normative reason to act accordingly, and if we collectively decide that some law applies to all of us, we generate a normative reason to act accordingly. That is the basic explanation to how, in a situation where we have no independent reason to prefer driving on the right, we have reason to do so. (See e.g. Raz 1990, Christiano 2008). In majoritarian systems, also the minority who loses the democratic contest is bound by the result. It would be pointless to make laws that only those who voted for the laws, and not others, would be bound by (Christiano 2008).[31] The demands of authority have *content-independent* justification: independently of the content of the democratic decision (or a demand by a superior) there is a reason to act in accordance with it. (Raz 1990). That is, in rough outline, the explanation for the successful cases. The central feature is that the authority has normative *power:* the ability to alter the normative landscape.

But why are not all cases successful? What, then, explains the *limits* of the authority of law (for example in the killing case)? Christiano (2008) cites two considerations: first, the collective decisions must not be too outrageously morally wrong in violation of the rights of individuals, and second, the collective decisions must not be too outrageously against what people have reason to do anyway (that is, not merely moral reasons). The idea is that within these limits, the requirements of the law generate typically normatively$_1$ good reasons.

Reasons and oughts are central to our interest in normativity: what we really want to know is what people ought to do, and have reason to do. And while that is the central interest in the normativity of law, we can ask whether law, and other social and institutional norms, are by definition normative even in the cases when they do not provide good reasons for action.[32]

---

31 Note however that it is not pointless to give the binding form of a law to something that everyone is doing anyway: they can e.g. externalize self-control by making something otherwise independently desirable also legally binding. Thanks to Renne Pesonen for the observation.

32 A related debate concerns morality: do we (always) have reasons to follow moral requirements? (I thank Jaakko Reinikainen for the comment). For example, Scanlon (1998) holds that moral impermissibility is an important and stringent reason against doing something, but like all reasons, can occasionally be outweighed.

4 Normativity$_2$: Norms, Expectations, and Demands

Let us continue the conceptual pursuit. Remember the two examples we used:
- The law demands me to drive on the right
- The law demands me to kill humans if they engage in blasphemous activity

Claims about what the law demands may be *by definition* normative in the sense that we can call normativity$_2$. Independently of normative reasons to act in accordance with the law, statements about what the law *requires*, or *demands*, seem on the face of it normative in some sense. According with norms or rules, that pose requirements or demands, seems normative$_2$ by definition, quite independently of whether one has reason to follow the norms or rules or not, i.e. quite independently of whether the norm is normatively$_1$ significant.

A rival view would have it that normativity$_1$ is all the normativity there is, and the statements are best seen as descriptive on their own. They merely tell what the law is, and what it isn't. But they differ from normal descriptions of the world.

The law is a rule that classifies drivings as those that are "in accordance with the law" (namely those that are drivings on the right) and those that are "in violation of the law" (drivings on the left). If *confers* to them the property of being lawful or unlawful (Ásta 2018). There is a constitutive connection between the law, and the properties of being lawful and unlawful. But further, there is a sense in which the lawful drivings are positively marked as "correct", "appropriate", or corresponding to the law – and *required* by the law. And with the unlawful cases, there is something amiss, some mismatch or failure. The relationship can be called "satisfaction" or "fulfilment" of the requirement.

There seems thus to be an obvious difference between descriptive features of the world ("A drives on the right side") and requirements: the law *requires* one to drive on the right side. The latter are rather *prescriptions* than descriptions, *imperatives* rather than characterizations. They do seem to have a feature of ought, or should, even in the immoral or unjustified cases. So perhaps there is another irreducible dimension of normativity, irreducible to the core normativity of reasons and oughts?

I have not seen these two senses of normativity distinguished in the literature (although e.g. Christine Korsgaard 1996 may have something similar in mind when stating that different theorists have different normative "words" or concepts; but even she thinks that each theorist has one view of normativity).[33] Some think that what the law requires is merely a descriptive fact (Fact 1 in the schema above), and they study whether and how the law manages to give good reasons for agents (see e.g. Raz 1990). By contrast, many think that normativity is a matter of accepted norms or rules, and the requirement to act in accordance to such rules and norms (see e.g. Brandom 1994; Glüer and Wikforss 2018). My suggestion here is that it can be both. In the more important sense of normativity, namely normativity$_1$, norms and expectations are not by definition normative, but they can be by definition normative in some other sense, normativity$_2$.[34] The benefit of this verbal distinction is that it allows us to pay attention to both phenomena, and to make more precise what different views ultimately disagree about.

Whether or not we think that normativity$_2$ is a genuine phenomenon, the question of when norms, expectations and demands create genuine reasons is an important one. Above we already saw that the concept of authority is central for this question. This authority of the other persons or institutions can be stronger or weaker, and so the strength of the generated reason can be stronger or weaker. In addition to authority in a literal sense, there can also be other kinds of standing, based on caring or identifying-with someone, where the source creates wishes or requests. Think of telling someone, that "your wish is my command" – the slogan captures the sense in which positive regard for the other, the special standing of a friend for instance, means that the recipient's positive attitude, or a positive mutual relationship, can strengthen the normative standing of the other's wishes and requests. It seems that different kinds of recognition (respect, love, esteem) go with different kind of standings (whether or not all of them are forms of "authority"). What is common to all these is that they are forms of (content-independent) exercise of *normative powers* by recognized authorities, experts, friends, and fellow humans as co-authors.

All humans are to be respected as what John Rawls (1972) called "sources of valid claims". Some special authorities may generate "exclusionary reasons" (Raz 1990), which exclude other reasons from consideration and take a

---

33 For a discussion of normative concepts, see Eklund (2017).

34 The relation between the expectation, claim or request, and the expected or requested conduct can be called "normative$_2$" – something is by definition normative if it includes a behavioural expectation. When a behavioural expectation can be satisfied by behavior, the expectation is in normative relation to the behavior, it creates a normative$_2$ pressure to conform to the behavior. "Heteronormativity" is a description of such expectations and felt pressure to conform.

monopoly of reasons in the situation, whereas arguably other "sources" (such as friends) generate merely reasons to be weighed together with other considerations (Scanlon 1998).

Normative power (had by an individual or collective) is the power to generate or construct a variety of expectations, claims, requests, by a variety of means, from mere mental states such as desires, or overt speech acts, to collective decision-making procedures such as meetings or votes, and it can be had by a variety of sources from oneself, to any human being, to one's friends, to fellow citizens bound by the same laws, to epistemic experts, and finally to binding authorities, such as one's superiors in a formal organization and recognized law-making authorities.[35]

Interestingly, exercise of normative powers has seemed to some a form of "bootstrapping" (lifting oneself up from one's own bootstraps), others thinking that bootstrapping is obviously bad news (Bratman 1987, Broome 1999), others thinking that on the contrary some kind of bootstrapping is indeed what is at stake, and good news (Brandom 1994, 2000). My suggestion is that both are right about some cases: valid exercises of normative powers (such as the power to make promises that all adults have, or the power to make joint commitments, or a variety of speech acts, or various acts in defined roles) are indeed ways of making genuine normative changes.[36] But there are also invalid attempts, where the normative powers are lacking (say, I am not your superior but try to give commands) or existing normative powers are being used out of bounds.

Normative$_1$ reality has two roots, then: some features of the world generate reasons independently of our activities, or "construction", and these include our actions and interactions as causal or descriptive features of the world (if you hit your head, I have a reason to help; if some convention has created a path in the forest, I have a reason to walk there). But as recognized holders of normative power, we construe an artificial layer of normativity on top of the independent practical reality, or rather, to the midst of the independent practical reality (in usual cases), or in special cases, to replace the independent practical reality (the case of exclusionary reasons).

Its normativity$_1$ – does the agent have good reason to satisfy the expectation – depends on five features: the content (and the independent reasons it

35 Hohfeld (1919) uses "power" for the capacity to alter the rights (claims and privileges) people have; I use "normative power" here more broadly for the capacity to create reasons and oughts, even when they do not result in rights, strictly speaking.
36 For an influential criticism of this kind of normativity, see Turner (2010).

generates); the kind of recognized standing the power-holder has (oneself, friend, binding authority, etc); the kind of request, expectation, requirement or decree in question (varying from optional recommendations which are at the agent's discretion to respond to, to binding commands or requirements) and the way of generating the expectation (from mental states to speech acts to collective expectations and official decisions); and whether or not it is an exclusionary reason, or to be weighed with other reasons (See Table 3).

Table 3: Aspects of exercises of normative power.

Content	Does the agent have independent reasons to pursue this content? Is the content of the relevant kind, given the standing of the power-user?	From independently reasonable valuable, moral pursuits to something that will be pursued only if requested, for the sake of the authority.
Standing of the person	What kind of standing?	From oneself, friends, to binding authority
Recommendation or requirement?	What kind of request, expectation, requirement or decree is in question?	From optional recommendations which are at the agent's discretion to respond to, to binding commands or requirements
Form of Address	By what means or method is the expectation generated?	From mental states to speech acts to collective expectations and official decisions
Exclusionarity?		Yes/no

So, there is great variety from the law requiring everyone to pay their taxes, to one's friend asking one to the movies tonight; from the heteronormative expectations in the locker room to the democratic decision to replace carbon-intensive forms of production by 2035.

The outputs are of two kinds: exclusionary reasons which replace all other reasons one has and pre-empt any need for deliberation, and ordinary reasons of different strengths which enter one's deliberation in a case-by-case basis. In that deliberation all the aspects make a difference (content, standing, requiredness, form of address). A full theory of normativity of law would then deal with these issues.

5 The Other Putative Normativities

For the rest of the paper, the research question is: do the putatively *other* forms of normativity boil down to the first one, or the first two?

As already suggested, the personal and interpersonal cases (cases 7 and 8) can be dealt with using the same normative powers – model as with normativity$_2$. That is, there is a possessor of normative power X, with recognized standing S, addressing in some form of address F (thought or speech or writing), someone (Y), expecting, requesting or demanding Y to do something Phi. In the personal case X and Y are the same person, but there is no doubt that (adult) agents have the normative power to bind themselves in promises and commitments. A full theory of exercises of normative powers would deal with these cases as well. To the extent that Normativity$_6$ is about subjective desires, it can be placed here as well: it is to be dealt with in the same manner as normativity$_2$.

But there's another aspect of the "direction of fit"-idea: independently of whether some desire is an adequate exercise of normative power (and thus leading to reasons), it *is* a desire and as such, poses a demand to the world to correspond to it. A belief poses no such demand, but rather expresses an aim to correspond to the world.[37]

Hegel, for example, anticipates this in writing about desires that there is a double "ought" (Sollen): on the one hand desire poses a demand to the world, a demand on how things ought to be, but on the other hand the desires themselves ought to be reasonable.

Central to the idea of "direction of fit" is the distinction between which ought to change, the mind or the world, in the case of discrepancy. In the case of beliefs, it makes sense to say that the believer, the agent, ought to change the belief (an "ought-to-do"). In the case of desire, the world, what is at stake seems to be that the world ought-to-be such-and-such (in relation to a subjective desire). This is clearly a conferred property, a bit like subjective "yuckiness" of certain foods. The food has the feature only in relation to a subject. Similarly, the world "ought to be" such and such only from the viewpoint of the desire. Whether anything normative follows, in terms of ought-to-do's, the explanation seems to be either the exercise of normative powers – route, or the independent reason-giving content – route. If the agent ought to change the world to fit the desire, it is either because the content is such that it does provide good reasons

37 In the "normativity of meaning"-debate the correctness of language is a thinner idea: it is merely the relationship of correctness (e.g. of a token use and a general rule), without a distinction of two ways to achieve the correspondence (by correcting the token, or by correcting the general rule).

for the desiring agent, or because the desire is recognized, say as expressing one's authentic selfhood, and so is something that one, if one wants to be authentic, should realize. Or perhaps, what follows is only a wide-scope normative requirement of the sort that one should either realize one's intentions and desires or drop them. So I conclude that the cases of normativity 6 included in the debates on direction of fit, is also reducible to the previous versions of normativity, 1–4. There is no separate sense of "normativity$_6$" anymore than separate senses of "normativity$_7$" or "normativity$_8$".

In debates on normativity of meaning it seems that there is no real sense of "normativity" at play. The idea of correctness, the putative normativity$_5$, is not really normative – this seems to be the majority opinion in the debates as well. What seems normative in the "direction of fit"-idea becomes visible in the case of discrepancies: it is either the mind or the world that ought to change, not both. Lack of correspondence is just a descriptive fact, it becomes normative only if one or the other of the relata ought to change, ought to be such, that the correspondence returns. In the case of individual usage of language and the general rules of language it is not clear, whether either the individual ought to change the usage to fit the general rules, or whether the general rules ought to change, to fit the individual usages. To the extent that there is such, it can be captured first on terms of ought-to-be's from which then ought-to-do's (to correct the usages etc.) can be derived. But then it seems that normativity$_5$ is either not normative at all, or if it is, it will be reducible to the other normativities 1–4.

But it is a live option that the four phenomena will remain different: reasons and oughts; exercises of normative powers resulting in norms and expectations; wide-scope normative requirements; and ought-to-be's. We have seen that the ought to be's are irreducible to ought to do's, and remain a distinct conceptual category. Similarly, the wide-scope undetachable oughts seem irreducible, and perhaps even constitutive of the exercises of normative powers. So not even a sophisticated model of exercises of normative powers is likely to catch these two senses of normativity: the model is meant to explicate whether and how normativity$_2$ results in reasons and oughts (normativity$_1$). It need not deny that normativity$_3$ or normativity$_4$ are real possibilities.

Ought-to-be's can concern artefacts which have functions: clocks ought to be such that they show the right time, even though they are not agents with duties. Same concerns robots, cars, computers. Ought-to-be's can also concern organisms: they ought to be healthy, flourish, and self-maintaining. And ought-to-be's can concern institutions: they ought to be just. These judgements are independent from judgements concerning who ought to do what, to see to it that the artefacts function, that the plants or animals flourish, or that the institutions are just. Ought-to-be's seem therefore separate from ought-to-do's (and thus from normativity$_1$).

It also seems that ought-to-be's are irreducible to merely evaluative statements of the form that "it is *good that* institutions are just". Typically, that something is of value is a separate statement from something being a reason (see, however Scanlon's buck-passing account). If so, we can acknowledge that ought-to-be's come with evaluative features (what ought to be is typically good) without reducing one to the other.

Ought-to-be's concern for example virtues: agents ought to be such that they willingly and skillfully do what they ought to do, for the right reasons; i.e. agents ought to be virtuous. They may not have a *duty* to become virtuous, because it may well be they cannot. By contrast, it seems that for each ought-to-do statement, an ought-to-be -statement trivially corresponds, but one must be careful in choosing which statement. From the fact that I ought to eat a cabbage, it follows that I ought to be such that I eat a cabbage, but it does not follow, concerning any particular cabbage, that that cabbage ought to be eaten. So I conclude, that normativity$_4$ seems to be an independent kind of normativity.

Concerning law, we can also see that this kind of normativity applies to legal systems as well: there are many ought-to-be's concerning legal systems: they ought to be just, for example.

What about Broome's "normative requirements" of rationality then? They seem to form a separate normative phenomenon, normativity$_3$. But it does seem that the routes towards detached oughts follow the two routes identified above. They result in detached oughts insofar as the premises are backed by independent reasons, or by valid exercises of normative powers. But on their own, they remain wide-scope considerations.

6 Conclusion

About ought-to-be's this chapter merely defended their irreducibility to ought-to-do's.[38] Legal systems ought to be fair, for example. The central sense of normativity concerns ought-to-do's and reasons. In this paper, that has been called normativity$_1$. Certain things we have independent reasons to do, thanks to the

38 In deontic logic, there has been some debate about the possibility to reduce ought-to-do's to ought-to-be's, the majority view being that it will not work. I thank Aleksi Honkasalo for the comment.

content alone. Certain other things we have reasons to do if valid exercises of normative powers lead to legitimate expectations that we do them. The latter route explains why and when the law, which is by definition normative$_2$, creates normative$_1$ reasons. And not only law, but a dizzying variety of requests and commands from a variety of sources, including oneself (and so the cases discussed as 6 to 8 above). These two routes together explain when and why normative$_3$ requirements result in detached oughts.

References

Anscombe, G. E. M. (1957). *Intention*. Oxford: Basil Blackwell.

Ásta (2018), *Categories We Live By. The Construction of Sex, Gender, Race, and Other Social Categories,* Oxford: Oxford University Press.

Bicchieri, C. (2006). *The Grammar of Society: The Nature and Dynamics of Social Norms*. Cambridge: Cambridge University Press.

Boghossian, P. (2003). "The Normativity of Content". *Philosophical Issues*, 13: 31–45.

Brandom, R. (1994). *Making it Explicit*, Cambridge MA: Harvard University Press.

Brandom, R. (2000). *Articulating Reasons*, Cambridge MA: Harvard University Press.

Bratman, M. (1987). *Intention, Plans, and Practical Reason*. Cambridge, Mass., Harvard University Press.

Brennan, G., Eriksson, L., Goodin, R. E., and Southwood, N. (2013). *Explaining Norms*. Oxford: Oxford University Press.

Broome, J. (1999). "Normative requirements". *Ratio*, 12, pp. 398–419.

Broome, J. (2005). "Does Rationality Give us Reasons?". *Philosophical Issues*, 15, 321–337.

Broome, J. (2007). "Is rationality normative?" *Disputatio*, 23: 161–178.

Broome, J. (2013). *Rationality through Reasoning*. Oxford, Wiley Blackwell.

Chisholm, R. M. (1964). "The Ethics of Requirement". *American Philosophical Quarterly*, 1: 147–153.

Christiano, T. (2008). *The Constitution of Equality: Democratic Authority and Its Limits*. Oxford: Oxford University Press.

Dancy, J. (1993). *Moral Reasons*, Oxford: Blackwell.

Dancy, J. (2000). *Practical Reality*, Oxford: Oxford University Press.

Dancy, J. (2004a). *Ethics Without Principles*, Oxford: Clarendon Press.

Dancy, J, (2004b) "Enticing Reasons," in Wallace, R. J., Pettit, P., Scheffler, S., and Smith, M., eds., *Reason and Value: Themes from the Moral Philosophy of Joseph Raz,* Oxford: Oxford University Press, 91–118.

Eklund, M. (2017). *Choosing Normative Concepts*, Oxford: Oxford University Press.

Fennell, J. (2013). "The Meaning of 'Meaning is Normative'". *Philosophical Investigations*, 36: 56–78.

Foot, P. (2001). *Natural Goodness*. Oxford: Oxford University Press.

Glüer, K., and Wikforss, Å. (2018). "The Normativity of Meaning and Content", *The Stanford Encyclopedia of Philosophy* (Spring 2018 Edition), Edward N. Zalta (ed.), URL = <https://plato.stanford.edu/archives/spr2018/entries/meaning-normativity/>.

Gregory, A. (2012). "Changing direction on direction of fit," *Ethical Theory and Moral Practice*, 15: 603–14.
Hartmann, N. (1925). *Ethik*. Berlin: De Gruyter.
Hattiangadi, A. (2007). *Oughts and Thoughts. Rule-Following and the Normativity of Content*, Oxford: Oxford University Press.
Hohfeld, W. N. (1919). *Fundamental Legal Conceptions*. New Haven: Yale University Press.
Humberstone, I. L. (1992). "Direction of fit". *Mind*, 101, 59–84.
Ikäheimo, H., and Laitinen, A. (2007). "Analyzing Recognition: Identification, Acknowledgement, and Recognitive Attitudes towards Persons", in Bert van den Brink and David Owen (ed.): *Recognition and Power*. Cambridge: Cambridge University Press, 33–56.
Ikäheimo, H. (2011). "Holism and normative essentialism in Hegel's social ontology". in Ikäheimo & Laitinen (eds.) *Recognition and Social Ontology*, Leiden: Brill, 145–209.
Kolodny, N. (2005). "Why be rational?". *Mind*, 114: 509–63.
Korsgaard, C. (1996). *The Sources of Normativity*, Cambridge: Cambridge University Press.
Kripke, S. (1982). *Wittgenstein on Rules and Private Language*, Cambridge MA: Harvard University Press.
Kusch, M. (2006). *A Sceptical Guide to Meaning and Rules. Defending Kripke's Wittgenstein*, Chesham: Acumen.
McNaughton, D., and Rawling, P. (2004). "Duty, Rationality, and Practical Reasons". In A. R. Mele and P. Rawling (eds) *Oxford Handbook of Rationality*. Oxford: Oxford University Press.
Millar, A. (2004) *Understanding People. Normativity and Rationalizing Explanation*, Oxford: Oxford University Press.
Moore, G.E. (1922). "The Nature of Moral Philosophy". in his *Philosophical Studies*.
O'Brien, L. (2019) "The Subjective Authority of Intention". *Philosophical Quarterly*. 69, 275, 354–373.
Parfit, D. (1997). "Reasons and Motivation". *The Aristotelian Soc. Supp*. Vol. 77, 99–130.
Parfit, D. (2001). "Rationality and reasons". in *Exploring Practical Philosophy: From Action to Values*, edited by Dan Egonsson, Jonas Josefsson, Björn Petersson and Toni. Rønnow-Rasmussen, Aldershot: Ashgate, pp. 19–39.
Parfit, D. (2011). *On What Matters*, volumes I and II. Oxford: Oxford University Press.
Peter, F (2019). "Normative Facts and Reasons". Forthcoming in *Proceedings of the Aristotelian Society*.
Platts, M. (1979). *Ways of Meaning*. London: Routledge and Kegan Paul.
Rawls, J. (1972). *A Theory of Justice*. Oxford: Oxford University Press.
Raz, J. (1990). *Practical Reason and Norms*. Oxford: Oxford University Press.
Raz, J. (1999). *Engaging Reason*. Oxford: Oxford University Press.
Raz, J. (2000). 'The Truth in Particularism'. in Hooker & Little.
Raz, J. (2010). "Reason, Reasons, and Normativity". In Russ Shafer-Landau (ed.) *Oxford Studies in Metaethics*, Volume 5. New York: Oxford University Press, pp. 5–24.
Robertson, S. (2012). "Introduction: Normativity, Reasons, Rationality". in his (ed.) *Spheres of Reason: New Essays in the Philosophy of Normativity*, Oxford: Oxford University Press, 1–28.

Searle, J. (1995). *The Construction of Social Reality*, London: Allen Lane.
Sellars, W. (1968). "Language as Thought and Language as Communication". *Philosophy and Phenomenological Research*, 29, 506–527.
Sellars, W (1991). *Science, Perception and Reality*. Atascadero: Ridgeview.
Scanlon, T. (1998). *What We Owe To Each Other*. Cambridge, MA: Belknap Press.
Scanlon, Thomas M. (2014). *Being Realistic about Reasons*. New York: Oxford University Press.
Schnädelbach, H. (1990). "Rationalität und Normativität". reprinted in *Zur Rehabilitierung des animal rationale*, Frankfurt a. M.: Suhrkamp, 1992, 79–103.
Shafer-Landau, R. (2003). *Moral Realism: A Defence*, Oxford: Oxford University Press.
Star, D, ed. (2018). *The Oxford Handbook on Reasons and Normativity*. Oxford: Oxford University Press.
Thomson, J. J. (2007). *Normativity*. Chicago: Open Court.
Tuomela, R. (2007). *Philosophy of Sociality*. Oxford: Oxford University Press.
Turner, Stephen P. (2010). *Explaining the Normative*. Cambridge, Polity Press.
deVries, Willem, "Wilfrid Sellars", *The Stanford Encyclopedia of Philosophy* (Winter 2016 Edition), Edward N. Zalta (ed.), URL = <https://plato.stanford.edu/archives/win2016/entries/sellars/>.
von Wright, G. H. (1963). *Norm and Action*, Routledge and Kegan Paul, London.
Wedgwood, R. (2007). *The Nature of Normativity*. Oxford: Clarendon Press.
Wedgwood, R. (2009). "The Normativity of the Intentional". *The Oxford Handbook of the Philosophy of Mind*, ed. Brian P. McLaughlin and A. Beckermann, Oxford: Clarendon Press, 421–36.
Whiting, D. (2013). "What is the normativity of Meaning?". *Inquiry*, doi: 10.1080/0020174X.2013.852132.
Zangwill, N. (1998). "Direction of fit and normative functionalism". *Philosophical Studies*, 91(2),173–203.

Rachael Mellin

The Metaphysics of Legal Organisations

1 Introduction

Legal organisations are a crucial element in Scott Shapiro's Planning Theory of Law. In order to see this and appreciate the relevance of the problems that will be developed throughout this paper, it will be instructive to look first at Shapiro's larger project (as set out in his 2011).

Working in the field of analytic jurisprudence, Shapiro is interested in the metaphysical foundations of law. He identifies the principal question of this field as the broad and ambiguous: *What is Law?* He suggests that there have been two main ways that people have tried to answer this question, depending on their understanding of the term 'Law'. The first approach that one might take is to inquire into the content of law, so that asking about the nature of law is to ask about e.g., the nature of legal norms. Alternatively, one might approach this question by examining the nature of legal systems since they are generally taken as instantiating law. Shapiro is of the view that an answer to the question *What is Law?* involves inquiring into the nature of both legal norms and legal systems. In fact, he thinks that in order to understand what laws are, we need an account of how and why legal systems produce them in the first place. But, he notes, the question *What are legal systems?* is also ambiguous because 'legal system' could refer to either a particular system of rules (e.g., the US Constitution), or it could refer to a particular organisation (e.g., the US Supreme Court). The distinction amounts to a difference in constitution of legal systems – either by *norms* in the case of the former, or *people* in the case of the latter.

Shapiro notes that historically analytic jurisprudence has examined legal phenomena in terms of the legal norms produced by legal systems and has focused on legal systems as particular systems of rules. Shapiro thinks that in order to understand particular systems of rules, we should first turn to the organisations that produce them. Once we know more about legal systems as particular organisations, we will be able to answer *how* and *why* they establish the systems of rules they do. We need this to give a full account of the nature of legal systems as systems of rules. Once we have such an account, we will have an answer to the question *What are legal systems?* and are in a position to then try to answer *What are legal norms?* If we can also answer this question, then we will have succeeded in answering the main question: *What is Law?*

https://doi.org/10.1515/9783110663617-010

Shapiro clarifies what he understands as inquiring into the *nature* of something by, again, distinguishing two questions that one may be asking. I think his formulation of these questions is very unclear and problematic, an issue that I will return to in **§4**. For now, I will present them as I understand them. Firstly, one may be asking about the *identity* of something, or *what is it to be that thing?* He calls this the 'Identity Question' and suggests that a correct answer to it for some object, *X*, will list the set of properties that makes *X* what it is. Alternatively, when inquiring into the nature of something, we may be asking *what necessarily follows from the fact that an object is what it is and not something else?* That is, we may be interested in determining which of the properties we identify *X* as possessing are necessary and which are not. Shapiro calls this the 'Implication Question'. As far as he is concerned, to give a full account of the nature of something, we need to answer both questions.

Based on Shapiro's clarification of the various questions motivating his project, as well as his distinctive approach to these, we can draw the following expectation. Answering the principle question of analytic jurisprudence – *What is Law?* – requires answers to both the Identity and Implication questions for law. This involves inquiring firstly into the nature of legal organisations in order to analyse the nature of the system of rules they create. The first step for Shapiro, then, should be to answer both the Identity and Implication questions for legal organisations. That is, to ask:

> **Identity Question for legal organisations:** What are the properties that distinguish legal organisations from other kinds of groups?
>
> **Implication Question for legal organisations:** Which of these properties are (not) necessary properties of legal organisations?

Throughout this paper, I will primarily be concerned with Shapiro's answer to the former question which, for simplicity, I will refer to as 'Identity Question'. I agree that answering this is crucial for giving an account of the nature of legal organisations. Yet, I contend that Shapiro does not do so since his conception of *identity* is limited partly because his notion of *nature* is inaccurate. To put it plainly, Shapiro does not give an account of the nature of legal organisations, nor does he fully answer the Identity Question for them. As a result, he cannot distinguish legal organisations from other, similar kinds of groups. This leads to several problems for his account. Most notably, it casts doubt on his methodological approach which claims that the nature of law can be analysed in terms of legal organisations. The purpose of this paper is to elucidate the identity problem in particular and suggest an answer to it by presenting a closely related objection advanced by Kenneth Ehrenberg (2016). Roughly, the objection is that Shapiro's characterisation of the nature of legal organisations (regarding their identity) is incorrect, and so fails to distinguish them from other similar kinds of groups. While I agree that this presents a challenge to Shapiro's thesis, I disagree with Ehrenberg's proposed solution that we see law as an abstract institutional artifact. In fact, I will argue that Ehrenberg does not provide a solution at all, rather, that he tries to avoid the problem by changing the focus from the nature of legal organisations to the nature of law. Moreover, I will argue that this attempt is unsuccessful as he still needs to give an account of the nature of legal organisations to answer some questions that arise from his own view. Finally, I will return to the original challenge and claim that Shapiro can answer this, as well as some other issues, firstly by revising his conceptions of *nature* and *identity*. I will suggest, secondly, that with a broader understanding of the latter, he can give a more promising account of legal organisations by using Brian Epstein's metaphysical framework for understanding the nature of groups (as developed in his 2015; 2017).

I proceed as follows: In **§2**, I will briefly outline Shapiro's Planning Theory of Law before focusing in some detail on his account of the identity of legal organisations as self-certifying, compulsory, social planning organisations with a moral aim. In **§3**, I will consider the objection advanced by Kenneth Ehrenberg that focuses on the property of self-certification before arguing that his proposed solution only adds complexity, and though it may seem that Ehrenberg can avoid giving an account of the nature of legal organisations, in order to answer questions which arise from the added complexity of his view, he cannot. In **§4**, I will return to Shapiro's legal organisations and present my diagnosis of the problem – that the issue is due to an incomplete account of their identity (partly owing to Shapiro's inaccurate conception of *nature*). Thus, I will argue that further analysis of this kind of group is required in order to overcome this problem. More specifically, I will introduce Brian Epstein's metaphysical framework for understanding the nature of groups in **§5**, and briefly suggest a modification of it which I take to illuminate the notion of *identity*. In **§6**, I refer to this framework to show just how incomplete Shapiro's account of the identity of legal organisations currently is and suggest that, by using it, Shapiro can give a complete account of the nature of legal organisations in a way that is in line with his project. **§7** concludes.

2 Shapiro's Planning Theory of Law

The main tenet of Shapiro's Planning Theory of Law is:

> **The Planning Thesis:** Legal activity is an activity of social planning. (Shapiro 2017, 2)

Simply put, the idea is that legal activity (the exercise of legal authority) is carried out by legal organisations (groups of officials) and the product of this activity are legal rules. Since, by the planning thesis legal activity is social planning activity, legal organisations are social planning organisations and legal rules are (social) plans.

Shapiro's argument for this thesis is extensive and I will not be able to present a full reconstruction of it here. Fortunately, the focus of this paper solely concerns his characterisation of legal organisations. Thus, for our purposes, we need only unpack his answer to the Identity Question for legal organisations.

From the above, we can see that part of Shapiro's answer is that legal organisations are social planning organisations. Let us begin by unpacking this, before considering the extra properties he takes legal organisations to possess.

For Shapiro, an organisation is any group that has the following three features:

(i) *The group must perform a shared activity.*
(ii) *The group must be official* – individuals acquire power, rights, etc. because of the role (the office) they occupy.
(iii) *The group must be institutional* – officials act by following formal procedures.

From this, and the Planning Thesis, legal organisations are social planning organisations since they are official and institutional groups which perform the shared activity of social planning.

But legal organisations have further properties. Shapiro identifies another three by comparing them with other similar kinds of groups. Firstly, he points out the compulsory nature of the law by comparing legal organisations with parents. Though parents cannot be said to be official or institutional groups, they do perform a shared activity, the results of which Shapiro thinks we can learn something from. He notices a similarity between parental authority and legal authority. The validity of each type of authority does not require consent from its subjects. That is, just like children are subjected to the rules of their parents regardless of whether or not they accept them, the subjects of legal authority are subjected to legal rules regardless of acceptance. As Shapiro (ibid., 17) puts it, "children cannot "quit" their parents" and the subjects of legal authority cannot quit the law. People may refuse to follow it, but they cannot quit it as the consequences of refusing to follow the law often show.

That legal organisations are compulsory social planning organisations is still not enough to distinguish them from other similar non-legal kinds of groups. To paraphrase Shapiro (ibid., 20), all legal organisations are compulsory social planning organisations, but not all of the latter are instances of the former. Shapiro considers the Mafia to demonstrate this point. The Mafia seems a good example of a compulsory social planning organisation, but we certainly do not want an account of legal organisations that includes the Mafia or to mistake their rules as laws! The difference between these two kinds of groups, according to Shapiro, is one of aim. Legal organisations necessarily have a moral aim while criminal organisations do not. Of course, a legal organisation can fail to achieve this aim, but it cannot fail to have it, or else it is not a legal organisation. There is no similar requirement that a criminal organisation have a moral aim.

Yet, Shapiro identifies another kind of group which qualifies as a compulsory social planning organisation with a moral aim but is still not a legal organisation. He considers a retirement community in Florida which establishes an official 'Condo Board' charged with the task of regulating the behaviour of its residents through creating rules and applying them in order to solve any moral issues that might arise. By comparing the legal system of Florida with the Condo Board, he determines that the third and final distinguishing property of legal organisations concerns their general presumption of validity by superior planning organisations. In this case, the US Federal legal system is superior to Florida State legal system, which is superior to the Floridian Retirement Community Condo Board: "US law pre-empts state law just as the state law pre-empts the rules of the Condo Board" (ibid., 24). Although state law is subordinate to federal law, "federal law automatically presumes that state law complies with federal law" (ibid.). The upshot of this being that Florida need not demonstrate the validity of its rules before enforcing them. However, the same cannot be said of the Condo Board. The Condo Board must seek approval from Florida before enforcing its rules because it does not enjoy the same presumption of validity:

> Even though both the Condo Board and Florida are required to comply with the rules of superior planning institutions, only Florida is presumed to be in compliance with those rules and, hence, only it is allowed to enforce its own rules without federal permission. (ibid., 25)

Shapiro calls this general presumption of validity the property of *self-certification*. For him, legal organisations are necessarily self-certifying. Since the Condo Board does not possess this property, it does not qualify as a legal organisation.

Though one may challenge any of the properties that Shapiro identifies as properties of legal organisations, this property of self-certification seems to be the most salient as well as the most contentious. I will presently consider Ehrenberg's challenge that this property is not exclusive to legal organisations.

3 Ehrenberg's Challenge

Ehrenberg (2016) argues not only that self-certification is an arbitrary feature of legal organisations that other non-legal groups may possess, but also that legal organisations do not seem to be fully self-certifying. I will briefly consider each of these points.

Firstly, while Ehrenberg does not provide an argument for the claim that self-certification is an arbitrary property of legal organisations, he uses Shapiro's analysis of his own example to argue that other, non-legal groups may possess it. Shapiro considers why, if Florida enacts a law forbidding skinny dipping from all pools, public and private, the Floridian Retirement Community Condo Board cannot remove skinny-dippers from their pool, but must contact the police who can do so without seeking further permission. As Shapiro (2017, 25) admits, this is because Florida law "does not permit owners to enforce their property rights through this form of self-help". Ehrenberg correctly identifies this as the crux of the issue and notes that this could have been different, and is different in other legal systems, and so self-certification does not seem to be a feature unique to legal organisations.

He reinforces this point by noting that, though it is true in the example above that Florida can be said to be self-certifying and the Condo Board cannot, this does not mean that in other instances the Condo Board is not self-certifying. Ehrenberg points out that many of the actions of the Condo Board do enjoy presumptions of validity (e.g., when to switch the TV off, or when to clean the communal areas, etc.) and so it is unclear that self-certification is a property that is exclusive to legal organisations. This problem arises, he thinks, because Shapiro has in mind too narrow a conception of the actions which may or may not be presumed valid. That is, Shapiro restricts his understanding of 'enforcement' to something more physical. In the case of the skinny-dipper, enforcing the rules against them, physical force in 'yanking' the skinny-dipper out of the pool is required. As Ehrenberg mentions, this can infringe on a right the individual has to bodily integrity. He argues (2016, 336) that other kinds of actions that do not threaten to interfere with such closely guarded rights are less likely to require prior authorisation.

Consequently, by broadening our view of what counts as enforcing rules and realising that many actions do not require prior authorisation, Ehrenberg concludes that self-certification is not unique to legal organisations. Furthermore, he uses some examples to argue that legal organisations do not always enjoy a presumption of validity and quickly dismisses two responses given by Shapiro. Let us briefly consider these in light of one of Ehrenberg's examples (ibid., 337). The system of government in some Commonwealth countries requires that the Governor

General (representative of the Crown) approves all acts of Parliament before they become law. Ehrenberg claims that this undermines self-certification. Shapiro offers two responses. The first suggests that in cases such as this, where a legal organisation is not presumed valid by a superior group, the former is a subsidiary of the latter – i.e., it is part of the same legal system. In the case of the Commonwealth country, "where the Governor General exercises real authority to withhold Crown approval, the system is simply a sub-part of the British legal system" (ibid., 337). Yet, as Ehrenberg points out, Shapiro takes State law as a distinct system, afforded the presumption of validity by Federal law, and so it is difficult to see where Shapiro draws the line between subsidiaries and distinct legal systems. Ehrenberg argues that Shapiro's only way to do this seems to be by using self-certification. But this is circular: Shapiro is trying to argue that what appears to be a non-self-certifying legal organisation is not a counterexample to the self-certification of legal organisations because the former is in fact a subsidiary of a superior, self-certifying legal system. Yet, that subsidiaries are not self-certifying is the only way we can identify them from legal systems. In other words, in order to argue for this property, we have to use it.

The second response given by Shapiro concedes that self-certification, as well as the other properties that constitute legality come in degrees. Consider, for example, the compulsory property of legal organisations. He qualifies a variation in strength by noting that certain groups are given the right to refuse to follow certain laws, e.g., conscientious objectors. Although imprisoned as a consequence of their refusal to take up arms, they are not forced to fight. They have the right to refuse to do so. As Shapiro puts it, they cannot quit the law entirely, but they can quit some part of it under certain circumstances. Just as this property comes in degrees, so does self-certification: some groups can be more or less self-certifying than others if more or less of their actions are presumed valid by a superior. We should expect that legal organisations are almost always self-certifying. From this, Shapiro suggests that legality itself also comes in degrees: "the more self-certifying or compulsory an organisation is, the more legal it should be considered" (Shapiro 2017, 27). However, the problem remains – this property does not draw a clear line between legal organisations and other similar, but non-legal groups since, as we have seen, some of the latter seem to possess a fair degree of self-certification. Appealing to the degree of this or any other property of a group is too vague since it is possible to have groups with a high degree of each property that still do not qualify as legal, and others with a lower degree which should. Short of fixing some ad-hoc threshold, Shapiro fails to give the clear-cut distinction he needs to separate legal organisations from other similar kinds of groups and Ehrenberg is correct to reject this as a satisfactory response.

So how can Shapiro respond to these objections? Can he revise his answer to the Identity Question and offer an alternative way of making the distinction he needs to for his project? I think he can, and I will gesture towards this in **§5**. But first, I will consider Ehrenberg's alternative.

Ehrenberg's suggestion is to abandon the focus on self-certification as it "is not what makes [legality] special" (Ehrenberg 2016, 340). Moreover, he claims that we no longer need worry about the Identity Question once we see that "the particular kind of plan that law represents is an institutionalised abstract artefact" (ibid., 338) and that "law is an expressly designed social institution for solving [. . .] social problems" (ibid., 340). What makes law special, argues Ehrenberg, is that "we make it special when we make it" (ibid.). That is, "we make it special by making it an institution with a special status, conferred when appropriately sourced norms are used to solve for the conditions of legality" (ibid.). Briefly, the idea is that artifacts are designed to perform a certain function and it is this function that gives a certain artifact its identity. So if we take law as being designed to perform a certain function, then the Identity Question answers itself: law is whatever performs this function.

I think there are several issues with Ehrenberg's approach here. Most notably, it is unclear what he means by 'law'. He uses it to make at least two different claims: he says that law is an abstract institutional artifact before drawing on Searle to say that "law is a specifically created status that provides for the institutional creation and assignment of other statuses" (ibid., 339). I think in this latter case, he means to speak of legality rather than law. Still, I do not understand what he means by 'law' when he claims that it is an abstract institutional artifact. It seems more likely that he is referring to law as legal system (e.g., as constituted by norms), but given what he says elsewhere about law as "an expressly designed social institution" (ibid., 340), he could mean that law as an institution is an abstract institutional artifact. This second notion does not make sense to me as I take institutions to be constituted by more than just rules and roles, but of people and objects as well, so that an institution cannot be an abstract artifact. Let us assume, then, that when Ehrenberg claims that law is an abstract institutional artifact, by 'law' he means system of legal rules.

Recall that Ehrenberg presents his view as an alternative way of answering Shapiro's Identity Question given the challenges he raises against Shapiro's own answer. He also intends for his solution to be compatible with Shapiro's Planning Theory of Law. However, this is not so much a solution to Shapiro's problem as it is an entirely different approach to the question about the nature of law. By suggesting that we instead see law as an abstract institutional artifact, Ehrenberg is shifting focus from (concrete) legal organisations to the (abstract) systems of rules they create. This will not give us an answer to Shapiro's Identity Question for legal organisations. Although Ehrenberg intends for his solution to be compatible with Shapiro's theory, for this reason, it is not. As we have already seen in **§1**, for Shapiro, legal organisations play a central role. He thinks that not enough attention has been given to them, with the majority of analytic jurisprudence focusing instead on legal norms to explain legal phenomena. Shapiro's approach is distinctive because his project changes this historical focus from legal norms to legal organisations: to give an account of the nature of law begins by analysing the nature of legal organisations. Thus, it is paramount for Shapiro to distinguish legal organisations from other similar kinds of groups because his account of law depends on whatever is his account of them. To abandon this in favour of an analysis of legal norms as Ehrenberg suggests is to undermine the priority Shapiro gives to legal organisations, which is to stray too far from the focus of his project.

Even if we gloss over this tangent, Ehrenberg's alternative raises more problems than it solves. The most immediate questions we might ask are as follows. What is an institution with a special status? How is it made? What is this special status that the institution possesses? And how does it come to possess it? What are appropriately sourced norms? How are they created? It seems to me that in order to answer all of these questions, we need an account of the nature of legal organisations. If this is the case, then Ehrenberg does not avoid the problem faced by Shapiro in trying to give such an account. He too faces the same challenge and we are back to square one. I will presently consider each of the above questions and show how I think legal organisations are, at least in part, involved in answering each one.

Firstly, *What is an institution with a special status?* Given that Ehrenberg takes 'law' (or, as I suggested, 'legality') as a status, it seems that another way to put this question is: *What is a legal institution?* While Ehrenberg does not give us any such account here, it seems that whatever he takes legal institutions to be, they partly involve Shapiro's legal organisations as we can see from his other description of law as "an expressly designed social institution for solving social problems" (ibid.). Social institutions created to solve social problems sounds familiar: for Shapiro, legal organisations are an expressly designed kind of social institution that solve social problems through social planning. If we want to know what legal institutions are, then we also need an account of legal organisations since they partly constitute them. We also need to say more about this special status.

Secondly, *What is this special status possessed by the institution?* This question asks what the 'legal' status amounts to when assigned to entities. Where an answer seems to involve certain properties such as powers and responsibilities that are held by the institution, individuals or objects within it. This also raises more questions, amongst them: *How* does an institution hold this status?

What exactly holds it? To answer these questions involves inquiring into the individual(s) who assign the institution this status, and an account of the powers and responsibilities enjoyed by the institution, its members, and objects within it. Given that legal institutions are partly constituted by legal organisations, we need an account of the latter's properties.

How do we make an institution with a special status, e.g., a legal institution? Again, this is a question that Ehrenberg does not answer. However, since legal organisations are part of a legal institution, to create the latter, we must know about the properties of the former and Ehrenberg cannot avoid giving such an account.

What are appropriately sourced norms? And how are they created? These two questions are closely related. The appropriate source of appropriately sourced norms seems to be tied to their creation. So what about the second question? According to Ehrenberg, such norms are abstract institutional artifacts, which means that they are collectively intentionally created. Therefore, to answer both questions, we need to know more about the group which creates them. We need to know about its existence, persistence, identity, and constitution conditions, powers and responsibilities, etc. Given the role of the source here in identifying certain norms, it is crucial that we can distinguish this source (i.e., a certain kind of group) from other similar sources (i.e., other kinds of groups). As for the second question, we need an account of the collective intentionality involved in creating these norms. I think that such an account will depend on the kind of group we are talking about, and so in both cases we need first a metaphysical analysis of the nature of this group.

Moreover, as he mentions, "there is some limitation on what kinds of social plans are candidates for legal plans, set both by *the methods by which they are created and adopted* and the purposes to which they are put" (ibid., 339, my emphasis). Clearly, we need to analyse the method by which they are created and adopted, which will partly involve an account of the group which creates and adopts them. Therefore, even with his alternative, by his own lights Ehrenberg cannot escape the need for an account of legal organisations. It seems, then, that we are back to Shapiro's project.

For all of these reasons, I wish to briefly present an alternative which can answer all of the above problems faced by Shapiro as well as those that I have directed at Ehrenberg. This approach is for those who wish to follow Shapiro in finding the distinction between legal organisations and other kinds of social planning organisations (e.g., similar, non-legal groups). It will also shed light on questions about group agency, which will help us say something more about the method by which legal plans are created and adopted. Most importantly, we will have a full account of the nature of legal organisations, leaving us with no doubt about which properties are most salient, which come in degrees, and which are simply shared by other similar kinds of groups.

4 *Nature* and *Identity*

Before offering this alternative solution to Shapiro's problem, it will help to clarify exactly what I take the problem and the root of it to be.

If I am correct, it seems that Ehrenberg's main objection against Shapiro concerns his answer to the Identity Question. In particular, Ehrenberg rejects self-certification as a defining property of legal organisations. He takes himself to have shown both that not all legal organisations possess this property and that some other non-legal kinds of groups do.

Even if Ehrenberg is correct that Shapiro's answer to the Identity Question is inadequate and that self-certification is not the correct property to focus on for making the distinction Shapiro wishes to, the next natural move is not just to deny Shapiro's whole project. Rather, it should be to try to offer a better account of the identity of legal organisations and see if some other property or properties can distinguish between different kinds of similar groups. The focus should remain on legal organisations – not to give up entirely on providing an account of their nature, which is consequently, to abandon Shapiro's project. It is not such a simple re-focusing of what makes legality special as Ehrenberg makes it out to be: we lose something important by re-focusing the project in this way.

I agree that Shapiro's answer to his Identity Question is inadequate. However, I think the main problem is that his conception of *identity* is incomplete which is partly due to an inaccurate notion of *nature*. Given this incomplete conception, we can hardly expect that his answer is enough to distinguish legal organisations from other, similar kinds of groups. Yet, I think such a project is possible once these notions are clarified. The purpose of the present section is to do exactly that, by elaborating on what I take to be the issues with Shapiro's conceptions of both *identity* and *nature*.

Let's consider, firstly, what Shapiro understands by *nature*. According to Shapiro, to give an account of the nature of something, we must inquire into both its identity and what necessarily follows from this. In other words, we need to determine its properties, paying close attention to those which are necessary (and those which are not). This idea is formulated into his Identity and Implication questions. I said in **§1** that I find his formulation of these questions unclear and problematic which I think is due to his incomplete and inaccurate conceptions of both *identity* and *nature*. His conception of *nature* is inaccurate because he separates out the necessary properties of an object from its identity, and phrases this as a separate question. But it is not a separate question: necessary (and contingent) properties are part of the identity of an object, so an answer to the Identity Question will also include a list of the object's necessary properties. This, then, is not a separate question with a separate answer; it is already answered by giving an account of identity. Of course, we may want to focus on an object's necessary properties – it is not problematic to highlight this as an important question. What is problematic, however, is to split the notion of *nature* in this way.

This is partly why I take Shapiro's conception of *identity* as incomplete. It is also unclear, though, I think this is a general issue when people mention *identity*. It seems that there are at least three different discussions which are often conflated. I think it is worth taking a brief clarificatory detour to consider these so that we can be clear with regards which of these discussions Shapiro engages.

Consider some object, let us call it *X*. When we ask *What is the identity of X?* we could be asking, (1) about the *properties* that constitute it, so that our question is something like 'What makes *X* the thing that it is?'. Alternatively, we might be asking (2) 'What kind of thing is *X*?'. An answer to this will involve using the properties noted in the first question to determine what *kind* of object *X* is. Or, (3) we may be looking for conditions to *individuate X* from other instances of the same kind, or to track *X* through time and possibilities. In this case, we are looking for a Criterion of Identity (a formula which logically expresses an identity relation). This provides extra conditions that *X* must satisfy in order to guarantee that *X* is one and the same object. Since we are trying to individuate *X* from other instances of the same kind, we must already have determined this kind. Thus, we will first need an answer to (1) and (2).

From this, it seems that Shapiro's project is something along the lines of (2). His thesis is that legal organisations are self-certifying, compulsory, social planning organisations with a moral aim. He considers himself to have shown this by presenting some properties that he takes legal organisations to possess. So by his Identity Question, it seems that he is trying to answer (1) for legal organisations in order to show that they are groups of a particular kind – self-certifying, compulsory, social planning organisations with a moral aim, which is to answer (2).

I agree with Ehrenberg that he does not achieve this goal. However, I do not think we can expect him to. As noted, Shapiro's conception of *nature* is problematic in a way that renders his notion of *identity* incomplete, and not just because an object's necessary and contingent properties are considered separately. It seems that it is also minus some other important properties that we can categorise in certain ways. Categorising properties in ways other than by modal characterisation is an interesting exercise, but seems particularly pertinent given Shapiro's project to show that legal organisations are a certain kind of group, distinct from other similar kinds. For example, the constitution, existence, and persistence properties of an object seems crucial to its identity. In the case of legal organisations, properties concerning norms, powers, responsibilities, etc. seem especially important to consider. Elaborating on this is the purpose of the next section. What is important here is to see that Shapiro's notion of *identity* is incomplete, partly due to a problematic conception of *nature*. Given that Shapiro's project is to identify the properties possessed by legal organisations in order to show that they are groups of a certain kind, it is no wonder that his answer is unsuccessful – it, too, is incomplete. It is to the task of suggesting how to provide a complete answer that I will now turn.

5 Epstein's Metaphysical Framework

In this section, I will present an alternative way for Shapiro to provide an account of the nature of legal organisations and I will use it also to demonstrate the incompleteness of his notion of *identity*.

Brian Epstein has recently developed a metaphysical framework for understanding the nature of groups. He promises that it will "help classify and categorise groups, and shed light on group agency" (Epstein 2017, 1) by considering the metaphysical features of specific kinds of groups as arranged into four complementary 'profiles'. These profiles are: *Construction profile*, *Extra-Essentials profile*, *Anchor profile*, and *Accident profile*.

Epstein considers four different kinds of groups in order to show how they can be characterised in terms of these profiles. Due to a lack of space, I will not go through his examples here. Nor will I be able to fully fill out these profiles for legal organisations, or any other kind of group. However, I think it will be enough to explain what is contained in each of these profiles in some detail, as well as to slot in the properties that Shapiro identifies legal organisations as possessing. By doing this, I hope to show just how much more is left to be said about the identity of this kind of group. I take it that such a demonstration will highlight the incompleteness of Shapiro's notion of *identity* and thus, his answer to the Identity Question for legal organisations. And so, the result, that he is unable to distinguish them from other similar kinds of groups, is unsurprising. Equally clear, I hope, will be my contention that filling in the rest of the profiles for legal organisations will result in a complete account of their identity, and so will allow Shapiro to also distinguish them from other similar kinds of groups. To see this, let us begin by looking more closely at each of the profiles.

For Epstein, the first task for understanding the nature of groups is to analyse how they come to exist (existence conditions), how they persist over time (persistence conditions), how they can be individuated or identified across time and possibilities (criterion of identity), and how they are built out of their members (constitution conditions). Together, these are characterised in the *Construction Profile*. Epstein develops formulae for each of these to be filled in for whichever kind of group is of interest. I will not present the formulae here, but I will briefly explain each of these components. Existence conditions concern how kinds of groups come to exist. Some come to exist when a particular activity is performed, while others require that individuals realise certain roles. Persistence conditions characterise what is required for kinds of groups to continue to exist. Some cease to exist when a certain activity is no longer performed, others can persist through breaks, and others must be officially disbanded. There are also some kinds of groups that can survive changes to members and others that can even exist for some time without any members at all. This feature is captured by constitution conditions, which also concern whether or not a kind a group requires its members to have collective intentions or to play certain functional roles. Finally, the last part of the construction profile is the Criterion of Identity which I already introduced in the previous section. For Epstein, the Criterion of Identity gives the minimal relation which must hold between two groups of a kind (or two stages of the same kind of group) in order to guarantee that they are the same group (or stages of the same group). Depending on the kind of group, the criteria may concern properties found in different profiles, e.g., constitution properties found in the *Construction Profile*. For two groups of a kind, e.g., g_1 and g_2, the Criterion of Identity to guarantee that $g_1=g_2$ may be that g_1 and g_2 have the same members across time and worlds. I will return to the Criterion of Identity shortly in order to suggest a minor modification to Epstein's framework. For now, I will continue outlining the rest of it.

Though we can find essential (or necessary) properties of kinds of groups in the construction profile, Epstein does not take this as an exhaustive account. He presents the *Extra-Essentials Profile* as including these additional essential properties that kinds of groups (and, in some cases, their individual members) possess, such as abilities, powers, rights, responsibilities, norms, as well as the limitations of these. Exactly how groups are designed (or set-up) is depicted in another profile (the *Anchor Profile*), soon to be discussed. The task of this profile is to characterise, for a certain kind of group, these various essential properties that apply to the group, as well as those that apply to the individual members. Epstein mentions that they can be deontic but are not always – groups may have abilities or powers without any obligations to use them. Moreover, some individual members may have powers or limitations that others do not – this accounts for groups with asymmetric structures, or hierarchies.

Another interesting question about the nature of groups concerns the source or metaphysical basis for them to have the properties they do. To provide an account of this is the job of the *Anchor Profile*. Let us consider Epstein's example of the kind of information we can expect from this profile. Take the conditions for membership (constitution) of a certain kind of group. We capture these conditions in the construction profile. But, we may ask, why are these the conditions for membership? And what makes them the conditions? To answer the first question, we need a causal explanation of the membership conditions– i.e., a history or genealogy for why the membership conditions were set up the way they were. For the second question, we need a constitutive explanation of what makes these conditions the membership conditions – i.e., certain intentions and actions. An answer to the former question will involve a causal story about the membership conditions, whereas with the latter will be the metaphysical reason that explains what makes these conditions the membership conditions.

As Epstein (ibid., 37) puts it, "[t]he anchor profile of a kind of group is a list of facts that metaphysically put in place various properties of that group. Even for a given kind of group, some properties may be anchored in one way, while others are anchored in a different way" (i.e., some properties may be anchored by causal explanation and some others by constitutive explanation). So we can ask what sets up each of the conditions of the previous profiles where our answers (those facts that set the conditions up as they are) are the anchors. That is, we can ask what anchors the existence, persistence, and constitution conditions, the criterion of identity, and the powers and restrictions of specific kinds of groups.

As both Shapiro and Epstein note, when we inquire into an object's (or in Epstein's case, a certain kind of group's) nature, we are not only interested in their necessary (or essential) properties: we are also interested in their contingent (or accidental properties). Epstein suggests that these properties, depicted in the *Accident Profile*, "can be equally or more important to understanding what groups are, and to classifying them or developing typologies" (ibid., 39). This profile gathers the accidental properties possessed by a group of a given kind, as well as those of its members. More specifically:

> Profiling the accidental properties of a kind of group might include anything at all. They can include properties that groups of the kind actually have in all or most cases, properties that members have, historical properties, size, location, and so on. Among the accidental properties are also various causal properties: the causes by which they came to exist, the causes for them to have the actual memberships they do, the causes for exercising various powers. There are also the causes for the anchors to be in place. (ibid., 40)

Now that each of the profiles have been presented, I wish to suggest a modification to Epstein's framework. I mentioned in the previous section that I take there to be three main discussions concerning *identity*. In Epstein's *Construction Profile*, he is clear which of these is involved: Criterion of Identity. While this is still an important part of a metaphysical framework, I think it is better left out of the profiles. The reason for this is that I think the discussions we are interested in when we look to the profiles concern a certain kind of group and its properties (e.g., (2) and (1)). That is our purpose for filling out the profiles. Moreover, we can only utilise the formula for the Criterion of Identity when we have such an answer (to (1) and (2)) since we need to have already determined the kind in question. It seems to me that, minus the Criterion of Identity, the rest of Epstein's framework (his profiles) gives us an account of the identity of kinds of groups in the sense of (1) – i.e., we have a complete list of a certain kind of group's properties. Perhaps we need this set of properties before confirming that the group is of this particular kind, or maybe we already know the kind and want a full account of its properties. Regardless, what we do not need for either task is the Criterion of Identity. Rather, the Criterion of Identity is only useful to individuate groups of a certain kind, or to track a particular group through time and possibilities. It does not contribute anything towards a group's properties or membership kind. By this, I do not mean that we should forget about the Criterion of Identity. I think it is a useful tool, but I do not think it does the same job as the rest of the components in Epstein's profiles, which is why I think it should be removed from the *Construction Profile*, but not from his framework.

If I am correct about this, then this modified version of Epstein's profiles will give us a full account of a group's properties. With this, or perhaps prior to this, we will also know which kind of group it is. Add to this the Criterion of Identity and we will have a complete account of its identity (i.e., (1), (2), and (3)). I take the *nature* of something to be equivalent to its *identity* in this broad sense, so that this modified version of Epstein's framework still gives an account of the nature of groups.

Let us consider what this means for Shapiro's project. I said earlier that it seems that Shapiro is only concerned with listing the properties of legal organisations in order to show that they are particular kinds of groups – self-certifying, compulsory, social planning organisations with a moral aim. As I contend, he does not give a complete account of identity due to a limited conception of it. I have tried to show that this conception is limited in two ways: first, he does not take into account Criteria of Identity and, second, he does not consider all of the different kinds of properties that we see above, contained in each of Epstein's profiles. I will presently gesture towards how consideration of the latter can help Shapiro's project.

6 Profiling Legal Organisations

Let us return to Shapiro's characterisation of legal organisations. According to him, they are self-certifying, compulsory, social planning organisations with a moral aim. Let us consider each of these features more carefully in order to see where they fit into Epstein's profiles. Shapiro takes all of these properties as necessary, so at first glance, it looks like most will feature in the *Extra-Essentials Profile*. This certainly appears to be the case with the self-certifying and compulsory properties. More specifically, they are extra-essential properties of the group itself rather than of the individual members. It may be possible to make sense of some members holding such properties, but this is something Shapiro does not consider, however important this might turn out to be. That legal organisations have a moral aim is also an extra-essential property. While others may argue that this is contingent and so belongs in the accidental profile, Shapiro clearly states that this is a necessary property of legal organisations. Recall in **§2** that Shapiro rejects groups without this property as qualifying as legal organisations. To put it otherwise, a "legal system cannot help but have a moral aim if it is to be a legal system" (2011, 215). Again, this is an extra-essential property of legal organisations rather than of individual members. Unlike for the other properties (self-certifying and compulsory), this property cannot be similarly extended to any individual members.

All that remains to be categorised is legal organisations as social planning organisations. To do this we need to know what social planning organisations are. From Shapiro's characterisation of organisations and his planning thesis, we saw in **§2** that social planning organisations are official, institutional groups which perform the shared activity of social planning. So how does this fit into Epstein's profiles? It seems that the official and institutional features, as understood by Shapiro, say something about the constitution conditions for legal organisations and so belongs in the *Construction Profile*. A separate but interesting question nonetheless concerns why they have these features as well as what makes this the case. These questions may be at least partly answered by Shapiro's 'Master Plan' (a shared plan which sets out authorisations as well as instructions for how authorised power should be exercised) which seems to act as the general anchor for many of the properties possessed by legal organisations. Where this would feature in the *Anchor Profile*.

Lastly, then, we still have to analyse the shared activity of social planning groups. For the purposes here (of finding where in Epstein's profiles such a property is located) we are *not* asking *how* they perform this activity or *what* it involves. Rather, following Shapiro, we assume *that* they perform a social planning activity (whatever is it and however they do so) and are asking how this feature should be profiled. For some, this may seem like a contingent feature of legal organisations, but as we know, from Shapiro's account it is an essential property and so it will be included in the *extra-essentials profile*.

The point of undertaking this task has been to illustrate just how much of Epstein's profiles remain to be filled in for legal organisations. The *Accident Profile* is empty with much more also to be said concerning the anchors of both the group properties as well as those of the members, i.e., the *Anchor Profile*. Similarly for the *Construction Profile*; perhaps we can gesture towards some answers here, but it is still mostly incomplete.

Of all of Epstein's framework, the only profile which appears to be closer to completion is the *Extra-Essentials Profile*. However, there is still much more work to be done here. Firstly, for this kind of group, we need to clarify which of these properties belong to the group itself and which are possessed by its members. Also, of the latter, we must determine of a property if each member possesses it, and if so, whether they possess it to the same degree. Secondly, we need to make sure that the properties listed here provide a complete account of the extra-essential properties of legal organisations. This involves analysing this kind of group further as well as social planning organisations so that we can be sure nothing is missing in our account of their nature.

7 Conclusions

In this paper, I have outlined an objection against Scott Shapiro's answer to his Identity Question for legal organisations, advanced by Kenneth Ehrenberg, and shown how important it is for his project that he answer it. If he cannot, he is unable to distinguish legal organisations from other, similar kinds of groups which is crucial for his methodological approach. I rejected a suggestion put forth by Ehrenberg that we should, instead, take law as an abstract institutionalised artifact, on the grounds that this approach is incompatible with Shapiro's project as it undermines the priority given to legal organisations in his account of the nature of law. Moreover, I argued that Ehrenberg's view raises more questions that to answer require, at least in part, an account of legal organisations. I suggested that a more accurate challenge to Shapiro is that his answer to the Identity Question is incomplete. This is unsurprising, I argued, since his notion of *identity* is incomplete, partly due to an inaccurate conception of *nature*. I suggested that once these notions are clarified, we can use a slightly modified version of Brian Epstein's metaphysical framework for understanding the nature of groups to provide a complete account of the nature of legal organisations which is compatible with Shapiro's project.

Acknowledgement: I wish to thank Miguel Garcia for several helpful discussions and comments which greatly improved this paper.

References

Ehrenberg, Kenneth (2016), "Law as Plan and Artefact", *Jurisprudence*, Vol. 7, No. 2, pp. 325–340.
Epstein, Brian (2015), *The Ant Trap*, New York: Oxford University Press.
Epstein, Brian (2017), "What are social groups? Their metaphysics and how to classify them", *Synthese*, https://doi.org/10.1007/s11229-017-1387-y.
Shapiro, Scott (2011), *Legality*, Cambridge, Mass.: Harvard University Press.
Shapiro, Scott (2017), "The Planning Theory of Law", *Yale Law School Public Law Research Paper*, No. 600, pp. 1–30.

Kirk Ludwig

The Social Construction of Legal Norms

1 Introduction

What are legal norms? What is the nature and extent of the authority that they have over us? What sorts of reason do they give us for action? What is their relation to other sorts of norms, and specifically moral norms?[1]

A legal norm applies only within the jurisdiction of a legal system. Legal norms are thus relative to legal systems. We can speak of widespread or even universal legal norms, but what we have in mind are similar norms in many or all legal systems. Legal norms are therefore the result of reflective human social activity. There were no legal norms in the state of nature in small tribes of hunters and gatherers. There were no doubt social norms of various sorts, and legal norms are social norms of a sort (as are the norms of etiquette), but the institutional structures for legal norms were not in place. Legal norms are an invention.

In this paper, I want to say something about the kind of invention that they are and how they are similar to and different from other sorts of norms, and specifically other social norms and moral norms. I approach this question not from a background in legal philosophy but from the theory of social action. The idea of the paper is to bring to bear on the topic of legal norms work on the structure of institutions and institutional agency.

In a nutshell, my proposal is that legal norms derive from rules *which specify role functions in a legal system*. Legal rules attach to agents in virtue of their status within the system in which the rules operate. The point of legal rules or a legal system is to solve large scale coordination problems, specifically the problem of organizing social and economic life among a group of people and their successors. This is not to say that every legal rule pertains to a coordination

1 I take norms in general to be expressed using 'ought' or 'should' statements and to be (intended to be) action guiding. There are norms of etiquette, practical norms, moral, and legal norms among others. Rights are correlative to duties: if one has a right to autonomy, others have a duty to or ought to or should respect it. Legal rules or laws generate legal norms. Some ascribe powers or give permissions or set limits. These are normative rules with implications for how others ought to legally act with respect to those given powers or permissions, but I am not counting them as norms *per se* since they are not specifications of what one ought or should do or not do legally.

https://doi.org/10.1515/9783110663617-011

problem. While the legal requirement that one drive on the left in the direction of travel solves a coordination problem for drivers, the speed limit and laws regarding wearing safety belts while driving and automobiles having air bags do not solve coordination problems, but rather have safety as their goal.

The framework for thinking about legal norms I describe is a framework for thinking about institutions and policies more generally. The idea is to show that legal norms are a species of institutional norm. There are two central ideas. The first is the idea of a role in an institution. The second is the idea of proxy agency. Proxy agency involves one agent or group acting under the authorization of another agent or group (perhaps subsuming it) in a way that makes the actions of the proxy count as actions (under a description) of the individual or group for which it is a proxy. We get the characteristic structure of a legal system by conceiving of an institutional group, itself conceived of as a set of interlocking roles realized in individuals, as having one or more roles for proxy agents who are authorized by the group to make policy for the group. The set of rules governing the basic constitution of the group and spelling out the powers of the policy proxies determine fundamental norms for the group with specific role responsibilities attaching to particular positions in institutional arrangements. The policies determine further norms whose force derives from the fundamental norms. We must then say some further things to distinguish institutions and policies which we wish to designate as legal.

In section 2, I introduce the conceptual machinery of constitutive rule, status function, status role, collective acceptance, substantive and formal acceptance, rights and duties associated with status roles, and proxy agency.[2] In section 3, I apply the framework to the explanation of legal norms, compare the account to the social practice theory and Shapiro's planning theory, explain its bearing on the debate between legal positivists and natural law theorists, explain what it tells us about the sort of authority laws have over its subjects, discuss the role of enforcement, Hart's (Hart 1961) distinction between primary and secondary rules, and a puzzle about laws that seem regulative rather than constitutive. In section 4, I sketch a preliminary and tentative answer to the question in what way a legal system differs from other institutions with a similar structure. Section 5 is a brief conclusion.

The upshot is that legal norms are socially constructed in a precise sense.

2 These ideas are developed in further detail in (Ludwig and Ludwig 2014, Ludwig 2017a).

2 Conceptual Foundations of Institutional Reality

Institutions come in (at least) two varieties. First, there are institutions as stable transferrable jointly intentional practices. Language and systems of bartering are institutions in this sense. Second, there are institutions in the sense of a set of transferrable roles inter-defined in terms of their functions established to collectivize behavior for one or another purpose. Clubs, teams, universities, corporations, general partnerships, city governments, and nation states are institutions in this sense. I am primarily concerned with institutions in the second sense and will henceforth use 'institution' in this sense.

Institutional roles are status roles. Institutional membership is itself a status role. Being university professor or student, a member of a club or the parliament, are status roles. A status role is a variety of status function. A status function is a function that an object has in an essentially intentional social transaction that it can perform only by its being collectively accepted, in a certain sense, that it has that function. Searle introduced the notion in his 1995 book *The Construction of Social Reality* in the following passage:

> The radical movement that gets us from such simple social facts as that we are sitting on a bench together or having a fistfight to such institutional facts as money, property, and marriage is the collective imposition of function on entities, which – unlike levers, benches, and cars – cannot perform the functions solely by virtue of their physical structure. . . . The key element in the move from the collective imposition of function to the creation of institutional facts is the imposition of a collectively recognized *status* to which a function is attached. Since this is a special category of agentive functions, I will label these *status functions*. (Searle 1995, p. 41)

Being a 10 pound note, a pawn or knight in chess, a crown, an official seal, a driver's license or passport, are all status functions. The curious thing about status functions is the requirement that they be collectively accepted as having a function in order for them to be able to perform it. This contrasts with other agentive functions (functions defined in terms of the purposes of agents) like a two man cross-cut saw. While a two man cross-cut saw can be used intentionally for its purpose only if it is recognized as a two man cross-cut saw, its function can be performed without its being intentionally being used for that purpose. In the woods a blind man may come upon the handle of a two man saw at the same time at which another blind man comes upon the other handle, while it is set against a tree. One pulls experimentally, the other pulls back, and soon they have felled a mighty oak, without realizing that they are doing so. But a ten pound note cannot be used for its function unless it is accepted as a certain unit of monetary exchange by those involved in the transaction. Status roles are the same. No one can function as the CEO of a company unless in the relevant community it is collective accepted (by most at least) that she has that function.

In the following, I explain why status functions have this special feature and what distinguishes status roles among other status functions. The key idea is that the functions in question are defined by *constitutive rules* which specify a role for something in a social transaction without specifying what is to fulfill the role. This presents those who intend to engage in it with a coordination problem. Solving it requires them to coordinate on the same thing, and, hence, to collectively accept it as playing the role, or having the function. Then, I will explain how norms associated with institutions arise from the definitions of the status roles that people occupy. I will explain in what sense the notions of rights and duties arise in connection with those functions – why this talk is apt. This will show that these notions of rights and duties are entirely socially constructed. This doesn't mean that they have no force, and it does not mean that they are not shaped by other non-socially constructed norms and values, but it does mean that in their nature they are entirely the product of human intentional activity and *have no status or force or authority beyond what we give them.* Then I will argue that this applies in a straightforward way to legal norms which have the same source and status.

Essentially Intentional Activity Types and Constitutive Rules

I begin with the concept of an essentially intentional activity type. These come in two varieties.

(1) Activities defined in terms of patterns of behavior (individual or collective) that are instantiated intentionally.
(2) Activities defined in terms of a goal intentionally pursued.

Examples of (1) are playing solitaire, shaking hands, having a conversation, playing a game of chess, writing and passing legislation. Examples of (2) are looking for your lost keys, waiting for the Second Coming, and checking your work for mistakes. I am concerned here only with the former.

A simple example is the playing of tic-tac-toe (noughts and crosses). The rules of the game describe constraints on a pattern of activity by two people. We can think of all the possible sequences of moves in a two player game constrained by the rules as defining a type of activity pattern. From the rules we can extract a description of the pattern. The description involves roles for two agents. The pattern can be instantiated in principle accidentally. In this case, it is not an instance of tic-tac-toe. For it to be tic-tac-toe, the rules must be followed jointly intentionally, with the agents playing agreeing on who has what role (this is part of the pattern that they intend to instantiate). In addition each agent must intend to win, where the winner is the one whose mark occupies three contiguous squares (including diagonals) in a three-by-three grid. The description of the activity pattern in terms of the alternating actions of the two agents engaged in it become rules for the activity when they are treated by them as guiding their behavior. Since playing tic-tac-toe requires that the pattern be instantiated intentionally by the agents, following the rules jointly intentionally suffices for playing tic-tac-toe.

A constitutive rule is a rule the (intentional) following of which brings into existence the type of activity it governs, whereas a regulative rule is one the following of which brings order into an activity type that can exist without the rule being followed, e.g., Robert's Rules of Order (RRO). Thus, we have an explanation of the status of constitutive rules for activity types. Constitutive rules are descriptions of activity patterns taken as a guide to behavior in relation to an activity type that requires that the activity pattern be instantiated intentionally (or jointly intentionally). Constitutive rules are not a special type of rule. They are only special in relation to an activity type whose concept requires not just that the activity be described neutrally with respect to whether it is produced intentionally, but also that it be intentionally instantiated. If this is right, then for every rule defining an activity pattern, there ought to be an activity type relative to which it is a constitutive rule. And this is clearly the case. Define a *parliamentary meeting* as one conducted in accordance with RRO. Then RRO are constitutive of parliamentary meetings. A consequence is that constitutive rules govern essentially intentional activity patterns.

Status Functions

What is the relevance of this to status functions? Shift the example to tournament chess. There are six types of pieces in chess. The number of each type and their initial positions on a board are specified by the rules. How each can then be moved is specified by the rules with the white player taking the first turn, followed by the black player, and so on, until one of the end conditions for the game is reached. The rules determine a pattern of activity involving the pieces. But what things in the world are pawns, knights, rooks, bishops, kings and queens? The rules don't tell us. What they give us are functional role concepts. What role a pawn, etc., is to play in the game. Thus, the constitutive rules for chess specify functions for items in a social transaction without telling us what things are to play the roles.

This presents two people who want to play chess with a coordination problem. To play chess, they have to settle *together* on what things are to play the roles specified by the rules. Of course there are standard chess sets. But anything will do. You can play chess with bottle caps and a checkered picnic tablecloth on a train trip as long as you and your opponent agree on what's what. Thus, in a sense, they have to collectively accept that these things are the pawns (black and white), the knights, and so on.

What is collective acceptance? Is it belief? Belief will typically be involved, but what is fundamentally required is that, in chess, e.g., the players' intentions directed at their playing chess together involve the same items in the same roles. Following the literature, I will call the intentions individuals have when they are participating in joint intentional action *we-intentions*. I do not mean by this to suggest that they have a special mode of intending (cf. (Searle 1990, Gilbert 2009)). My view (Ludwig 2016) is that what distinguishes we-intentions from I-intentions is their content, and that the concepts involved are already in play in our understanding of individual intentional action (see (Bratman 2014) for another reductive view and (Tuomela 2005, 2013) for a view on which the content of we-intentions contains irreducible concept of shared intentional agency). What is special about my view is the particular structure of the content. A taxonomy of views is given in Figure 1.

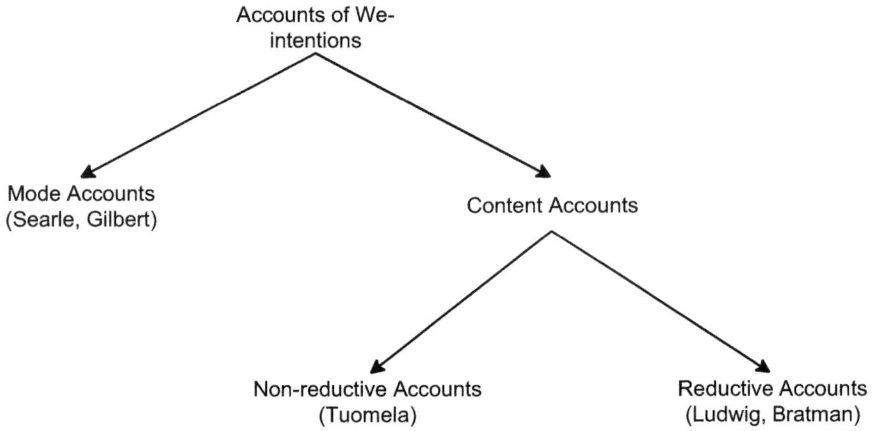

Figure 1: Types of Accounts of We-intentions.

For our purposes it won't matter what the analysis is, though it does matter that we take shared intention, for example, our shared intention to play chess, to be a matter of each of us we-intending to play chess, that is, we treat shared intention as a distribution of individual intentions with appropriately interlocking contents (and a special mode as well on some views). So collective acceptance of something as having a certain function, specified by constitutive rules for an activity type that do not specify what is to serve the function, is a matter of the members of the group having we-intentions directed at the same objects in the same roles with respect to the activity. This is what it is to impose a status function on an object. This does not have to be a reflective exercise, and for types of activities which we are familiar with we may just fall naturally into a salient coordination without discussing it or thinking much about it.

If we play chess with bottle caps and a checkered tablecloth as a one off, then what matters is just that we direct our we-intentions at the same tokens we press into service in various roles. Often, we want to settle on the same things, or more broadly things of a certain type, as playing the roles, anticipating an open-ended number of occasions on which we might wish to play chess (and so for other such activities). In this case, we have generalized conditional we-intentions to play with the particular items in the roles or with types of items in the roles whenever we engage in the relevant type of social transaction. These generalized conditional we-intentions sustain a convention with respect to the use of the items or types of items. Thus, standing status functions for particulars or types are sustained by conventions in the relevant community. These are practices that are stable, social, arbitrary, and reciprocal and they meet the Lewisian standard of solving coordination problems (Lewis 1986).

Status Roles

Status roles are a particular type of status functions. They are distinguished from status functions generally in being (a) status functions assigned to agents who (b) are to exercise their agency in fulfilling at least some of the functions of the role. Examples are being a university professor, senator, member of the House of Lords, Supreme Court justice, club president, Prime Minister, grocery store clerk, student, criminal defendant, attorney, barrister, judge, prisoner of war, enemy combatant, and so on. Status roles can be assigned to groups as well as individuals: the Supreme Court, the Parliament, the Intergovernmental Committee on Climate Change, a member of the United Nations, and so on. The functions assigned to groups however are carried out by its members (or enough of them doing it well enough) carrying out theirs.

What status roles have in common is that in the relevant community it is collectively accepted that those possessing them are

(i) to give or accept directions or permissions to or from others, given their status roles, or
(ii) to play certain roles or do certain things in joint activities or types of social transactions (see below for a further specification of the range of things),
  (a) on certain conditions obtaining or
  (b) at their discretion or
  (c) upon the exercise of their judgment about certain matters

  which all parties to the arrangements are to act in conformity with, in accordance with their own status roles.

Status roles like status functions in general are possessed by agents by virtue of their being collectively accepted as having those roles, where this is a matter of enough members of the relevant community having appropriate generalized we-intentions with respect to action plans involving interacting with the agent with the role.

We can call a role that involves directing others in virtue of their roles a command role (a general in the army, a manager in a firm), and a role that involves taking direction from others (a private, an employee), in virtue of their roles, a compliance role. Status roles may and often do combine both of these elements, but need not involve either.

The *powers* that agents may have in virtue of their status roles include
(i) directing or
(ii) giving permissions to others,
(iii) exercising rights,
(iv) making findings that have an official status that others must conform their behavior to,
(v) issuing rules (which are generalized directives), and
(vi) conferring status roles on others or status functions on things.

These are real powers. They effect constitutive changes to the fabric of social reality. They make a difference to the causal evolution of the world. But they reside entirely in the collective acceptance of the relevant community that those with those roles have those powers. Thus, they supervene on the conditional we-intentions of members of the relevant communities. It comes to this: when we confer on someone a status role that involves the exercise of a power, we are committed to engage as appropriate in collective intentional behavior in which that person plays the relevant role. A simple example is one person committing himself to following another's directions. This confers a power on the other, but it resides entirely in his willingness to follow through on his commitment and the other to accept the arrangement. The same goes for the fully articulated interlocking roles and institutions of modern life. The practical difference lies in the individual having very little ability to affect the basic structure of social reality by withdrawing acceptance of large-scale institutional arrangements because of how many others would have to cooperate.

We can distinguish between two basic types of status roles. The first sort I will call agent status roles. Agent status roles presuppose that the person to whom they are assigned is party to the collective acceptance that imposes the role on her. The second sort, I will call subject status roles,[3] in contrast, are assigned to agents independently of whether they accept the role. Being a university professor is an agent status role. Being a prisoner of war or persona non grata are subject status roles. Even functions of subject status roles involve their possessors exercising their agency in those roles in the sense that they are supposed to recognize the roles assigned to them and recognize that roles as such involve behaviors on their part in various circumstances. However, they need not participate in the collective acceptance that assigns them the role (e.g., prisoners of war), and there is no presumption that they will willingly fulfill the role assigned, hence, the need to make provisions for various forms of coercion.

Some status roles have a hybrid character in the sense that they are in certain conditions assigned without the presumption that their assignee is party to the collective acceptance that she has that role but also on the basis of the assignee explicitly accepting the role. Citizenship is a hybrid category in this sense because it is assigned by birth right as well as naturalization, and because until citizens reach their majority, they are not assumed to have fully accepted their roles as citizens (and the associated rights and responsibilities). It is important for our discussion though that when citizens reach the age of majority, they are presumed to be party to the collective acceptance in accordance with which they are citizens.[4]

3 In previous work I have called these "patient status roles" after the distinction in linguistics between the thematic (or case) roles of agent and patient (actor and thing acted upon). In the context of this discussion, "subject status role" has the advantage of emphasizing the role of the exercise of power to ensure conformity of behavior to the assigned role.

4 This might be and has been disputed. But it is important for the thesis I want to develop about the authority of the law that this is the default assumption. It is, it seems to me, part of the ideology of citizenship. I will offer a few supporting remarks later, but I will not try to offer a full defense of the assumption in this paper.

Substantive and Formal Acceptance

Agent status roles are designed for agents who are party to the collective acceptance by which they have the role. They are assumed to be sincerely engaged, when appropriate, in the kinds of joint activities defined in part by the someone performing the functions of the role. Having the role may be defined in terms of the agent's being party to the acceptance, so that absent accepting it, the agent does not genuinely have the role.

This may be appropriate for small scale organizations. However, in larger scale organizations which have roles to play in relation to other large organizations, it becomes more important that organizations can rely on someone not to capriciously opt out. For these purposes three innovations are necessary.

> The first is that we allow for a distinction between formal and substantive acceptance of a role. Formal acceptance of a role is a public acceptance of the role that represents oneself as committed to fulfilling the role's functions.
>
> The second is provision for the relevant status role to attach to someone in virtue of formal acceptance, with further provisions for when the person can be said no longer to have the role.
>
> The third is provision for incentives to fulfill the duties of the role in the form either of punishments for failure or rewards for fulfillment or a combination of both.

Thus, one may possess a role in an organization by formally accepting it (it being collectively accepted in the community that one thereby has it) without being sincere, though it is presumed that you are party to the collective acceptance by which you assume the role. Then performance in the role, until the formal conditions for discontinuance obtain, is expected, and provision made for what steps to take if performance is inadequate, the type of response calibrated to the degree and dimension along which the performance is inadequate.

This is an evolution of the idea of a pure agent status role under pressure from the real-world conditions under which human agents make as if to sign on to them.

Rights and Duties

The design functions of status roles specify how their possessors are to interact with others in virtue of their assigned status roles. The possibility of a gap between assignment of role and performance provides scope for evaluating the role occupant for adequacy of performance. The gap arises from two sources. First, from the possibility of failures of competence or performance in the role. Second, from the possibility of possessing the role even in the absence of substantive acceptance of it, that is, by virtue of not having commitment to fulfilling the functions associated with the status role (or even having commitments to subverting it). Given the possibility of a gap between function and performance, the design specification serves as a standard of evaluation. This is what provides scope for the use of the language of rights, on the one hand, and duties or role responsibilities, on the other, in relation to status roles. A role occupant has rights against others in virtue of their role responsibilities with respect to him in virtue of his status role. He has duties or responsibilities with respect to performance of functions in the role in essentially collective intentional activities with others in virtue of their status roles.

Thus, to touch briefly on the legal sphere, a defendant at a trial, willing or not, has both rights and responsibilities. Their source is the design specification of the various roles he occupies and the roles occupied by those whose actions in those roles constitute the conduct of the trial. The defendant has, e.g., the right to be confronted with the evidence against him and to offer a rebuttal. This right derives from the role responsibilities of prosecutors and judges. The defendant has responsibilities as well, e.g., to be present for the trail, to answer questions truthfully, etc. Of course, given that the nature of a trial is adversarial, provision is made for failure of a defendant to fulfill his responsibilities.

Role responsibilities and rights based on occupancy of a role are not moral responsibilities and duties. First, in the case of subject status roles, e.g., that of POW, it is clear that POWs do not have a moral responsibility to fulfill the role of POW. Second, even in the case of agent status role, the functions assigned may themselves be things which in themselves or in some circumstances are morally proscribed. For example, the official torturer has the duty to extract information from suspects under the threat of torture, but this duty is not a moral duty, but instead violates a moral duty. Similarly, the concentration camp commander fulfils his role responsibilities by committing mass murder, but these are not moral responsibilities, but instead responsibilities whose execution involve the violation of his moral responsibilities.

One may have moral responsibilities to fulfil one's role responsibilities. These can arise from two sources. First, from explicitly placing oneself under an obligation by promising or agreeing to perform them. Second, by generating expectations of performance in others by one's accepting the role, where their reliance on one in the event of failure of performance will disadvantage them. Even in these cases, of course, the moral responsibilities will be pro tanto, and they are distinct from the role responsibilities as such, understood, that is, in terms of the standard provided by the design function. Here it is interaction of the circumstances of acceptance of the role with general moral principles which generates a moral responsibility to fulfill the functions of the role. But this is no different from simply giving someone reason to expect performance in a cooperative task in general and then failing to do one's part, or promising or agreeing in general and then failing to fulfill one's promise or to do what one agreed to do.

Proxy Agency

There is one more concept central to understanding many institutional transactions which we need to get on the table, namely, that of proxy agency. In proxy agency, what one agent or group does counts as another agent or another group, or a subsuming group, doing something. A paradigmatic example is the spokesperson, who in speaking in her role, delivering a sanctioned message, performs an act which counts as her principal's, e.g., announcing something. Other examples are the United States declaring war by way of Congress passing a declaration of war, a corporation filing for bankruptcy by way of its lawyers filing papers, a university awarding a degree by way of a clerk in the registrar's office approving paperwork, the legal system sentencing a defendant by way of a Judge's doing so.

What is proxy agency? How is it possible for what one person does to count as another person or a group doing something?

The basic idea is that the proxy agent occupies a status role whose function is to signal commitment by a group to act in certain ways. The group counts as an agent of an event of so signaling because the group authorizes the agent by assigning to her the relevant status role (where the agent in these cases is supposed to accept the role as well). So while the proxy performs individual acts, they are of a type that performs a role in a social transaction with others because of the fact that the proxy has been assigned the role.

Let's take the spokesperson as an example. Focus on the simplest case in which, say, a club is deciding on a method for communicating commitment to various audiences with respect to its official actions. We can imagine the members casting about for a method. They want some public event to be recognized as their making a commitment of a certain sort. It could be that they formulate a message and they all read out one word of it in turn in front of their audience after telling them what the significance of it is supposed to be. But that is awkward and inefficient. A better solution is to convey to the audience that what one member of the group chosen by them says, as a result of being chosen to say it, is to convey that they are committed to acting in accordance with what is said. This is basically the device of the spokesperson, who is authorized to speak in the name of the group. This is a status role. What the spokesperson says in that role, e.g., in the assertive mode, conveying a message agreed upon by the group, is both an individual speech act (though not an individual assertion), and a speech act, in an extended sense, by the group, a status function it has in virtue of it being produced by the spokesperson acting in her role. See Figure 2 for an illustration.

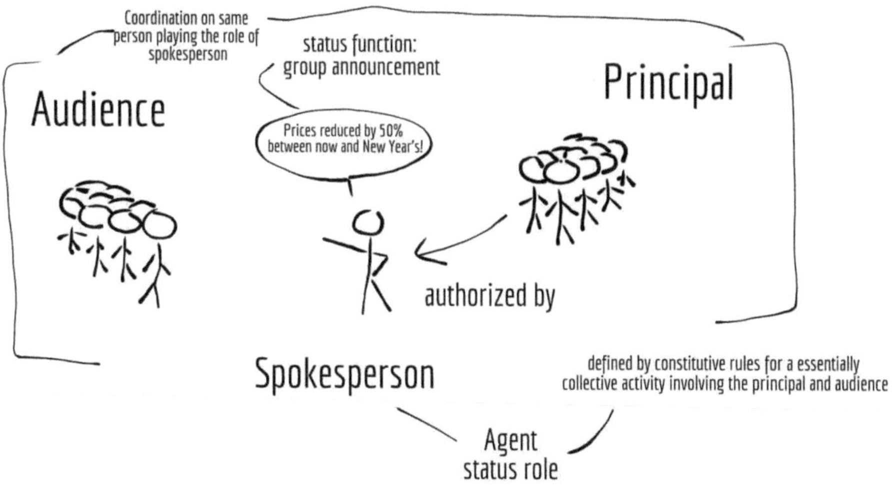

Figure 2: Spokesperson as Proxy Agent.

The two keys to understanding proxy agency then are the authorization relation (which is the assignment of the role to the proxy) and the idea of a status role part of whose function involves conferring on something – an event, an object, a process, etc. – by an act of a certain sort in the role, a status function in a social transaction with others (individuals and groups). The community in which the proxy functions includes not just the group that authorizes the proxy but also the consumers of the act, some of whom may be those it is directed on or at, and others indirectly in virtue of the relevance of the status function conferred to their status role functions.[5]

Proxy agents may be assigned many powers to act in the name of the group, including assigning other proxy agents, formulating group policy, issuing orders, interpreting rules, making judgements, undertaking investigations, etc. Authorization is transitive, so the group that authorizes an agent to assign

5 See (Ludwig 2017b) and (Ludwig 2017a, ch. 13) for more on proxy agency; see (Ludwig 2020) for a more detailed discussion of the case of the spokesperson and complications and extensions of the simple case.

further proxies authorizes those further proxies as well, who also act in the name of the group. A group that authorizes proxies to make policy for the group thereby endorses the policies adopted as governing their actions.

Proxy agents are representatives of the groups that authorize them. They act in the name of the group. This is more than just acting in their behalf, which is to act in their interests. For the proxy to act in the name of the group, to be a representative of the group, is to express the agency of the group in her role as a proxy. In many cases, the assignment of proxy roles is itself assigned to someone or some group smaller than the whole group that the proxy represents. The proxy represents the whole group because other members accept the arrangements (which is not to say that they may not work to change them) by which the proxy is assigned. Accepting the arrangements is an indirect form of authorization for whoever acts in the role to act in their name as a part of the group. Though those whose functions do not give them an explicit role in the assignment do not participate in the formal assignments of the roles, they nonetheless authorize whoever plays the relevant roles to represent them because they sign on to the arrangements. What is crucial for representation is not participation in the formal procedures of assignment but participation in the whole system of roles that sanctions the formal procedures of assignment.

3 Application to Legal Norms

Legal Norms are Role Constitutive Norms

Legal norms apply to those who are in the jurisdiction of a legal system. A legal system is an institution realized in a set of interdefined status roles. Typically a legal system has jurisdiction over a geographic territory and a community largely composed of those who typically live in the territory whose behavior and interactions the laws are designed to govern, though the laws apply to them whether they are in the territory or not. These are members of the relevant polis, citizens in the case of the laws of a sovereign state. Similarly, the laws apply, typically, to everyone in the territorial jurisdiction whether or not they are members of polis, e.g., visitors, or transients. The definition of the scope of a legal system is internal to the legal system itself. The maintenance of a legal system is a massive collective intentional activity. The effectiveness of the definitions of the categories of person to whom the law applies relies on there being enough people who collectively accept what the law says about people who fall in these categories for them to function in accordance with the design of the institution. Thus, these are status roles.

In US Law the basic statuses recognized are Alien, US National, US Citizen, Immigrant, Non-immigrant, Undocumented Alien. Within these categories US law recognized more specific status roles, of course. For example, varieties of visas determine more specific status roles for non-immigrant aliens in US territories. Citizens are subject to Federal Law in the category of citizen (which includes rights not extended to non-citizens). They are typically subject to additional subordinate systems of law at the state, county, township, and city level depending on residence, with rights attaching to state citizenship in addition when further conditions are met.

Thus, in the general case, being a member of a polis, subject to its legal system, is having a status role. These are hybrid status roles typically. They are conferred often by a birth right, or a right of residence, or in the case of nation states by naturalization, which involves taking an oath. However, though one may be a member of the polis by birthright, upon one's majority one is expected to understand and accept membership. Thus, to focus on citizenship as an example, the status of full citizenship with its rights and duties presumes that the role is accepted substantively. Whether or not this is so, one is recognized as having the status, and subject to the norms attaching to it in virtue of the legal regime governing the status.[6]

The status of the norms that arise from being subject to the rules of a legal system as a citizen are no different from those attaching to any status role. To be subject to a legal system is to have a status role. The norms are derived from the design functions of the role. Norms can be conditional or unconditional. A norm is unconditional if it applies in any context. For example, the requirement that one not interfere with the lawful activity of others is unconditional. A norm is conditional if it applies relative to a context or condition. The norms governing contracts apply if one enters into a contract, and more specific legal obligations arise from the details of what is contracted. Typically status roles are layered. In the army, one is a soldier, which is the basic status role. Then one has a rank, which in conjunction with organizational position, determines the chain of command, those from whom one ought to accept directions from when acting in their official roles and those, if any, to whom one has the right and obligation to issue directions acting in one's role, and who in term are required

6 I am here concerned with norms attaching to official legal status roles. There can be unofficial norms governing practices, including legal practices, in a community governed by a legal system.

by the design function to accept those directions. Further specifications of the role are determined by one's position in a unit and the functions assigned in joint activities. *Citizen* is the basic status role in a nation state. Further status roles are determined by residence, employment, licensing, club membership, offices, contracts, calls for jury duty, tickets, arrests warrants, and so on.

An immediate consequence of identifying legal status with having a status role is that this gives one role related rights and duties. These are legal rights and duties, and the norms that arise from these are legal norms and duties. Their ontological status is exactly the same as for rights and duties attached to status roles in general. They exist because there are enough people who collective accept that agents have them for them to function (at least roughly) in the ways they were designed to. In this sense, the roles, and the accompanying rights and duties, are socially constructed. They are socially constructed in exactly the same sense that a pawn is socially constructed, that is, that something is a pawn is determined wholly by the we-intentions and policies (generalized conditional we-intentions) of agents with respect to its function. I will call this *the status role account of legal norms.*

Brief Remarks on Relations to Practice Theories and Shapiro's Planning Theory

Among positivist theories, practice theories of one sort or another have been most common. Varieties of these are represented by (Austin 1971, Hart 1961, Hayek 1969). For Austin, it was the habit or custom of obedience to a sovereign. Austin's thesis that laws were imperatives issued by a sovereign was famously criticized by Hart. Among other points are that not all laws involve imperatives, for example, laws making provision of marriage or contracts more generally, and it makes the authority of law (to the extent that there would be any) rest on the threat of punishment. Yet Hart also held that legal norms rest on customs, specifically amongst legal officials (and more on this specifically below). Hayek held that legal norms arise from abstraction of rules from customs which then serve as a standard of behavior.

At the heart of the view that I am presenting is the idea that legal norms arise out of specifications of role responsibilities in a legal system. These are sustained by a large scale social practice. But the practice is not a mere custom. It is a large scale joint intentional activity directed at sustaining a system of interlocking institutional roles and realized in both generalized conditional we-intentions and appropriate actions. Customs include such things as eating with knives and forks or with chopsticks, sleeping on mattresses or on tatami mats, or in hammocks, men wearing pants and women wearing skirts, and so on. Although these kinds of customs are collective (in the sense that they involve a community of agents) they are not essentially jointly intentional. The special character of legal norms does not derive, on the status role theory, from an observed regularity which has given rise to expectations which assume a critical-reflective character, but from the content of the intentions which sustain the systems of roles and associated patterns of joint intentional activity. We act in those roles in accordance with rules that define their functions, and thus the patterns of activity generated are generated by participants following constitutive rules for a kind of activity type. Calling this a social practice is not wrong, but fails to capture essential structure. The relations are illustrated in Figure 3.

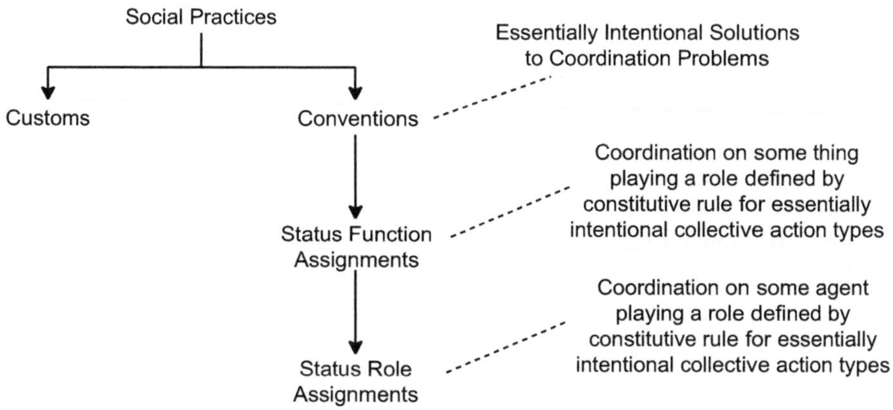

Figure 3: Crucial Distinctions between Customs and Status Role Assignments.

Shapiro (2011) has argued for what he calls the planning theory of law. The planning theory is inspired by the work of Michael Bratman on collective action and shared intention. Like the present account, it sees the maintenance of a legal system as a large-scale collective enterprise. “Legal systems are institutions of social planning and their fundamental aim is to compensate for the deficiencies of alternative forms of planning in the circumstances of legality” (Shapiro, 171). Laws and legal norms are on this view plans, specifically plans regarding the organization of life in a society.

The difference between the planning theory and the status function account lies in the way the latter brings to center stage (i) the idea of a status role as the concept essential to understanding institutional structure, (ii) identifying norms attaching to status roles as arising from their design function, and (iii) identifying legal statuses as status roles. A legal system does embody a plan for the organization of social and economic life. While the specification of actions in an action plan are not *per se* norms, from an action plan you can extract *hypothetical* norms, if the plan is the only or the best plan for doing something. If [. . .] is the only plan you can adopt or the best plan you can adopt for driving to the store, then we can say: if you want to drive to the store, you ought to [. . .]. If [. . .] is an action plan for driving to the store, but there are other equally good action plans for driving to the store (two routes that take the same time, etc.), then all we can say is: If you want to drive to the store, you can [. . .]. But if there is a range of equally optimal plans, we can say: if you want to drive to the store, then you ought to adopt plan A or plan B or . . .. These are norms of practical rationality relativized to goals. We could think of legal systems in a similar way. If we want to organize social and economic life, we ought to implement such and such a legal system or some legal system. This leaves out something important, however, about the source and nature of legal norms. If the status role account is correct, the norms attach to status roles. They are not hypothetical in form. They are not norms of practical rationality. They rather fall out of the design specification for the roles. We get to say that someone who has a legal status role ought legally to do something, if that is required by the role, not just if she wants to do it. (This does not mean that that ought-statement has practical force for her without her being committed to fulfilling the role, but that is why the norms are not just practical norms.) These status roles do play a part in specifying an action plan for implementing a legal system. But the norms are rather like standards for something's being a good knife or a good hammer. Their content is specifiable in terms of a function assigned to the role independently of talking about what anyone wants. This is still essentially connected with human purposes – like tools, status roles have agentive functions. But the standards are at one remove from simple hypothetical norms.

Natural Law Theory and Legal Positivism

The status role account of legal norms is a version of legal positivism, according to which laws are posited or decided on or defined by social practice – in a word, socially determined, or, as I have been putting it, socially constructed. The law is a social fact that is in principle independent of considerations of its merits or value with respect to other standards of evaluation, and, in particular, moral standards. As John Austin put it:

> The existence of law is one thing; its merit and demerit another. Whether it be or be not is one enquiry; whether it be or be not conformable to an assumed standard, is a different enquiry. (Austin 1971, p. 157, first published 1832)

What is special about the view is the story about the nature of the social construction, that it comes down to the definition and collective acceptance of the imposition of status roles (or the conditions sufficient for having them), and what follows from this about the status, ontology, and authority of the law. We invent legal systems. We sustain them. Their content is up to us. Their norms are standards pertaining to design functions of roles that people accept or have imposed on them. Role responsibilities have to do with what the role occupier is to do *qua* role occupier. What those responsibilities are, whether of the social worker or concentration camp guard, are internal to the definition of the role. Insofar as this is the case, there is no essential connection with the moral. Reasons we have to act in accordance with the law either derive from our reasons for being party to the collective acceptance by which the system is sustained or from considerations external to their constitutive norms, whether they are prudential (e.g., connected with mechanisms of enforcement) or moral. Legal reasons themselves are not *per se* motivators or practical reasons in the sense being input into practical deliberation.

Is this opposed to Natural Law Theory? It is not opposed to the view that in accepting status roles we acquire moral responsibilities. It does not insist that this is so because the role duties may themselves be proscribed by moral law. But in many circumstances, the application of moral principles to acceptance will generate moral duties connected with the role. It is not opposed to the view that morally we ought to design legal systems to promote moral good, even if not every element of the law is directed toward the moral good. It is not opposed to the view that legal systems in bringing order and stability to social interactions, which is arguably one of their central aims, also thereby promote morally valuable ends. It is not opposed to the view that law may be made that makes reference to moral considerations, even making what is morally wrong be the criterion for what is legally wrong (though this would be fraught with difficulties). It is not opposed to the view that judges may bring to bear moral considerations in adjudicating cases, and even properly so by the lights of the legal system itself. It is opposed to the view that it is intrinsic to the nature of law and legal norms that they involve moral standards. Moral standards are on this view standards external to the law with respect to which the law may be judged, but by moral standards, not standards internal to the law. In sum, though it does not prohibit moral considerations entering into the content and practice of law, the concept of law does not require the deployment of moral concepts in its analysis.

I mention briefly a maneuver one may apply here to set it aside as verbal. That is the idea that by law we mean socially constructed norms of behavior designed as a comprehensive framework for organizing social and economic life backed by force *and guided in their formulation by the moral law.* This concept of course does include moral considerations constitutively, but it is an entirely verbal maneuver because it consists in adding to a non-moral conception of the law the additional requirement that its formulation be guided by morality. This is equivalent to arguing the physicians are intrinsically moral by adding to the standard conditions for being a physician that one is also morally good.

Law's Authority

What is the nature and source of the law's authority on this view? In saying that the law has authority over those to whom it applies I mean that they recognize that they have a reason to obey the law that does not depend merely on the threat of sanction by the mechanisms of enforcement maintained by the legal system if they do not. On the view advanced here, the law has authority in this sense over those who are committed to maintaining the legal system (at least as a whole), that is, those whose conditional we-intentions sustain the status roles in terms of which the law is defined. The authority then is an authority ceded to the law by those who are subject to it. At root it rests on the practical commitment to accept the law and the whole system of status roles in terms of which it is understood. The basic structure is exhibited in Figure 4.

Commitment to maintaining the legal system as a whole is consistent with not obeying all the laws all the time (speeding, non-reporting of some income on tax returns) and with civil disobedience. Indeed, civil disobedience, aiming at non-violent change in the law, presupposes a commitment to maintaining the legal system as a whole. In accepting the role of citizen one gives the law its authority over you even when you violate it. This does not mean that you are irrational whenever you violate a law. While it comes with an internal tension, considerations in favor of obeying any given law in virtue of a commitment to the legal system are not overriding.

Not everyone to whom a legal system applies its laws have in this sense ceded authority to the laws. In their case, the law has no authority over them in the sense just articulated. Instead, they only have reasons to obey the law that derived from the risk of sanctions if they do not. They are like POWs in this

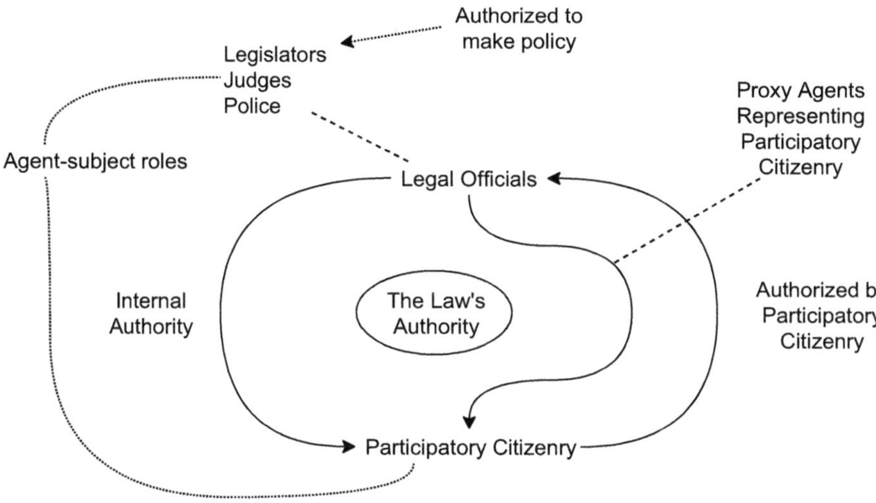

Figure 4: Internal Authority of the Law.

sense. POWs are not POWs by having agreed to be. They obey rules in POW camps because of the threat of sanction if they do not. The authority of the rules imposed on them is given to the enforcers by themselves. It is recognized by them, but not by those on whom they impose the rules.

We can say that:

(1) a rule has *internal authority* over someone iff the person is committed to its guiding their actions independently of whether they will be subject to sanctions if they follow them;
(2) a rule has *definitional authority* iff it applies to one by virtue of the assignment of a status function to one when one is not a party to the collective acceptance by which one has it;
(3) a rule has *external authority* iff it gives one reasons only by virtue of the threat of sanctions if one does not follow it.

POWs are subject to camp rules that have definitional authority over them and external authority over them but no internal authority over them. Definitional authority is thin. It provides external reasons that are not motivators, nor practical reasons. External authority provides internal reasons in the sense of practical reasons, but nothing that those subject to it recognize as in itself worth pursuing. The difference between POWs and citizens (as ideally conceived) is precisely that for citizens the law has internal authority: they recognize and accept its authority over them independently of the threat of sanctions if they don't conform.[7]

On this view, it is internal to the concept of law that it has internal authority over its target subjects, those for whom it is designed, though it allows for its application without universal acceptance, and that, in any case, for the roles that realize a legal system there must be a significant proportion of those subject to it for whom it has internal authority – who are, I will say, in another sense, its (proper) subjects. This means that where rules govern a subjugated or oppressed people who have only external reasons to obey them, while the rules may have the status of laws in the ruling group, those subject to them against their will are not properly its subjects. This is so even if they are called 'citizens', for they are in name only, and in fact have a status akin to prisoners (though *prisoner* is not quite the right flavor). De facto they occupy what I called above subject status roles. Thus, a regime may look as if it exercises a legal system that has as its subjects a population, when in fact they are not its subjects at all but only subject to it. It extends a façade of legality over its operations in pretense of a legitimacy that it lacks. In a sense, no one in such a system plays their designated roles (the guards, and maybe prisoners too, pretend that the guards are not guards and the prisoners are not prisoners).

It follows from this conception of the force and authority of the law that the legal system is not simply an organization of officials, judges, legislators, prosecutors, police, etc., that is, legal officials. They play special institutional roles in the formulation and administration of the law, but they also represent the citizens (or self-conscious citizens) in general. They function as proxy agents for the self-conscious citizenry. Their authority derives from the whole community (or enough of it) for which the legal system is designed collectively accepting (for the most part) the arrangements, which include the arrangements for roles in which special authority is vested to make and change law, to adjudicate cases, to interpret law, and to determine fact and enforce its provisions, including sanctions for breaking the law. On the view of the law on which the legal system is sustained by a special class of officials (the Hartian tradition), the rest of the citizenry are conceived as like POWs, agents assigned a status role by the officials and who are provided external reasons to conform. On that view, the authority of the law with respect to citizens is external authority not internal

---

7 This is, I think, one of the primary reasons we should recognize the concept of full citizenship (assumed upon one's majority) as including the concept of participation in the sense of being party to the collective acceptance by which the legal system defining it is sustained. For this is what distinguishes being a citizen from being something analogous to a prisoner of war on parole.

authority. This is, I submit, a mistake, once we have in view the possibility of proxy agency and see the role of citizen on majority being to participate in the system and accept the laws that define citizenry in its various contexts as responsibilities internal to their roles as citizens. This is not invalidated by the fact that not everyone who is a citizen will be committed or fully committed to the law. This is just a reflection of the possibility of a gap between role defined functions and performance in the role. What is necessary is only that enough people do participate to ensure the continued stable functioning of the relevant institutions.[8]

Enforcement

Enforcement looms large in our conception of the law and much of the apparatus of the law is concerned with enforcement and adjudication. Enforcement is the result of the intersection of the design of rules that are to be accepted by those subject to them with the real-world conditions in which they are to be applied, in which the rules are to apply to jurisdictions large in both area and population, to self-interested human beings for whom following the law is not always in their immediate or even long term interest, and to successive waves of citizens regardless of whether they officially sign on to the institutions, as well as to agents temporarily in the intended jurisdiction who are not members of the relevant polis. Enforcement itself requires rules governing it, and these are rules that define status roles for those involved in enforcement and adjudication (police, judges, prosecutors, attorneys, etc.), and it is a distinctive feature of all real world legal systems. Nonetheless, it is a mistake to think that enforcement of rules over a population constitutes the essence of law or we could not distinguish ourselves from POWs.

Primary and Secondary Rules

Hart famously distinguished between primary and secondary rules.

- Primary rules are ordinary laws.

8 What about corrupt or evil regimes or countries that have been conquered and occupied? In these cases the citizens, if they act in conformity to law only under the threat of punishment, accord the law only external authority, and are in the relevant sense like POWs.

- Secondary rules are rules about rules:
  - rules of recognition (what are the criteria for something being a law),
  - rules of modification (how to change the law, including the introduction of new law),
  - rules of adjudication (how to settle the application of law in particular cases).

  In Hart's words: "rules of recognition, rules of change, and rules of adjudication" (Hart, 76–77).

On the account sketched here,

> these are all rules that define status roles and their relations to one another.

Actual legal systems all have a long and complex history. Some arise out of the explicit adoption of a constitution, but even in those cases there are often background legal systems or sets of rules within which the writing and adoption of a constitution takes place. If we think abstractly about the origination of a legal system, it is clear that functionally there need to be rules that (i) define basic roles in the system about who makes (additional) rules, and (ii) who decides on their correct application to cases, and (iii) how they are to be enforced (though we can conceive of communities in which buy-in is universal and enforcement unneeded). Rules of recognition and modification have to do with the first set of roles. What counts as law is what rules are (a) agreed upon in the initial framing in the basic institutional roles and (b) rules that are subsequently promulgated by the appropriate authority without being changed or rescinded in the meantime. The distinction between primary and secondary rules is not fully captured by the distinction between rules that define the basic roles in the system in its origin story, for these may also be subsequently revised. The rules in question here are rules defining the relevant network of institutional roles, some of which are role categories which allow, for example, for the expansion of the polis by the inclusion of additional agents in the relevant roles but some of which are fixed in number (at least at a point in time).

The rules specifying the basic network of status roles are constitutive rules. They say what it is to be engaged in this kind of joint intentional activity. Then there has to be a collective acceptance among those who realize the network of roles (or enough of them) for the network of roles to be realized in a population. Thus, this approach to understanding legal institutions solves the problem of the original authority of law without an infinite regress (or appeal to the presupposition of a Basic Norm (Kelsen 1960)). We conceptualize a system of roles; we then realize it; it includes provisions for roles whose function is to promulgate additional rules; these rules are further articulations of the role responsibility and rights of those subject to them; their authority derives from the acceptance of most members of the group of the institutional arrangements by which the lawmaker roles are defined and realized.

Hart said that the basic structures were supported by a social custom. As noted above, this is in the ballpark but not quite right. Collective acceptance of a set of status roles that is transmitted over time is a sort of social practice. But the method of reproduction is not imitation of a social practice reinforced perhaps by some social benefit as for social customs. It is rather that the roles are institutional roles and are designed to be successively occupied by different agents. The perpetuation of customs is external to their content. The perpetual succession of organizations is internal to their design. This refinement gives us a more articulate account of the grounding of legality.

Hart's rule of recognition is on this account simply an articulation of a constitutive rule for officials and citizens with respect to what defines at any time the responsibilities attaching to various roles in the legal system. The responsibility is to accept as role duties those specified by rules recognized as meeting relevant criteria.

A Puzzle about Constitutive and Regulative Rules

On my account, status roles are defined by constitutive rules. These rules define forms of joint intentional action. They specify functions that agents play in those action types. They don't specify which agents fill the roles. In this lies the possibility of institutions designed for perpetual existence together with rules for when agents occupy the roles. I have said that legal norms arise from the design function of legal status roles. Laws define role responsibilities. Thus, it seems, laws are to be conceived of as constitutive rules. Yet, some laws, it seems, are clearly regulative rules. For example, traffic laws regulate traffic but don't constitute traffic. There would be traffic (and is traffic) even if the traffic laws don't exist or are not obeyed. So how can they be constitutive rules? The answer is that constitutive rules are constitutive relative to certain activity types. In this case, it is the type: legal behavior. It is not the type: traffic. So rules that are regulative relative to one activity type may be constitutive relative to another.

4 What Makes an Institution a Legal Institution?

I have assimilated legal institutions to other sorts of institutions and argued that legal norms are a species of the norms that attach to any formal status role in virtue of the ever present potential for a gap between performance and role function. But what makes a legal institution a legal institution? Recognizing that this is a large question that many people have had a stab at, I want to hazard a tentative characterization. As the concept of a legal system is apt to be a family resemblance or prototype concept, what I aim at is the characterization of a prototype in relation to which we evaluate institutions as legal or not. A legal system is (paradigmatically) an institution, $\mathscr{L}$, that

(a) makes provision for
   (i) an institution (which may be a group with its own internal structure or an individual in the limit case) as a component of $\mathscr{L}$ that makes rules for a group of agents ("citizens" or "subjects") on the basis of the statuses in the larger institution who themselves invest it with the authority to do so, i.e., as a proxy agent for them;
   (ii) an institution (which may be a group with its own internal structure or an individual in the limit case) as a component of $\mathscr{L}$ that determines the application of the rules in light of the facts and which settles issues of interpretation;
   (iii) an institution (which may be a group of agents with its own internal structure or an individual in the limit case) as a component of $\mathscr{L}$ for the enforcement of the rules by the imposition of sanctions where there are certified violations of the rules (optional but typical);

(b) where the rules of $\mathscr{L}$
   (i) have authority over every agent in a designated territory;
   (ii) have authority over all who meet certain conditions such as being born in the territory or born to parents who are subject to the authority of the rules, meeting residency requirements, etc.;
   (iii) some significant number of whom are party to the collective acceptance by which $\mathscr{L}$ is realized;

AND

   (iv) take priority over rules and policies issued by other institutions within the territory;

OR

   (v) are recognized by a legal system $\mathscr{L}^*$, whose authority is recognized by $\mathscr{L}$, that governs a territory that subsumes $\mathscr{L}$'s territory as taking priority over all other rules and policies issued by other institutions within the territory excepting those of $\mathscr{L}^*$ which take priority over those of $\mathscr{L}$.

This is a recursive definition that allows for a hierarchy of legal systems in a territory divided into smaller units within which legal systems operate within the set of rules determined by a system that is not so subject to a subsuming system of rules.

This allows state, county, and city legal systems as genuine though their rules do not take priority over all rules that their territories are subject to in virtue of their authority being recognized ultimately by a sovereign legal system. It rules out church rules (canon law – which is merely operational policy for the church as an institution) which do not attach to a territory and the Mafia with its code which governs only its members (like the rules of a club) and not a territory.[9]

5 Conclusion

Legal norms attach to legal statuses, which are a species of status role. The norms are constitutive rules for the roles. To be governed by the rules is to perform the role as designed. Having the role does not require fulfilling the function. So though the role of citizen on majority is conceived of as an agent status role, the role attaches independently of whether one accepts it or performs its functions perfectly or even passably. It is this gap between role function and performance that give rise to the use of the language of duties and rights. The norms specify the regulative ideal. The norms are socially constructed in this sense. Realizing a set of status roles is something that people do together

9 The recursive characterization offered here is intended to answer a challenge issued by Scott Shapiro that motivates his "Moral Aim Thesis," namely, that "the fundamental aim of legal activity is to remedy the moral deficiencies of the circumstances of legality" (Shapiro, p. 213), namely, that otherwise we cannot distinguish the law from other institutions of planning like those of a criminal organization. That law has essentially a moral aim would seem to be refuted by the observation that it makes sense for a society of high functioning psychopaths to institute a legal system with robust mechanisms for enforcement, transparency, and checks and balances for practical purposes, for the order which such a system brings into economic and social life that supports self-centered pursuits that would otherwise not be able to flourish. One might say that even such a system solves moral problems, if one regards "questions about ownership, contractual obligations, . . . proper levels of taxation, limitations on public power, legitimacy of state coercion" as moral problems, except that it is not regarded by its realizers as having that as its goal. They are not trying to solve moral but practical problems. If I help save a drowning child, I do what is morally right, but my aim need not be to do what is morally right: I may do it expecting a reward, or an accretion to my reputation which I expect to gain an advantage from.

intentionally. Absent a network of status roles being realized by a set of agents acting together under the conception of the network as instantiating a legal system, there are no legal status roles, and, hence, no legal norms (or none that apply to anyone). Other norms that might attach to occupancy of legal positions are derivative from extra-legal norms and the circumstances of occupying the relevant legal position. The authority of legal norms derives from those subject to them authorizing those who promulgate them to determine and modify status roles that they occupy. The authority rests in the commitment of those canonically subject to them to realize the network of institutions that realize the legal system. They have internal reasons to obey the law. Those whose reasons for conforming to the law consist in fear of sanctions are not properly a part of the group that sustains the institutions. They have only external reasons to obey the law.

In summary, we can list some of the advantages of the status role account of legal norms:

- It grounds the law in large scale collective intentional action vindicating, and giving precise content to, the social fact theory of legal norms and the claim that legal norms are socially constructed.
- It exhibits legal institutions as continuous with other institutions and explains legal norms in the same way as norms attaching to status roles in general.
- It explains the requirement that laws be general.
- It is flexible enough to encompass as wide a range of rules as may govern, guide, restrict, and promote behavior and the assignments of powers, rights, duties, permissions.
- It explains why law should be written so that it is acceptable to its core subjects, since they are (by design to be) party to the collective acceptance by which legal officials have their roles and in virtue of which they are representatives of the laws core subjects.
- It explains why those subject to the law are not analogous to POWs.

References

Austin, John. 1971. *The Provice of Jurisprudence Determined*. London: Weidenfeld and Nicolson.

Bratman, Michael. 2014. *Shared Agency: A Planning Theory of Acting Together*. Oxford: Oxford University Press.

Gilbert, Margaret. 2009. "Shared Intention and Personal Intentions." *Philosophical Studies* 144 (1):167–187.
Hart, H. L. A. 1961. *The Concept of Law*. Oxford: Clarendon Press.
Hayek, Friedrich. 1969. *Law, Legislation and Liberty*. London: Routldge and Kegan Paul.
Kelsen, Hans. 1960. *Reine Rechtslehre*. Vienna: Deuticke.
Lewis, David. 1986. *Convention: A Philosophical Study*. Cambridge: Harvard Univ Press.
Ludwig, Kirk. 2014. "Proxy Agency in Collective Action." *Nous* 48 (1).
Ludwig, Kirk. 2016. *From Individual to Plural Agency: Collective Action 1*. 2 vols. Oxford: Oxford University Press.
Ludwig, Kirk. 2017a. *From Plural to Institutional Agency: Collective Action 2*. 2 vols. Oxford: Oxford University Press.
Ludwig, Kirk. 2017b. "Proxy Agency." In *The Routledge Handbook on Collective Intentionality*. New York: Routledge.
Ludwig, Kirk. 2020. "Proxy Assertion." In *Oxford Handbook on Assertion*, edited by Sanford Goldberg. Oxford: Oxford University Press.
Searle, John. 1995. *The Construction of Social Reality*. New York: Free Press.
Searle, John R. 1990. " Collective Intentions and Actions." In *Intentions in Communication*, edited by Philip R. Cohen, Jerry Morgan and Martha E. Pollack, 401–415. Cambridge, Mass.: MIT Press.
Shapiro, Scott. 2011. *Legality*. Cambridge, Mass.: Harvard University Press.
Tuomela, Raimo. 2005. "We-Intentions Revisited." *Philosophical Studies* 125:327–369.
Tuomela, Raimo. 2013. *Social Ontology: Collective Intentionality and Group Agents*. New York, NY: Oxford University Press.

Pekka Mäkelä and Raul Hakli

Identity of Corporations: Against the Shareholder View

1 Introduction

Corporate agents, corporate action, and socially responsible corporate actions are topics of multidisciplinary discussion and debate in social sciences aiming at social relevance. Corporate agency and corporate action are ubiquitous in social life. In the globalization debate it is pretty much taken for granted that in today's world the role of corporations is growing as corporations are taking over some roles and responsibilities traditionally attributed to a state (see, e.g, Sorsa 2008). Understanding and being able to explain them are crucial for understanding the object of study in various social scientific fields, such as economics, political science, and sociology.

From a theoretical and philosophical point of view there are many questions concerning corporations yet to be answered including such as: How to conceptualize corporations? If we see corporations and firms as purely economic organizations, how should we go about their analysis? If we understand, like for instance some sociologists in the Marxist camp, corporations as not only economic organizations but as political institutions as well, how should we go about their analysis? What are the implications of the various alternative ways of understanding corporations? How are they to be evaluated? It seems that the rules of the game are slightly different depending on the stance we take on the economic vs political organization issue?

Corporations are part of the socially constructed world. From this it follows that they could "be" in many ways depending on how the relevant "we" ends up constructing them. If so, it makes sense to ask what would be a good way to construct them? What are the success criteria for answering this kind of question?

On the one hand, as hinted above, it seems that we can analyse corporations from a neutral perspective or at least from a point of view that does not take a normative or political stance explicitly. Having done that we can then try and squeeze out the potential implications, if any, for normative or political debates. We can then check the compatibility of such implications with the implicit background assumptions of the analysis.

On the other hand, it seems that we can openly start with a sociological, normative or political stance and use these views to locate the functions and

https://doi.org/10.1515/9783110663617-012

roles of corporations, and then proceed to providing an analysis of the entities fulfilling these roles and functions.

In this paper we discuss Kirk Ludwig's (2017) approach to corporations, which stems from the arguably normatively and politically non-committal discussions and debates in, to a large extent, overlapping fields of collective action theory, collective intentionality, and social ontology. Here we very briefly try and give an overview of the landscape of that literature. In a broad sense the subject of study of these fields is collectively intentional phenomena such as collective action, collective intentions, collective beliefs, collective goals, social groups, social structures and social institutions etc.

The background of the collective intentionality literature again in a general sense is in the single agent action theory and the generic conceptual apparatus used is the folk-psychology or agency framework. Unsurprisingly, one of the central questions in the collective intentionality literature is, analogously with the single agent action theory: What is a collective agent? Agents in general can be understood roughly as entities that can act and function intentionally. Can collectives be agents, and if so, how? What about corporations, can corporations be agents, and if so, what kind of agents would they be?

The question of agency is obviously an interesting metaphysical question in its own right but it also has practical relevance, e.g., from the point of view of legal and moral responsibility. Indeed, the debate concerning collective moral and legal responsibility is one of the central and rapidly growing areas in the collective intentionality literature.

The discussion of collective agency and collectively intentional phenomena more generally has historically been divided into two broad camps: individualism and collectivism. In their extreme forms, individualism claims that only individuals can be agents and all agency is individual agency whereas collectivism claims that both individuals and collectives can be agents, and hence there is both individual and collective agency. However, as the study of these phenomena has progressed and become more subtle and sophisticated the use of such labels as "individualism" and "collectivism" is perhaps more misleading and confusing than enlightening. The field has become rather fine-grained and such a coarse dichotomy has become uninformative. One might say that most of the positions in the field in their peculiar ways, and with their distinctive subtle twists, gravitate towards some form of interrelationism that is individualistic in the sense that only individuals can be agents but admits various kinds of adjustments or extensions to that basic position in order to account for a phenomenon of joint agency that springs from individuals acting together, in particular, in order to achieve collective goals. This is not to say that flat-foot individualists or stand-up collectivists are non-existent.

Well-organized collectives or social groups with a decision-making structure are strong candidates for collective agents over and above individual agents. They are among the hotly debated objects in this literature. One way to analyse corporations is in terms of the analysis of social groups. As they are ordinarily understood, groups consists of members, they collectively accept group's goals and other intentional states for the group, and this enables talk of group attitudes like group beliefs and group goals. Their existence in turn enables the group members to pursue these group goals in light of the group's beliefs, thereby creating forms of joint agency. There can be both organized and unorganized groups. In organized groups, members have various roles, positions, duties, etc., and there are rules and decision-making mechanisms that govern the actions of the individuals in their roles, creates coherence in their endeavours, and gives them their identity as a group. These roles, positions, etc. are socially constructed, and hence, organized groups, such as corporations, can be seen as social institutions. Investigation of institutions and institutional facts is one of the core issues of social ontology that, broadly taken, studies and analyses the nature of the man-made reality. The study of institutions and institutional facts was kicked off by Searle's 1995 book *The Construction of Social Reality* (Searle 1995).

Searle's path-opening account of institutional facts was built on three core elements: collective intentionality, status functions, and constitutive rules. On the basis of these he introduced the "magic formula" of the construction of social reality, namely "X counts as Y in C". Status functions are collectively imposed functions on an entity such that the entity in question could not have the function in virtue of its physical or inherent properties but only in virtue of collective acceptance, which is an instance of collective intentionality, by the relevant collective for which the entity will fulfil the function in question, e.g., a traffic post. Constitutive rules, roughly, are rules that not only regulate but enable new forms of behaviour, e.g., chess playing.

In what follows we will focus on an account of corporations presented by Kirk Ludwig, who in the agency question is one of the most sophisticated and convincing representatives of the individualist position. In developing his account, he also draws on and modifies Searle's position of institutions and status functions.

2 Kirk Ludwig's Shareholder View of Corporations

Ludwig (2017) considers whether corporations are agents and presents a deflationary account of corporate agency. He takes corporations to represent the strongest case for a collectivistic understanding of group agency because corporations have certain special features that suggest that talk about their agency and attitudes cannot be reduced to talk about the agency and attitudes of their members. In the account of collective action presented in his recent book (Ludwig 2016), only individuals are agents, and discourse about corporate agency and corporate attitudes can be analysed individualistically. His paper aims at showing that such an analysis can be extended to the case of corporations. If successful, this would constitute a strong argument against collectivism as corporations are commonly taken as the most plausible case of collective agents.

Ludwig's strategy is to start from platitudes about corporations that his account should explain. To give some examples, this includes such commonplace ideas that (1) a corporation is designed for perpetual existence that is not determined by the existence of those individuals that realize it at any time, (3) a corporation may undertake projects that last longer than the lives of any of those who play a role in its realization, (5) a corporation is a legal person, (11) corporations can engage in actions which it does not make sense to speak even of groups of people engaging in, such as merging with other corporations, and (12) talk about what the corporation intends, says, or believes, or its interests, is evidently not a matter of saying what all its employees, or managers, or shareholders intend, say, believe, or what their interests are, individually, or as a group (Ludwig 2017, 266–67).

The machinery he employs consists of Davidsonian logical analysis of plural action sentences, the idea of social construction including constitutive rules, status functions, and status roles, and the idea of proxy agency. Roughly, according to his analysis, sentences attributing plural action to groups can be understood in terms of individuals performing their part-actions with an intention to bring it about that we act according to a shared plan to act together. Action sentences about institutions, in particular, corporations, differ in certain ways from ordinary plural action sentences, but at the end of the day, they admit a similar individualistic analysis. This requires understanding membership in institutions to be socially constructed, along broadly Searlean lines: Institutions are systems of status roles, designed for coordinating joint action in pursuit of collective goals over time (p. 275). A status role is a collectively accepted status function ascribed to a person, such that, the person accepts it, possibly tacitly, along with others and that requires and enables them to exercise their agency in specific ways in specific circumstances (p. 274). Corporations as certain kinds of institutions are constituted from the inside via such a collective acceptance of status roles.

Viewed from the outside, the existence of corporations requires as a constitutive element a legal recognition that is codified in the corporate law. A corporation is formed by an individual or a group filing articles of incorporation. According to Ludwig, this legal act does not bring into existence a new entity but rather a new status for the individual or the group incorporating. The new status enables the individual or the group to manage the assets set aside for the purposes of the corporation (in a legally protected manner, i.e., entity shielding: priority rules covering the treatment of creditors, liquidation protection, and limited liability). The initial owners of the corporation are its first shareholders. Their investment in the company constitutes the assets it is to manage.

Typically corporations are hierarchically organised. The shareholders may employ managers and officers who work for the corporation. In the case of large-scale corporations it is common to have a two-tier management system with a board of directors (tasks and function) and officers who constitute the highest level of day-to-day management of the corporation. The board and officers, managers and employees are proxy agents for the shareholders. The shareholders are, according to Ludwig, strictly speaking the corporation.

According to Ludwig's account, when a corporation acts, it is indeed the shareholders acting through their proxies. That is the board, officers, managers and employees qua proxies act in the name of the shareholders who constitute the corporation. A somewhat surprising fall out of Ludwig's account as to the intentional actions of a corporation is that when a corporation performs an action intentionally, it does not act intentionally under the description under which the proxies, via whose actions the corporation acts, perform their acts but rather only under a much more general description such as maximising return on shareholder investment. This seems like an action theory characterisation of the well-known shareholder value doctrine. According to this doctrine of corporate governance, corporations should be run primarily in the interests of shareholders. (For history and critique, see, e.g., Lazonick and O'Sullivan 2000; Hillman and Keim 2001.)

In the end, what we get is that:

1. We can explain "platitudinal" sentences without postulating corporate agents *qua* agents of their own, that is, individualism about corporate agents.
2. According to Ludwig, he can construe an argument to the effect that corporations are to be identified with shareholders, on the basis of above machinery.
3. Legal fiction claims, according to which the idea of corporations as legal persons need not be taken literally but can be understood as a "legal fiction". Ludwig writes: "While corporations have their life only within a larger institutional setting, namely within a legal system, nonetheless they are individuated by their origins and in particular by the act that brings them into existence in the eyes of the law, the filing of papers of incorporation. The filers are the incorporators and their identity determines the identity of the

corporation across possible worlds. If another group had beaten a particular group in filing articles of incorporation in a given jurisdiction with an identical name, business address, corporate purposes, registered agent and stock information, it would be a distinct corporation."

4. Analysis of corporate attitudes in terms of collectively accepted statements or goals that the members of the corporations are committed to in their actions specified by their status roles – in contrast to real mental states requiring something like a collective mind.

3 Criticism of the Shareholder View

As to Ludwig's methodology, his starting point is agreeable and reminiscent of that of Frank Jackson (1998) applied to the study of corporations: We should collect together the central platitudes concerning corporations to be employed in the identification of the central functions of corporations as they are commonly understood. This is required in order to identify the target of talk about corporations. Perhaps, due to his main aim concerning the agency of corporations, Ludwig's view on central platitudes used in the identification of the "thing" we want to study is narrower. A broader class of platitudes would include facts about the societal functions of corporations and the constitutive role of law in the existence of corporations and corporate actions.

Corporations as entities should be located and seen as embedded in the institutional web of democratic societies, and their functioning on multiple levels should be seen as interaction with other agents and agencies in such a web. On the one hand, corporations enjoy the facilitation by democratic societies, e.g., roads and educated employees, etc., and, on the other hand, they contribute to the functioning of the society: By way of providing work, they contribute to the factors constitutive of people's identity. In addition they contribute to the economy by paying taxes, providing goods and services, etc. Corporations are not functioning in a morally free zone.

One dimension of the features of embeddedness and interaction within societies is that law is an essential institution in democratic societies. Citizens in democratic societies through and by their democratic decision-making procedures create and make the law. Law is created by the people for the people. Law is also constitutive to the existence and recognition of corporations. Without the recognition of law they could not function as actors in societies, for instance, they could not make any binding contracts nor agreements. If there was no such mechanism of recognition the rest of the society could not make agreements and contracts with such actors. There would not be a single action of corporations without law. Hence, law is constitutive of corporations as agents.

Ludwig also thinks that "corporations are creatures of the law": they are created by the law and they are recognized as persons by the law. However, according to him, to treat a corporation as a person for the purposes of contract law is to engage in "legal fiction". This is one standard position in the discussions concerning corporate personhood. It is one thing to commit oneself to the fiction theory as to the corporations as legal persons. It is another thing that the role and the function of the law, in the constitution of corporations or corporate agents, be they ontologically whatever, is fictitious. We can live with the idea that when it comes to the legal personhood of corporations, the fiction theory is possibly right, but when it comes to the existence and reality of corporations, it is hard to see the role of the law as fictitious. Law has concrete effects on people's lives: If a contract is void because it did not satisfy the relevant legal clauses they may end up in prison or pay the corporation's debts themselves.

Furthermore, it is not clear how Ludwig can drive the wedge between the legal aspect being a fiction and the socially constructed institutional aspect being non-fiction. To say the least, it seems that if the legal construction is fiction, then everything else that is socially constructed is fiction as well. From where we stand, these institutional and socially constructed aspects seem to be on a par.

What we are hoping to do in the further development of this project is to provide the basis for identifying corporations in such a way that it is consistent with and communicates with empirical research on corporations in the social sciences.

Kirk Ludwig's reasoning and argumentation aims at defending a sort of individualism with respect to corporate agents. That seems to be the primary aim of his paper. His analysis of collective and corporate action sentences reveals that we can talk about collective and corporate action without being forced to accept the existence of collective or corporate agents with "minds of their own". However, as a fallout, he is also offering an account of corporations that identifies corporations to the set of their shareholders. Here we are not criticizing the main claim of his paper, it is the identification of corporations to the shareholders which worries us.

At face value, the identification claim comes across as counterintuitive, even anti- empirical, as one might say, in light of the following kinds of common-sensical "facts" about corporations: Attributions of actions and attitudes to corporations are often made from an external perspective, on the basis of actions and expressed attitudes of the managers and employees. Moreover, most of the actions of the corporations are constituted by actions of the managers and employees. Shareholders do not necessarily participate in the corporation's activities, or even be aware of them. Also from the point of view of political and legal institutions, actions and responsibility are attributed to proxies and the legal person instead of shareholders: Moral and criminal responsibility falls on individuals in constitutive roles of actions attributed to the corporation.

The identification claim is not insignificant but has interesting consequences due to its close connection to the shareholder value doctrine mentioned earlier. It would be useful to meticulously study what is Ludwig's argument for it. Somewhat surprisingly, in our view, Ludwig does not provide an explicit argument with a conclusion stating that corporations are to be identified with their shareholders, but rather a story to tell, a story about how corporations are created and how they are to be understood in terms of constitutive roles and proxy agency. The implicit argument in the background seems to be that of an argument to the best explanation: Ludwig's individualistic story is capable of explaining the platitudes concerning corporations and is ontologically more parsimonious than competing collectivistic accounts that postulate a stronger notion of group agency.

3.1 Individuation of Corporations

What are the individuation criteria for corporations? Should we aim at fitting corporations into our general (reductive or Occamian) ontology, as Ludwig seems to be doing, or make sense of them in terms of a constructivist approach that accommodates the external perspective and takes into account legal aspects and societal functions of corporations? Obviously, this is not a politically or normatively innocent choice but can have several normative implications. Ludwig's account seems like a good match with the shareholder value doctrine. Given that corporations are identical with their shareholders, a corporation's interests can be identified with the shareholders' interests. Hence, it is in the best interest of a corporation to maximize "shareholder value", that is, to act in order to maximize the value of the shares of the corporation.

However, it has been argued from a societal perspective that corporations serve many other functions or have social responsibilities over and above shareholder value maximisation. In addition to the contributions they make and are expected to make to their local communities discussed above, such functions and responsibilities can be seen even more important in the world of globalisation in which multi-national corporations take over tasks and duties traditionally ascribed to the state. For example, pharmaceutical companies are expected to donate drugs and vaccines to Third World countries, and manufacturing companies are expected to comply to more demanding norms concerning child labour than those that are in force in the local communities in which they operate (see, e.g., Hillman and Keim 2001).

From the perspective of such societal functions, the shareholder value doctrine has sometimes been argued to be detrimental to the corporation considered as an entity of its own (see, e.g., Chang 2010). For instance, it can be understood to be detrimental to the number and well-being of the employees, investments for the future, quality of products and services, reputation, etc. Such matters, however, are relevant for the long-term interest of the corporation. If this were the case, it might seem easy to construct a conceptual argument to the effect that if the interests of shareholders can be different from the interests of the corporation, these two entities cannot be identical with each other. However, this would be too quick, because one could still understand the set of shareholders to be extended in time so that future investments can be seen to eventually profit the shareholders even though they don't benefit the current set of shareholders.

However, even if we understand the set of shareholders to be temporally extended, the shareholder value doctrine has been criticised by arguing that the survival and long-term profitability of corporations depends also on their capacity to fulfil their social tasks to distribute value and wealth to a larger set of primary stakeholders that includes not only shareholders but employees, suppliers, customers, community residents, and the governments and communities that provide infrastructures, markets, and regulations (Clarkson 1995). The idea is that effective management of relationships with primary stakeholders can contribute to these stakeholders' willingness to continue their relationship with the corporation and, moreover, it can create intangible social resources that may enhance corporations' competitive performance in the long run. As Clarkson (1995) says: "[. . .] the corporation itself can be defined as a system of primary stakeholder groups, a complex set of relationships between and among interest groups with different rights, objectives, expectations, and responsibilities. The corporation's survival and continuing success depend upon the ability of its managers to create sufficient wealth, value, or satisfaction for those who belong to each stakeholder group, so that each group continues as a part of the corporation's stakeholder system."

Such claims have been supported by empirical studies that show a positive correlation between stakeholder management and shareholder value creation and, furthermore, suggest that the causal direction is from the former to the latter (Hillman and Keim 2001). This is in contrast to proponents of the shareholder value maxim who argue that increased wealth of capital investors will eventually spread to the larger community.

Of course, in spite of the compatibility between the shareholder value maxim and Ludwig's identification of corporation to its shareholders, we are not claiming that Ludwig is committed to the shareholder value maxim. He can maintain that even though a corporation is identical with its shareholders and hence whatever is in a corporation's interest must be in the interest of its shareholders, the policy recommendation assumed by the maxim does not follow: Just as narrow egoism may not be the best policy for an individual to pursue her interests, also the narrow goal of maximizing shareholder value may not be the most fruitful corporate policy in the long run.

Hence, even though what is said above by no means constitutes a knock-out argument against Ludwig's identity claim, however, it seems to us to underline and emphasize the surprising nature of Ludwig's claim and raises the question how well it coheres with empirical studies of corporations. Whereas the approach identifying corporations with a broad class of social functions seems to do justice to both our platitudes concerning corporations and empirical studies concerning well-functioning corporations. The identity claim is evermore surprising as Ludwig himself has the tension between his strong identification claim and his constructivist view on that nature of corporations as systems of status roles: As he writes, "[. . .] organizations in general, including corporations, considered as types, are types of types of systems of status roles." This presupposes a constructivist point of view to which we turn next.

3.2 Constructivist Argument

The ontology of corporations can be understood along constructivist lines: corporations are part of the man-made institutional reality. This aspect of construction involves two perspectives, an internal and an external. From the internal perspective, the institutional elements of a corporation are determined and maintained by shareholders and other operative members, typically employees. From this perspective we can understand the internal organisation of a corporation and its nature as a system of status roles. Corporations can also be viewed from an external perspective: The existence of corporations presupposes multiple layers of institutions, law, market economy, etc. Corporations are maintained by the collective acceptance of the relevant community: The capacity of corporations to function in their societal role is facilitated and enabled by the institution of law – a corporate arrangement must satisfy a definite set of conditions to be able to make legally binding contracts, for instance.

Ludwig very well explains the internal perspective, but perhaps to an extent neglects the external perspective. It is not possible for the shareholders and other operative members to create a corporation and the status roles it requires by its own collective acceptance alone. The recognition by law of institutional elements (structure) of a corporation justifies and enables the constitution relation between the actions of the operative members and the actions attributed to the corporation. To make sense of the agency of corporations we need collective acceptance of different "we"s, the internal "we" of a corporation and the broader "we" of a society collectively accepting the law for itself. Agency in the case of corporations seems to presuppose both an internal perspective and an external perspective.

Law is a part of the external perspective, and law is a *sine qua non* for the intentional capacity of corporations. From this it seems to follow that Ludwig's account identifying the corporate agency with the collective agency of shareholders is wanting. Also his understanding of corporate personhood as "legal fiction" suggests that his account does not do justice for the social reality of corporations understood in terms of their societal role and their legal individuation: Societal recognition of corporate agency is constitutive of such agency.

4 Conclusion

From a normative point of view, the constructivist story can be seen as emancipatory and optimistic. Corporations are dependent on laws which are socially constructed, maintained, and renewed by a large collective of people. This means that corporations can also change and be changed by a collective effort. This applies not only to actual corporations, but also to the nature of corporations: What counts as a corporation in a given society depends on the collective acceptance of the society's members. The rest of the society is not at the mercy of corporate agents as long as the law is setting the bar for such agents as corporations to function. This provides the rest of the society with an opportunity to set the bar higher for corporate agents. For instance, the society may demand real social responsibility in place of white wash and set high requirements for conditions of corporate citizenship, and this may indeed be in the interest of citizens if corporations are taking over the duties of the state.

All this is not to say that changing the nature of corporations is practically easy or even doable, but ontically speaking it is a live possibility, and suggestions to that effect have already been made, for instance, by Isabelle Ferreras (2017). She has argued that corporations face what she calls a "bicameral moment". They should grant the same rights to "labour investors", that is, employees, as the ones held by capital investors. She proposes a democratic model of corporate decision-making where 50 per cent of votes is assigned to workers and 50 per cent to owners of corporations. This model, albeit not in use as far as we know, is certainly conceivable, and as such it undermines Ludwig's account which identifies corporations with their owners. Hence, Ludwig's account cannot be a conceptual truth about the nature of corporations.

Acknowledgement: This research has been supported by the Academy of Finland.

References

Chang, Ha-Joon. 2010. *23 Things They Don't Tell You About Capitalism*. Penguin Books Limited, London, England.

Clarkson, Max E. 1995. "A Stakeholder Framework for Analyzing and Evaluating Corporate Social Performance." *Academy of Management Review* 20 (1). Academy of Management Briarcliff Manor, NY 10510:92–117.

Ferreras, Isabelle. 2017. *Firms as Political Entities: Saving Democracy Through Economic Bicameralism*. Cambridge: Cambridge University Press.

Hillman, Amy J, and Gerald D Keim. 2001. "Shareholder Value, Stakeholder Management, and Social Issues: What's the Bottom Line?" *Strategic Management Journal* 22 (2). Wiley Online Library:125–39.

Jackson, Frank. 1998. *From Metaphysics to Ethics: A Defence of Conceptual Analysis*. Oxford: Oxford University Press.

Lazonick, William, and Mary O'Sullivan. 2000. "Maximizing Shareholder Value: A New Ideology for Corporate Governance." *Economy and Society* 29 (1). Taylor & Francis:13–35.

Ludwig, Kirk. 2016. *From Individual to Plural Agency: Collective Action (Vol. 1)*. Oxford: Oxford University Press.

Ludwig, Kirk. 2017. "Do Corporations Have Minds of Their Own?" *Philosophical Psychology* 30 (3):265–97.

Searle, John R. 1995. *The Construction of Social Reality*. New York, USA: The Free Press.

Sorsa, V.-P. 2008. "How to Explain Socially Responsible Corporate Actions Institutionally: Theoretical and Methodological Critique." *EJBO Electronic Journal of Business Ethics and Organization Studies* 13 (1):32–41.

Michael Schmitz

Of Layers and Lawyers

1 Introduction

How can the law be characterized in a theory of collective intentionality that treats collective intentionality as essentially layered and tries to understand these layers in terms of the structure and the format of the representations involved? And can such a theory of collective intentionality open up new perspectives on the law and shed new light on traditional questions of legal philosophy? As a philosopher of collective intentionality who is new to legal philosophy, I want to begin exploring these questions in this paper. I will try to characterize the law in terms of a layered account of collective intentionality such as the one I have sketched in some earlier writings (Schmitz 2013; 2018). In the light of this account I will then discuss a traditional question in the philosophy of law: the relation between law and morality.

I begin by giving a brief sketch of a layered account of collective intentionality in the next section. Collective intentionality should be understood in terms of experiencing and representing others as co-subjects, rather than as objects, of intentional states and acts on different layers or levels. I distinguish the nonconceptual layer of the joint sensory-motor-emotional intentionality of joint attention and joint bodily action, the conceptual level of shared we-mode beliefs, intentions, obligations, values, and so on, and the institutional level characterized through role differentiation, positions taken in role-mode, e.g. as a judge or attorney, and writing and other forms of documentation. In the third section I introduce a set of parameters for representations such as their degree of richness, of context-dependence, of density and differentiation of representational role and of durability and stability, which can be used to more precisely distinguish different layers or levels. I also put forward the hypothesis that these properties are connected and tend to cluster, and that higher levels can only function and determine conditions of satisfaction against lower level ones. In the fourth and final section I critically discuss the sharp positivistic separation of morality and the law according to which whether something is a law is completely independent of its moral merits. I argue that this only seems plausible if we take an observational stance towards the law, but not towards morality. When we treat them the same way, it rather appears that the moral attitudes of the co-subjects of a society will determine whether and to what extent they will accept its legal order. I conclude by proposing to think of the law as being itself an institutionalized form of morality.

https://doi.org/10.1515/9783110663617-013

2 Layers of Collective Intentionality

Let me use a toy example to illustrate the idea of different layers of collective intentionality. Imagine some kids who evolve a game, a practice of kicking a ball around. Let us further imagine, a bit, but hopefully not too artificially, that this only happens at what I will call the "sensory-motor-emotional" level or layer, without yet involving concepts and language. They kick the ball around and respond to each other's kicking emotionally. In this way the point of the game – if there is such a thing – can be established in their joint interactions, and also what are good and admirable moves, what are rude ones, and so on. Of course, the game can only be roughly delineated in this way. Many things will remain indeterminate. But the players may still develop some sense of what they should do and what not. However, they may still be unable to conceptualize this sense, or may in any case not have done so yet. They may not think, they may not reflect about the game yet. And so their sense of what's right or wrong in the game may remain tied to the context of actually playing it.

Their understanding of the game and its normativity takes place on the pre-conceptual level. I think we should also take seriously the fact that they have not yet formulated rules for the game. Philosophers (and linguists, psychologists and others) often tend to take for granted that rules would have to be involved in such scenarios, especially when we speak of normativity. Terminologically of course it is quite sensible to assume that normativity should involve the presence of rules. But it is said too easily that rules are being followed "implicitly" and "unconsciously" when they have not yet been formulated. This is at best handwaving: it says that what is going on is in some way like what is going on when rules are being followed, but it does not tell us in which way. Worse yet, talk of unconscious rule following can suggest that we can just subtract consciousness from rules, but leave their intentionality (and causality) unchanged. And it may tempt us to disregard what is actually going on in consciousness at this level of social interaction – our sensory-motor -emotional experience. We often just operate on a sense of what is right or wrong which is manifest in this experience: in our perceptual experience of what others are doing, and our actional and emotional experience of our responses to it. We sense that something is right or wrong, but are often unable to articulate a relevant rule and to conceptualize the situation. I emphasize this because there is a deep-seated tendency in philosophy, but also in psychology, cognitive science and common sense, to conflate the conscious with the conceptual and therefore to disregard non-conceptual forms of consciousness (for more discussion see Schmitz 2013; 2011).

In light of this we may want to reserve the term "normativity" for competencies that involve the actual use of rules and instead use the term "protonormativity" at the sensory-motor-emotional level. What is crucial though is that, first, even at this level already action-guiding representational states such as having a sense of what's right or appropriate are in play, and that, second, such states may also have a social and collective dimension. Again, this dimension need not and at this level does not come in through conceptualization. At this level it is just manifest in that we experience others as co-subjects, as members of our group, and that this experience brings with it or triggers dispositions for joint action and a sense of how things are done in this group. We often operate on the basis of such a sense of what is appropriate in certain groups, but not others. There is a sense of how we do various things for various we's. For example, Alex may play with the ball differently when he plays with Harry and Peter than when he plays with Tom and Terence because these groups have evolved different games. (Of course, this is not to deny the importance of exchange between groups, often mediated through individuals who are members in both.) Experimental data show that from an early age, children are sensitive to the different normative constraints imposed by different co-subjects of joint action. The very same objective stimulus can trigger different action schemata when it comes from different co-subjects, depending on which if any joint activity the co-subjects have been engaged in. For example, in a study by Liebal et al. (2009) one-year old infants, who had been cleaning toys into a basket with an adult, put a toy into the basket when this adult pointed at it. But when a different adult performed the same pointing action, they mostly just handed the toy to him (see also Tomasello 2014, 55; and Schmitz 2016 for discussion).

At the next level, patterns and practices are conceptualized and become the object of deliberation, of debate, thought and reflection. Various relevant concepts such as "goal", "free kick", "penalty", "penalty box", "offside" and so on, will be introduced, and rules will be formulated and negotiated. A name for the game may likewise be introduced, and perhaps various versions of it may begin to be distinguished, as we now distinguish football – what Americans call "soccer" – from American and Australian football. This also means that the co-subjects of these versions – the people who play by their rules – can be identified conceptually – as "footballers" – and not just in the immediate context of joint action, as we just imagined. Relevant concepts also include concepts for various roles within the game – "goalie", "midfielder", "striker" etc., but also "referee". Such concepts will reflect a prior specialization or role differentiation, but they will also tend to promote and further such role differentiation as e.g. when teams are asked who their striker or midfielder is.

One important function of concepts is that they allow us to anticipate scenarios that haven't yet been encountered in practice. In fact, concepts almost force us into this, through the generality of thought that they bring with them and the fact that they tend to be parts of whole systems of concepts. In this way, conceptual thinking is very conducive to creating a whole system of rules for a game that is formulated in terms of interlocking concepts.

So far, I am assuming that we are talking about concepts and rules as passed on in the oral tradition. Another important step occurs when people start to write down rules. This makes it possible for the rules to be much more stable and to be distributed more widely. It is also an important amplifier of the power of conceptual thought. Writing the rules down makes it much easier to systematize them and to make them consistent.

Codifying the rules is not the only important function enabled by writing. Writing also makes various forms of documentation possible: e.g. the referee may be required to write and sign a report of the game; a team to list its players, who in turn may have to be licensed by the league in which they are playing or by some other supervisory body. The committees who run these bodies will document their meetings and the status of its members. The incredibly rich and elaborated institutional structure that we find in contemporary sports organizations such as, for example, the international football body FIFA, is certainly inconceivable without writing and other forms of documentation.

Given this rough sketch of an example of different layers of collective intentionality, where should we say that the law begins here? I've used this example so that certain patterns become discernible without immediately bringing in charged questions associated with central instances of the law and its application. For purposes of this question, our example can be taken in a straightforward and literal as well as in a more metaphorical sense. That is, we may ask: "where does sports law begin?". But we may also ask: "if we find an example of collective intentionality of a structure analogous to what I have described as our second layer, the layer where concept application begins, but in a domain which is a central domain for the application of legal structures such as, for example, the domain of marriage, would we think of this as sufficient for the existence of a legal system?" That is, if a society has certain concepts concerning marriage and a more or less elaborate system of corresponding rules, some of which may be connected to sanctions, and this system is passed on in the oral tradition and functions in the context of and against the background of the customs, traditions and practices of a people, should we say then that they have a proper legal system concerning marriage?

If we go by the first interpretation of our question, I suppose the answer is that we would speak of sports law only in the context of an elaborate system of sports bodies that certainly requires writing and other forms of documentation. And some philosophers such as Maurizio Ferraris (2015) have taken a general position in the theory of institutional reality – of which the law certainly is a prime example – according to which institutional reality and even collective intentionality in general depend on documentation. On such a view a legal system would also generally require documentation.

Such a view seems rather radical though. There certainly appear to be e.g. practices of treating something as somebody's property which do not require written documentation of property and perhaps not even a concept of property. Common law marriage would also seem to provide a counterexample. Common law marriages are legally recognized in some jurisdictions without a marriage ceremony and written documentation, solely on the basis of having lived together for a specified amount of time and presenting as man and wife – same-sex relationships are not recognized as common law marriages. Presenting as such surely includes referring to themselves as such with relevant concepts. Similarly, the Gender Recognition Act in the UK enables the legal recognition of the gender of transgender people who have lived in this gender for at least two years and who present themselves accordingly.

One might still try to argue that only the recognition by the authorities of the marriage or gender – which does involve documentation – is a proper legal act. But the claim that a proper legal system requires writing and documentation would be counter to the practice e.g. in anthropology where legal systems are ascribed to many preliterate societies. My aim here though is not to decide this kind of issue and defend a specific definition of the notion of "law". I believe the boundaries of this concept could be legitimately drawn more narrowly or more widely depending on what one is interested in. My purpose is rather to situate the law in a theory of layers of collective intentionality and to argue that key parameters which can be used to identify such layers in the theory of intentionality and intentional content can also be used to identify the dimensions which are crucial for questions of this kind. That is, I want to show that wherever one may want to draw the line between morality and a legal system, properties of this kind are crucial. Moreover, such properties cannot only be used to define a boundary between legal systems and morality, they can also be used to determine how elaborate and advanced a legal system is. Before I come to this, however, I need to say a bit more about the structure of collective intentionality on these different layers.

I believe the key to understanding collective intentionality is in terms of co-subjects jointly taking theoretical and practical positions towards the world in a self-aware way (Schmitz 2018). This happens on different layers of collective intentionality which correspond to the three layers I roughly distinguished in the football example.

1. The level of the mode of joint attention and joint (bodily) action. On this level the intentionality of co-subjects is non-conceptual sensory-motor-emotional intentionality. They non-conceptually experience themselves as jointly attending to objects in the world and acting on them. They also experience different kinds of emotional bonds that connect them. I believe that jointness on this and other layers necessarily includes at least a disposition for joint action. That is, what makes joint attention joint cannot be understood in terms of perceptual states and dispositions alone, as some philosophers have tried. Otherwise it cannot be distinguished from mutual observation (see Schmitz 2015 for discussion). There must be an emotional bond, however transient, involved in sharing, which disposes the co-subjects to seek, maintain and re-establish joint attention. Moreover, joint attention is typically geared towards joint action, for which it is an essential prerequisite.
2. The we-mode level of joint intention, shared belief and other conceptual level intentional states. In the we-mode, co-subjects represent states of affairs and other objects in the world from a position of identification with a group and its ethos. The we-mode is best seen as a further modification of an I-consciousness, the modification where this I represents the world from the perspective of a we-subject, in a mode of identification with it. It's important that sometimes positions I take in such a mode of identification with the group may differ from positions I take for myself, as a private person. It's further important that we-mode intentionality can misrepresent. For example, I may be in a mode of we-intending, but if my supposed co-subject has in the meantime abandoned our shared plan, I represent a joint position which does not exist anymore.
3. The institutional level, where individuals and groups take positions in what I call "role-mode", that is, for example, as a judge or as a committee, and at crucial junctures, in a written or otherwise documented form, or at least in a context which essentially employs documentation. "Institution" is here taken in the narrower sense where it refers to an organization. Like we-mode intentionality, role-mode intentionality should be seen as a further modification of I-intentionality, respectively of both I-and we-intentionality, as in such cases as when a we-subject makes a decision in its role as a committee. In such a case, an I-subject represents the world from a perspective of a we that in turn takes up the perspective of a body, which represents the world from a perspective informed by the role of this body in the organization of which it is part. Again, it is crucial that the positions co-subjects take in their roles can be different from the positions they take or would take in different roles or as

private people. For example, a judge may acquit somebody she privately thinks is guilty, and a politician may sometimes take a different position as leader of her party than as chancellor of her country.

To briefly address an objection[1]: it is true that people already take role-specific positions below the level of institutional reality, where these roles are either merely conceptually or even non-conceptually constituted and represented. For example, a mother will respond to her child as a mother on the basis of a role-specific emotional bond and/or role-specific conceptual level expectations and prescriptions. But it seems to me that the combination of increasing role differentiation and writing/documentation is an especially potent one that justifies thinking of them as being jointly characteristic for the level of institutional reality, and in the next section some reasons why this may be so will emerge. In any case, as I emphasized earlier, the tripartite distinction is more for purposes of rough orientation. More precise characterizations are possible with the help of the parameters/dimensions that I will now introduce. Some of these dimensions I have taken from the literature on nonconceptual content (e.g. Gunther 2003). So, I will sometimes begin with examples from their original domain and then present examples from the domain of collective intentionality in general and the law in particular.

3 Criteria for Distinguishing Layers

I will begin by introducing the following dimensions / parameters:
a) richness of content / from concrete to abstract
b) degree of context dependence
c) density / gestaltlike character / differentiation of representational role
d) degree of durability / stability / externalization / standardization

I will then go on to explore some hypotheses concerning relations between these criteria and between layers.

A) Richness of content / concrete to abstract
In the perceptual and actional domain, think about the richness of experience and the fineness of grain in perceptually discriminating shades of red vs. conceptualizing them, or the richness and fineness of grain in experiencing dance

1 Thanks to Judith Martens for pressing this objection on several occasions.

movements vs. the conceptual level instructions given by your dance teacher. For the application to collective intentionality and the law, think about the richness of experiencing an emotional bond vs. conceptual and institutional representations of this bond. For example, think about experiencing one's mother (as one's mother) in immediate emotional interaction vs. applying the concept "mother" to her (which will be partially shaped through the larger culture one is part of) vs. an official documenting her legal status as your mother in a family registry, or about the emotional reaction to a crime and its perpetrator vs. its representation in the legal language of a court.

B) Degree of context-dependence

Richness and efficacy of content often (causally) depends on presence of object or co-subject. The full richness of the experience of, say, the colors of a sunset may only be possible in the immediate presence of this sunset, not through memory, though imagination may come close. In CI, many co-subjective relationships depend on face-to-face, sensory-motor-emotional for their establishment and maintenance. Other relationships feel more abstract and official, like for example, most encounters with law enforcement. To maintain relationships with a higher degree of context dependence requires conceptual or even documental forms of representation. For example, the police officer will have an ID as well as other markers of their status such as a uniform, and the population will have a conceptual understanding of what a police officer is and does.

Context has many dimensions and accordingly distance from the context and the degree of independence from it can mean many different things. For example, the degree of context independence may sometimes be fruitfully measured in terms of spatial and temporal distance from a perceptual context. In this way, animal psychologists have studied the context-independence of an elephant's ability to use tools. Would Kandula use a box to stand on to reach fruit in a tree, even if the box had been placed in a different section of the yard, out of view when the elephant was looking up at the tempting food? "Apart from a few large-brained species, such as humans, apes, and dolphins, not many mammals will do this, but Kandula did it without hesitation, fetching the box from great distances" (De Waal 2016, 16; based on Foerder et al. 2011).

When it comes to morality and the law, a crucial dimension of context-independence is the independence of the behavior of upholding norms and defending them against violators from emotional bonds, familial connections and immediate shared interests with the victim. Will I support somebody against a norm violation only when they are a family member, a friend, or a business partner, or will I also support a random person out of an abstract sense of justice and the allegiance to a much wider community of co-subjects such as a nation, humanity, or even all my conscious co-creatures?

C) Density / gestaltlike character / representational role differentiation
A simple example for the density or gestaltlike character of basic representations is the fact that in visual experience color and shape cannot be represented separately, though they can be separated at the conceptual level in thought. Similarly, in certain monkey warning calls theoretical, mind-to-world direction of fit aspects – "there is a leopard here!" – and practical, world-to-mind direction of fit ones – "Get on the trees!" – are not differentiated. Ruth Millikan, who calls such representations "pushmi-pullyu"-representations, mentions representations of the moral rules or customs of a society such as "No, Johnny, we don't eat peas with our fingers here" as another example (Millikan 1995). As I shall discuss more extensively later, this also includes some representations of the laws of a society such as "The law says to drive on the left side of the road".

Moreover, as has often been pointed out, in primitive societies the law itself is not yet differentiated from moral and religious notions. Jürgen Habermas describes such an elementary understanding of justice as follows: "The concept of justice lying at the basis of all forms of conflict resolution is intermingled with mythical interpretations of the world" (Habermas 1988, 264). Habermas further characterizes the corresponding basic gestaltlike understanding of crime as follows:

> The severity of the crime is measured by the consequences of the act, not by the intentions of the perpetrator. A sanction has the sense of a compensation for resulting damages, not the punishment of someone guilty of violating a norm. This concretistic representation of justice does not yet permit a clear separation between legal questions and questions of fact. It seems that in those archaic legal processes, normative judgments, the prudent weighing of interests, and statements of fact are intertwined. (ibid., 265)

So, at this level of understanding, the severity of the crime is not yet differentiated from the damage done. A more differentiated legal system does this by taking into account the perpetrator's intentions, among other things. Such a system may also evolve a clear separation between a determination of the facts and the determination of their legal consequences, for example by assigning them to different phases of a trial.

This can also be seen as an instance of representational role differentiation. The most basic form of representational role differentiation is the move from the continuous flow of sensory-motor-emotional experience to the discontinuous propositional structure of language. Language comes in articulated units, sentences, and that is essentially connected to the fact that a sentence consists of elements such as verbs, nouns and adjectives, which have distinct representational roles within it. Such a differentiation of elements with distinct roles cannot yet be found in sensory-motor-emotional experience. The concept of representational role differentiation is wide and applies in many different contexts. To illustrate, the development of different text types such as, in the legal domain, briefs, opinions, and law review articles, is also an instance of representational role differentiation.

D) Degree of durability / stability

Conceptualization, documentation and institutionalization are all about making things more durable and stable so that one is able to manage disruptions and crises. They also enable integration with larger communities. For example, the relationship of a couple may first be solely or primarily based on their immediate sensory-motor-emotional interactions. Then they start to conceptualize it e.g. as love, which integrates it with the conceptual knowledge and expectations of their culture and make promises to each other. If they fight and want to break up, they might be told that there are ups and downs in any relationship. They might remind each other of their promises. If they get married, their relationship gets documented, certified by the institutional structures of the tribe, church or state, which will also tend to serve to protect it and make it more durable.

These functions are also enabled by the durability and stability of the relevant representational states, acts and artefacts. Written language and documentation are more durable and more easily repeatable and shareable than spoken language, which explains their importance for the process of institutionalization.

To these parameters let me add two more, which one would not ordinarily think of as being about representations, but which do essentially involve them and are essentially connected to the other parameters. The first is the differentiation of institutions themselves, e.g. the already mentioned separation of the legal sphere from morality and religion, or the differentiation of the legal sphere into sacred and secular law or criminal and civil law. The second is the attendant differentiation of institutional roles, which creates an ever increasing number of specialists. So instead of the mediators in some tribal societies we now have judges, attorneys, clerks, jurors, and so on.

A central hypothesis of my version of a layered account is that the parameters described all tend to cluster and thus correlate with one another. Let me try to make this plausible with the following brief narrative. We first react to moral infractions in an immediate, context-dependent and concrete way, notably through emotionally charged responses such as so-called reactive attitudes (Strawson 1962). Such representations are also dense and gestaltlike, because they are responsive to many features, without separating and singling them out for attention. What upset me so much about this behavior, why did it seem such a betrayal? It may take a lot of reflection to conceptualize the situation – even assuming we already have relevant concepts at our disposal. When we do have appropriate moral concepts, the gathering of knowledge of instances, which may deviate from the central, prototypical ones in different ways and the striving for systematization will lead to further differentiation of our conceptual apparatus. For example, was it theft or robbery, homicide or murder? And once the legal sphere becomes more clearly separated from others and institutional roles are further differentiated, this will further accelerate conceptual development. More and more specialists can focus on it and will produce ever more abstract and elaborate conceptual frameworks. Documentation and writing make the legal order and legal statuses much more durable and context-independent and further enhance legal reflection, which is built through centuries through consideration and systematization of ever more cases, also leading through a proliferation of different forms of legal texts, thus increasing representational role differentiation.

It is a central assumption of a layered account that such diachronic phylogenetic structures are also reflected in the synchronic structure of the mind, mediated through the extent in which ontogeny recapitulates at least some stages of phylogeny. In trying to capture this layered structure, I think we need to strike a balance. On the one hand, layers are really separate from another, that is, they have a certain degree of autonomy. This is also necessary if they are to fulfill their function of creating order and stability and managing disruption and crises created at the lower, more volatile layers. (Recall our couple and their fight.) This is especially true for the law. On the other hand, higher layers also depend on lower ones. They can only function against the background of lower level capacities. To illustrate this dialectic of autonomy and dependence, consider what is usually called the belief independence of perception (Evans 1982), but which also might be called the autonomy of belief. I form the belief that the lines in the Müller-Lyer illusion are of equal length even though perceptually they persistently appear to differ in length. At the same time my capacity to form beliefs about the world and to think about it depends on my capacity to perceive it. Normally I accept the deliverances of my senses, and I can only ascribe illusions to myself on the basis of other perceptions – like when I take a ruler to the Müller-Lyer lines (Schmitz 2019). And generally, my conceptual thoughts can only determine conditions of satisfaction against the background of lower-level, non-conceptual capacities (Schmitz 2012).

In the next and final section of this paper I will argue that this kind of relationship also holds between the legal system of a society and the moral attitudes of its members. The law has a certain degree of autonomy relative to these attitudes, but it is not completely independent of them either. Not every law will be consistent with the moral and other attitudes of all or even a majority of its members. Some laws are introduced against the will of a significant part of the population, others may lose the support of the people over the course of their existence because moral attitudes have changed. (One interesting manifestation of this is that laws will cease to be enforced and applied even though they remain on the books, like laws against sodomy and oral sex in some US states.) But it still remains true that the legal system of a society, like its institutional reality as a whole, depends on the acceptance of its members, and I think it is safe to assume that moral attitudes play an essential role in determining this acceptance. This will also be true regardless of where exactly we draw the line between morality and law. E.g. what degree of separation between the legal and religious sphere is required for us to speak of the legal system of a collective? As I said earlier, it is not obvious where this line should be drawn, but wherever we draw it, we will find that legal rules only function against the background of lower level attitudes.

Just like intentional states and acts in general, legal statutes also only determine conditions of satisfaction against the background of lower level capacities. To see this, consider the fact that they are often formulated using abstract concepts which cannot determine their conditions of application independently of common sense, including common sense moral attitudes. This point has been especially stressed by the tradition of legal realism, but it is also made by the great legal positivist H.L. Hart, who uses the example of a legal rule that forbids to take a vehicle into the public park: "Plainly this forbids an automobile, but what about bicycles, roller skates, toy automobiles? What about airplanes? Are these, as we say, to be called "vehicles" for the purpose of the rule or not?" (Hart 1958, 607). Or, we might add, what about scooters and the electric scooters that have recently become popular, but did not even exist when this rule was written? The law is typically written based on a gestaltlike apprehension of central cases, where many relevant properties cluster. But when we move to what Hart calls the "penumbra" of less central cases, these often can only be decided based on some understanding of what "the law ought to be" (ibid.: 608), and as Hart acknowledges, this means that uncodified, broadly moral considerations will be involved.

What then are layers? Talking about layers of intentionality is a way of talking about relations between representational states, acts and artefacts such that higher level representations emerge later in phylogeny and ontogeny than lower level representations and depend on them for their functioning. However this dependence is holistic – not every belief is based on a perceptual state, though the capacity to form beliefs generally depends on perceptual capacities – and allows for a certain degree of autonomy, so that there can even be conflicts between layers, as when my belief overrides my perceptual experience, or my legal thinking in my role as a judge overrides my gut feeling, even my belief, that the defendant is guilty, and I still acquit her, say because the evidence that moves me personally is legally inadmissible. And as I have argued, the representations on different layers can be ordered in terms of degrees of such parameters as concreteness, context-dependence, density and representational role differentiation, and durability and stability.

4 The Law as Institutionalized Morality

So far, I have approached the issue of the relation between morality and law in what one might think of as a broadly naturalistic, perhaps even positivistic spirit. That is, I have looked at law as a social practice, and though I did not try to draw a sharp boundary, I have tried to describe (some of) the parameters which may turn a (merely) moral practice into a legal one, as when it gets further developed, differentiated, codified and enforced by specialists. I have also claimed though that higher-level representations such as legal ones can only function effectively and determine conditions of satisfaction against the background of lower-level ones such as moral attitudes. While, as we have noted, at least the last point is also accepted by a legal positivist such as Hart, the resulting picture seems to be in tension with the positivist account of the relation between morality and law. In this last section I therefore want to explore traditional issues about this relation further in light of the account of collective intentionality that I have sketched. As we shall see, not only the layered aspect will be important for this, but also the emphasis on the distinction between representing others as co-subjects vs. representing them merely as objects.

I take the core claim of legal positivism to be that whether something is law does not depend on its merits – where by "merits" we mean moral merits – but on its sources, the social structures and processes that have originated it and maintain its existence, its being in force (e.g. Gardner 2001; Green and Adams 2019). Legal positivism rejects both the ideas of the natural law tradition that something could be law 'naturally', without a proper social, institutional context, and that something properly situated in such a context could fail to be law. So, whether something is part of the law is the question whether a certain social fact obtains.

Accordingly, when people express their opposition to certain prescriptions by saying that they are not, or not really, law, the positivist will think that they express this (typically morally motivated) opposition in a confused way. They are mixing up the question whether a certain social fact obtains with the question of whether it should obtain. So, they fail to properly separate law and morality. We have to recognize that – unfortunately – the law is not always just and morally right.

This is certainly true, but does it establish the separation of law and morality that positivism requires? Obviously, this depends on what kind of separation positivism requires, and different philosophers will give different answers to that. I believe that we should not be transfixed by labels such as "positivism". In what follows I will argue from the point of view of the layered account that law and morality still remain essentially connected. In fact, I will suggest that the best way to think of the law is as being itself an institutionalized form of morality (where morality is taken in a broad sense which includes mores, conventional ways of doing things). This view will combine positivist with not-so-positivist sounding claims, and I will leave it to the reader to decide how, if at all, it should be labelled.

While it is often pointed out that laws can be immoral, the corresponding observation about morality is much less often made. That is, while it has become routine to acknowledge that laws can be unjust, the claim that morals can be immoral may still sound paradoxical to some. But just as I can criticize a law as unjust on the basis of moral ideas and even as illegal because it violates other laws, so I can criticize a moral code as immoral on the basis of my own, different moral code. Of course, when calling a person (or action) immoral, people sometimes mean that they are not sufficiently governed by a moral code, or even that they lack one entirely. However, the latter claim is hardly, if ever, true. It's much more often the case that we are too outraged by moralities different from ours to even recognize and understand them as such. In our (genuine or faked) outrage, we fail to recognize the morality and thus the humanity of others.

The reason I emphasize that moral codes can be criticized as immoral just as laws can be, is that we must be careful not to confound the distinction between morality and law with the distinction between two different perspectives that we can take towards both, namely the perspective of the observer or theoretician with the perspective of the participant or, to put it in the terms I have been using, the co-subject. When we consider the law as philosophers of law, we naturally take a theoretical perspective or position as observers. When we then judge, or imagine judging, a law to be immoral, it is tempting to do so from the point of view of one's personal morality, or of one's morality as a member, a co-subject of a group one identifies with, without taking a corresponding theoretical perspective on this morality. That is, while one considers the law as an object of theoretical inquiry, a domain of social facts, morality is here construed subjectively in the sense that it is part of the apparatus with which we investigate this domain of facts, rather than as itself an object of inquiry.

Taking this perspective, it seems obvious that the existence of laws and legal facts must be completely separate from their moral merits, because it is certainly independent of whether the theoretician morally approves of a law, legal act or legal system, especially when we consider the laws of societies far removed in space, time and moral outlook, as we will tend to in such contexts. But the real question of course is whether the existence of laws in a society can be independent of the moral attitudes of the members, the co-subjects, of that society. For example, the Jim Crow laws in the US existed even though we now regard them as profoundly immoral. But could they have been the law of the land at the time if the attitude of the population then had been as it is now? That already looks like a rather implausible claim.

The corresponding general thesis in the philosophy of institutional reality is that institutional facts – of which legal facts are a species – are, as, John Searle put it in his seminal book *The Construction of Social Reality* (Searle 1995) observer- or belief-dependent or observer-relative, in contrast to ordinary facts, which of course are belief-independent. I think that Searle is right that institutional reality in general and legal reality is mind-dependent, that its existence depends on the collective acceptance of the society whose institutional reality it is. But we can't think of acceptance here as a mere theoretical attitude, a belief that something is the case. If all members of a given society, including the legal officials, only had relevant beliefs about the relevant states of affairs, if they knew what the others were doing, what their roles are, who they had been appointed by, and so on, but were practically and morally indifferent or even hostile towards these arrangements, I don't think we could say that these laws were really the legal system of that society.

Acceptance in the relevant sense must include practical attitudes. To accept the order of a society, whether moral or legal, is not merely to have beliefs that people have certain roles etc. including even beliefs that others believe this as well: it must include a recognition of this order as legitimate and binding. And this in turn must mean at least some disposition to comply with that order, to defend it and to have other pro-attitudes such as approval towards it. Therefore, the collective attitudes that are constitutive of legal reality can't only be attitudes of belief, at least if by belief we mean a purely theoretical, mind-to-world direction of fit attitude. (It is presumably for reasons of this kind that in his later work Searle often speaks of the intentionality- or participation-relativity of institutional reality rather than of its observer-relativity or belief-dependence (e.g. 2010, 17).)

I suggest that a basic kind of attitude among those that are constitutive of legal reality are the already mentioned pushmi-pullyu representations, representational acts or states that essentially contain mind-to-world and world-to-mind direction of fit aspects, though in an as yet not clearly differentiated form, like in Millikan's example "No, Johnny, we don't eat peas with our fingers here". A typical utterance of a sentence like this is not a mere description of the customs of a group, but has prescriptive force. It's a way of telling Johnny that he should not eat peas with his fingers either. "The law says that we must stop at the junction" will normally be meant and understood in just the same way. So, our basic way of relating to the law is one that acknowledges it as a reality, but at the same time recognizes it as something that has prescriptive force over our actions, with these two aspects not yet being clearly differentiated. The clear separation of description and prescription and thus the representation of legal facts as mere facts belongs to a higher level of understanding. This level is not as such constitutive of the existence of legal facts. It is rather a level on which we reflect on these facts as entities that exist independently of us as observers. But at that same level we also have to recognize that these facts do not exist independently of the attitudes of the co-subjects of this society, and that these attitudes have an irreducibly practical aspect, so that they represent the law not as a mere fact, but as somethings to be respected and followed, at least generally and under normal conditions.

This way of accounting for institutional reality is importantly different from Searle's superficially similar account in terms of his notion of a declaration, which (also) is supposed to have both directions of fit. The crucial difference is that on Searle's account the declaration both makes it the case that a state of affairs is a fact and represents it as a fact. That is, the very same representational act is supposed to have world-to-mind and mind-to-world direction of fit with regard to the same state of affairs. But it is highly questionable whether the very same representation can both create a fact and represent it as being the case at the same time (cf. Laitinen 2014 for criticism). This idea is in tension with realism. In contrast, the Millikanian account more modestly only claims that pushmi-pullyu representations represent a state of affairs as having prescriptive force with regard to other states of affairs, respectively actions. There is nothing mysterious about that. It is grounded in the fact that we perceive situations so as to immediately mandate certain actions, in basic cases even without clearly differentiating description and prescription. It is also grounded in the well-known tendency of humans, especially children, to imitate the actions of their fellow creatures, in particular members of their own group and be guided by them. The respect for the law of one's group is a higher-level manifestation of the same basic tendency, because the law is a codification, a more context-independent way of representing ways of behaving that are to be imitated, respectively that are prohibited.

Another way of making what is essentially the same point is to say that groups exist in virtue of subjects identifying with the other group members, their co-subjects. Already at the sensory-motor-emotional level this means, as argued earlier, that jointness cannot be reduced to perceiving the same things and being mutually aware of that, but must include an emotional identification with the other, imitative tendencies and at least a disposition for joint action. Analogously, at the conceptual level of we-mode intentionality, co-subjects must not only share beliefs and be aware of that, but must identify with what Raimo Tuomela calls the "group ethos" (e.g. Tuomela 2013). At the institutional level this means that being a member of communities ranging from tribes to nation-states or even supra-national units such as the EU requires a certain level of identification with these units and that also means an identification with their goals. This is not only, but particularly true for those who have official roles within those institutional contexts. For them, it means that the role-constituting intentionality I call "role mode"-intentionality cannot consist merely in beliefs about that institutional structure, the role one has been appointed to, and so on. There must be at least some degree of identification with the ethos and the goals of the relevant institution. In role mode, the subject takes theoretical and practical positions towards the world from the vantage point of the role, that is, shaped through the ethos of the organization and the function of the role within it.

Of course, it is still possible that somebody takes up such a role who does not identify with it and its ethos – for example, think of a spy, who only pretends to. Similarly, obviously not all co-subjects of a given collective will agree with all of its laws. We are here trying to explain the normal, proper functioning of laws and layers. As I have emphasized, these institutions are made for durability. They are generally able to survive laws and lawyers that do nothing or very little to promote justice and the common good. However, there will be a point where the institutional structure collapses, or is abandoned, when the disconnect between its rules and its officials and the moral and other attitudes of the rest of the population becomes too severe. The collapse of the East Bloc countries in the annus mirabilis 1989 is only one of the latest and most spectacular of many instances of this kind of phenomenon. Moreover, as we discussed, even in its normal functioning the law depends on moral thinking to determine its application to the penumbra of non-central cases.

While it is thus true that not all laws of a society have to agree with the outlook of all of its co-subjects, the existence of the legal system as a whole still depends on their acceptance. And this in turn means that it will depend on their moral attitudes, which will surely essentially contribute to determining this acceptance. I conclude that while the existence of a specific law or other specific legal facts is independent of their moral merits in the eyes of a mere observer, this cannot be said of the existence of the legal system as a whole in relation to the members or co-subjects of the relevant society. If these members cease to accept it, it will become idle and void and at same point will cease to be their law. Therefore, what the law of a society is, does ultimately depend on its moral merits in the eyes of the members of the society.

Once we clarify that the dependence of the legal system on lower level moral attitudes is holistic, I confess that to me it seems to be sort of obvious – how could the acceptance of a legal order not at least also be shaped by moral concerns? But is there anything that we could do say to convince a skeptic?[2] First, to block a possible misunderstanding, let me emphasize that quite often people are mere objects of legal systems. For example, an occupying force may impose legal statuses on the occupied population. But as long as they do not accept the occupying force, they would not be co-subjects of the relevant society and thus not a counterexample to my claim. (Of course, precise boundaries between acceptance and mere domination are hard to draw, but this does not mean either that this distinction is not vital, or that acceptance is not morally motivated.) Second, the question of the acceptance of legal and institutional structure is a political question and we have a lot of evidence that political attitudes are connected with moral attitudes. For example, in the present political situation proponents of the social justice movement – which is obviously a morally motivated movement – will tend to sympathize with left-wing parties, while adherents of more traditional, religiously shaped forms of morality will tend to sympathize with right-wing parties. Jonathan Haidt (2012) has collected an impressive body of evidence that in the US Democrats and Republicans have importantly different moral outlooks along similar lines.

It may be objected that this only shows that partisan politics are connected to moral outlook, while what we really need is evidence that moral outlook is connected to attitudes shared across party lines such as acceptance of the legal and institutional structure. But it still supports the notion that political attitudes are generally connected to moral ones. Further evidence is provided by the fact that the political and legal culture of a country generally reflects its moral and intellectual culture. For example, the culture in Anglophone countries tends towards empiricism and a winner-takes-all mindset, and this is reflected in their common law tradition and their political system.

It seems to me that therefore any satisfactory account of the law must explain both how the emergence of a legal system is a very important step that can transform a society and that it remains essentially connected to the moral attitudes of its members even if it is not consonant with them at every point.

---

2 Thanks to Miguel Garcia and Amin Ebrahimi Afrouzi for prompting me to say more on this.

I want to conclude by suggesting that the best way to do this may be by thinking of the law itself as consisting of institutionalized, codified moral rules. Again, this claim is independent of where exactly we may want to draw the boundary between (non-legal) morality and law for certain theoretical or practical purposes and accordingly of whether we interpret institutions broadly so as to include all customs and traditions, or more narrowly as referring to organizational structures, as I did in the tripartite distinction between layers introduced above. In fact, it seems to me that the very fact that it is not obvious where this boundary should be drawn, which degree of context-independence, systematicity of conceptualization, codification and documentation, separation from other spheres and role differentiation is required for a practice to count as a proper legal system, itself supports the idea that law is continuous with and itself an institutionalized form of morality, similar to how science is continuous with common sense observation and knowledge and an institutionalized form of it. There is nothing magical that happens to a moral rule when it is codified and enforced by a sphere of specialists that completely changes its character, just like a piece of knowledge still remains knowledge when it becomes scientific knowledge. This is quite consistent with how the rule of law can transform a society, just like science can.[3]

References

De Waal, Frans. 2016. *Are We Smart Enough to Know How Smart Animals Are?* New York: WW Norton & Company.

Evans, Gareth. 1982. *The Varieties of Reference*. Oxford: Clarendon Press.

Ferraris, Maurizio. 2015. "Collective Intentionality or Documentality?" *Philosophy & Social Criticism* 41 (4–5): 423–433.

Foerder, Preston, Marie Galloway, Tony Barthel, Donald E. Moore III, and Diana Reiss. 2011. "Insightful Problem Solving in an Asian Elephant." *PloS One* 6 (8).

Gardner, John. 2001. "Legal Positivism: 5 1/2 Myths." *Am. J. Juris.* 46: 199.

Green, Leslie, and Thomas Adams. 2019. "Legal Positivism." In *The Stanford Encyclopedia of Philosophy (Winter 2019 Edition)*.

Gunther, York H. 2003. *Essays on Nonconceptual Content*. Cambridge, MA: MIT Press.

Habermas, Jürgen. 1988. "Law and Morality." *The Tanner Lectures on Human Values* 8: 217–279.

Haidt, Jonathan. 2012. *The Righteous Mind: Why Good People Are Divided by Politics and Religion*. New York: Vintage.

Hart, H. L. A. 1958. "Positivism and the Separation of Law and Morals." *Harvard Law Review* 71 (4): 593–629. https://doi.org/10.2307/1338225.

3 Thanks to the editors Miguel Garcia and Rachael Mellin and to Amin Ebrahimi Afrouzi for very helpful written comments on an earlier draft.

Laitinen, Arto. 2014. “Against Representations with Two Directions of Fit.” *Phenomenology and the Cognitive Sciences* 13 (1): 179–199.
Liebal, Kristin, Tanya Behne, Malinda Carpenter, and Michael Tomasello. 2009. “Infants Use Shared Experience to Interpret Pointing Gestures.” *Developmental Science* 12 (2): 264–271.
Millikan, Ruth G. 1995. “Pushmi-Pullyu Representations.” *Philosophical Perspectives* 9: 185–200.
Schmitz, Michael. 2011. “Limits of the Conscious Control of Action.” *Social Psychology* 42 (1): 93–98.
Schmitz, Michael. 2012. “The Background as Intentional, Conscious, and Nonconceptual.” In *Knowing without Thinking: Mind, Action, Cognition and the Phenomenon of the Background*, edited by Zdravko Radman, 57–82. Basingstoke: Palgrave Macmillan.
Schmitz, Michael. 2013. “Social Rules and the Social Background.” In *The Background of Social Reality*, edited by Michael Schmitz, Beatrice Kobow, and Hans Bernhard Schmid, 107–125. Dordrecht: Springer.
Schmitz, Michael. 2015. “Joint Attention and Understanding Others.” *Synthesis Philosophica* 58: 235–251.
Schmitz, Michael. 2016. “A History of Emerging Modes?” *Journal of Social Ontology* 2 (1): 87–103.
Schmitz, Michael. 2018. “Co-Subjective Consciousness Constitutes Collectives.” *Journal of Social Philosophy* 49 (1): 137–160.
Schmitz, Michael. 2019. “The Good, the Bad and the Naive.” In *The Philosophy of Perception*, edited by Christoph Limbeck-Lilienau and Friedrich Stadler, 57–74. Berlin: De Gruyter.
Searle, John R. 1995. *The Construction of Social Reality*. New York: Free Press.
Searle, John R. 2010. *Making the Social World: The Structure of Human Civilization*. Oxford: Oxford University Press.
Strawson, Peter. 1962. “Freedom and Resentment.” In *Proceedings of the British Academy, Volume 48: 1962*, edited by Gary Watson, 48:1–25. Oup Oxford.
Tomasello, Michael. 2014. *A Natural History of Human Thinking*. Cambridge, MA: Harvard University Press.
Tuomela, Raimo. 2013. *Social Ontology: Collective Intentionality and Group Agents*. Oxford: Oxford University Press.

Bei Fragen zur Produktsicherheit wenden Sie sich bitte an:
If you have any questions regarding product safety,
please contact:

Walter de Gruyter GmbH
Genthiner Straße 13
10785 Berlin
productsafety@degruyterbrill.com